JA

Death in
Washington

Death in Washington

The Murder of Orlando Letelier

by
Donald Freed
with
Dr. Fred Simon Landis

*Introduction by
Dr. William F. Pepper, Esq.*

Lawrence Hill & Company
Westport, Connecticut

Freed, Donald.
    Death in Washington.

    Bibliography: p.
    Includes index.
    1. Letelier, Orlando--Assassination. 2. As-
sassination--Washington, D.C. 3. Townley, Michael
Vernon. 4. Phillips, David Atlee. 5. United
States--Foreign relations--Chile. 6. Chile--
Foreign relations--United States. I. Landis,
Fred Simon, joint author. II. Title.
F3101.L47F73   364.1'524'0924   50-52434
ISBN 0-88208-123-3
ISBN 0-88208-124-1 (pbk.)

ISBN clothbound edition: 0-88208-123-3
ISBN paperback edition: 0-88208-124-1
Library of Congress Catalog Card Number: 80-52434

The Pablo Neruda poems which appear in this volume are
translated by Fred Simon Landis. Editor Losada, S.A.,
owner of the copyright for all books by the author in the
Spanish language, has renounced economic benefits from
the special edition, published during the Allende presidency,
in which these poems appeared.

First edition November, 1980

1 2 3 4 5 6 7 8 9 10

Lawrence Hill & Company, Publishers, Inc.
Westport, Connecticut 06880

To "H.E.O.," who gave his life
so that the part of this story
he knew could be told.
And to J.R.M.A., who defected
in time from the DINA,
the Chilean secret police.

Contents

viii   Contents

Foreword

DONALD FREED AND THE CITIZENS RESEARCH AND INVESTIGA-
TIVE COMMITTEE have uncovered new, and while not surprising,
significant information surrounding the assassination of former
Chilean Ambassador to the United States, Dr. Orlando Letelier.
Those findings, published in this book, *Death in Washington*,
point to yet another illicit involvement of the government of the
United States with complicity on the part of not only some named
public officials, but also here, for the first time, reveal the role and
relationship of two famous sons of a prominent American family.

This work is important not merely as a rebuttal to an "official"
history now being prepared by those who may have orchestrated
aspects of the cover-up, but also because, in my judgment, it
relates to a far more pervasive problem in the United States today,
which constitutes perhaps the most substantial threat to liberty—
that is, the conscious utilization by government and quasi-govern-
mental structures of mass media techniques and institutions to
shape public opinion and attitudes with respect to significant
historical events.

The extensive use of media campaigns and opinion-molding
strategies and techniques to produce desired public reaction and
opinion has been developed over the last twenty years in the
United States with a sophistication unparalleled in the history of
either politics or communications. The toleration of the First
Amendment, by the forces of private and public power, seems
more than ever to rest upon their understanding that on critical
issues media instrumentalities will, by and large, keep dissent
within acceptable limits. In actual practice, then, in every significant instance of sensitive news coverage and commentary, power-
related media professionals, well placed in editorial and management positions, report, analyze and manage the news in protec-

tion of what they perceive to be their (and, of course, the nation's) vital interests.

This management of information extends from the most powerful mass television networks to news services, newspapers, periodicals, network and local radio stations, and, of course, film, book publishing, and theatre. In fact, the increasing interrelationship of many of the above within conglomerate structures makes collaborative news management even more efficient, though not readily apparent. Mr. Freed refers to Carl Bernstein's 1977 article, in which the latter maintained that over four hundred "agents" were working in key media positions, and that every major publication and broadcasting station, as well as many smaller ones, were infiltrated. Individuals named, such as DeToledano, Lardner, O'Leary, Hobbing, Hendrix, and the Buckleys, may be seen as comprising the tip of a vast iceberg of misinformation sponsored by the intelligence and multinational corporate community. The assassination of former Chilean Ambassador Letelier, carried out in broad daylight on a street in the nation's capital, and the investigation which followed, resulted in the maximum use of this capability.

This was predictable. Letelier stood for a former government deemed inimical to American private and public interests.

The work of Donald Freed and Fred Landis in this area is important because it discloses facts that might otherwise remain hidden. As such, *Death in Washington*, stands in a long line of independent, investigative writing projects, and in that tradition it serves only one master—the truth.

In the last twenty years, Americans have become all too used to the official tactics of whitewashing employed by both government and the private sector. These efforts have been prominently with us from the Bay of Pigs disaster, the war in Vietnam, the assassinations of the Kennedy brothers and Martin Luther King, Watergate, industrial assaults on individuals and the environment, mind and behavior control experimentation by intelligence agencies and the military on unknowing human guinea pigs, and so on, *ad nauseam*. The involvement of the Central Intelligence Agency, associated private intelligence organizations and personnel, and American multinational interests in the overthrow and assassination of Salvador Allende, and the subsequent coverup, were typical of many such efforts by American public and private interests to impose their will upon a foreign people, and deceive the American people.

I suggest that the official whitewash of the American orchestration of the replacement of Allende with the Pinochet regime in Chile is still persuasive with most Americans.

The problem ultimately resulting from Allende's overthrow was that Orlando Letelier obtained political asylum in the United States and became a very visible public figure. His presence and espousal of a free Chile threatened not only the Pinochet dictatorship, but was also potentially embarrassing to those Yankee interests behind the entire sordid adventure. The promise of the populist Allende government, subverted, first economically, and, finally, militarily, under the C.I.A.'s baton, lived on in the commitment and work of Orlando Letelier.

Consequently, it was inevitable that a time would come when those he opposed would act to silence him.

Donald Freed reveals and documents the fact that, contrary to official reports and the scapegoat convictions of three persons (two of whom, the record reveals, were not in Washington at the time, did not plant the bomb, and may well have their convictions reversed on appeal, while the third, Michael Townley, should walk in 1981), it was not the Chilean DINA that must bear primary responsibility for the control and management of the assassin Michael Vernon Townley. Freed establishes that from a much earlier time, Mr. Townley has been under the ultimate control of the C.I.A. and superagent David Atlee Phillips (also named in an extensivelyy documented new work by Anthony Summers as the "handle" of Lee Harvey Oswald in the Kennedy assassination). This is an important revelation, though by itself is certainly not surprising.

On the other hand, ramifications stemming from the involvement of the prominent Buckley brothers, and the public relations on behalf of the anti-Allende forces by William F. Buckley, should not only raise a few eyebrows, but result in the convening of a federal grand jury. This body, at the very least, could inquire into the documented visits of assassin Townley to the New York office of former U.S. Senator James Buckley exactly one week prior to the assassination.

A grand jury might also take a long hard look at William Buckley himself as an apparent unregistered agent of the Chilean dictatorship, as well as the possible role of former CIA agent Edwin Wilson (the first ever indicted for murder) in providing Townley with the necessary explosives.

In fact, such a grand jury might uncover a new perspective on the role of the Department of Justice and the FBI in investigating the assassination and prosecuting the case and obtaining the three convictions. On the surface, it is possible to discern an impressive degree of co-operation and collaboration extending from investigation to conviction and beyond into public information control and revisionism. The collaboration provided a solid public relations and disinformation front for the official government line disseminated through ongoing press releases, articles, and editorials, and even a soon-to-be-published book and movie emanating directly from the prosecutor's office. Thus we come full cycle— from the actual making of history to the writing of the official historical account.

At Mr. Freed's request, some months ago, I agreed to serve as counsel to him and the Committee. I was soon participating with them in a paper chase, begun months earlier. The object of the correspondence was to seek a receptive hearing at the Department of Justice for the new information and facts that the Committee had uncovered. Ranging from Donald Freed's first correspondence with Attorney General Griffin Bell on July 4, 1979, through my initial correspondence with Deputy Assistant Attorney General Philip B. Heymann, beginning on January 3, 1980, up to the present, we have been unable to find anyone at the Department of Justice who appears to be seriously interested in sitting down and discussing the documented, new information contained in this book.

In sum and substance, there appears to be very little official interest in new details. This, despite Philip Heymann's letter of August 3, 1979, stating that there is a "continuing investigation of this case . . ." (Our last request is reprinted below.)*

The Letelier assassination provides us with a good example of governmental techniques and the development of an official scenario in such a case of this sort. Fortunately, courageous and inquisitive minds are not easily fooled or deterred. Thus we all owe a debt of gratitude to the Citizens Research and Investigative Committee, and to Donald Freed and Fred Landis for their work in connection with *Death in Washington*. Without this effort, those who have regard for the truth in such matters concerning the functioning of our government, and equate it with liberty, would be poorer, more isolated and alone.

In the final analysis, then, such private efforts such as this—woefully underfinanced and unappreciated—bring us together. They are the quintessential reminders in self-centered times that we exist not for ourselves alone but share (*non nobis solum nati sumas*), the great binding tie of the people throughout the ages who have treasured individual freedom.

WILLIAM F. PEPPER
New York, New York

Sources

First came the idea (to assassinate Orlando Letelier). Then came the act, on September 21, 1976. Then came the *idea* of the act. The wheel of casuality, in Nietzsche's words, "doth not roll between them".

What W. B. Yeats called "gyres" of meaning warp and mystify the Letelier affair. The motives and actions of at least five secret organizations intersect and overlap the killing ground in Washington, D.C.: 1) Chile's secret police, DINA; 2) the anti-Castro Cuban underground, the "White Hand"; 3) the United States Federal Bureau of Investigation, which first let the crime take place, then helped to solve it, partially; 4) the U.S. Central Intelligence Agency, whose former officers and agents, deeply involved with the convicted killers, laid a noisome screen of lies across the trail of the murderers, after the fact; 5) rogues and renegades retired or fired from the CIA after the great purges of 1974-75 who have formed front organizations to carry out their Cold War clandestine agenda of antidemocratic activities.

The idea or ideology of these covert apparatuses before the murder, and their "disinformation" and lies after, are the severed strands of meaning, the shattered mosaic that must be painstakingly pieced together, no matter how disturbing the pattern. Indeed, so convoluted, one might almost say incestuous, is the relationship between the Central Intelligence Agency and its various "assets," clients, contract agents, "agents of influence," fronts and conduits, that we have felt it necessary to provide a glossary of names and groups.

These secret combinations, involved in this crime and in its cover-up, wind like snakes through the entrails of the Cold War toward Embassy Row and their victims on September 21, 1976. Again and again, the same faces and names flash into focus in the aperture of the murders. The montage of the Letelier-Moffitt assassinations is a time-capsule of secret war: Guatemala and Indonesia, Havana and the Bay of Pigs, Santo Domingo and Saigon, Iran and Zaire, Rio, Langley, Washington, and Santiago—the Watergate and Dallas.

The deeply concerned and gifted independent investigators, enumerated below, who worked against steady odds on the Washington killings, differ with each other at critical points on interpretation. This is inevitable, since in order to penetrate the conspiracy that exploded on Embassy Row it is absolutely essential to have informants from one or more of the above secret agencies. Freelance analysts and historians have no subpoena power over suspects, can administer no oath; they depend on information *voluntarily* given. And information voluntarily given is, by definition, self-serving. In the sometimes almost impenetrable thickets of truth and lies in this case, the lies are as revealing as the truth. In the end, a good portion of what each ambivalently connected secret group says *about the other* is mainly true.

The problem is that there is no pure truth waiting, like a smoking gun, to be found under the Freedom of Information Act. The CIA, for instance, has come down on several sides of the case. Can conflicting CIA statements and off-the-record confidences be equally true? Yes. Because there are at least two warring factions *within* Central Intelligence, and they believe in and say different things. So the disparity is not simply one between an official-line handout at Langley and a private disclosure on a dark country road.

Whichever disc or gyre of this underworld you find first will influence, from then on, your angle of refraction into this overdetermined political crime that took the lives of Orlando Letelier and Ronni Karpen Moffitt. It is perhaps a virtue, then, that this study depended on unofficial and *competing* sources as well as government material acquired under the Freedom of Information Act. There are, of course, the generally available documents, the paper trail of the case. Then there is that other trail of blood-red footprints leading away from Embassy Row: a path that crosses decades of deceit—from Dallas to the Watergate. We have tried to follow that trail.

When Orlando Letelier's automobile exploded virtually in front of the Chilean Embassy in Washington, D.C., and destroyed him and his colleague, Ronni Moffitt, her husband, Michael, who had been thrown from the vehicle, screamed up at the Chilean Chancery that the fascist junta of that country was responsible for this act of violence. Michael Moffitt had solved the case within twenty seconds—or a part of the case. This book is concerned with the other parts.

Acknowledgments*

The following individuals and groups made this investigation and its record possible.

- Fernando Faura is an award winning Puerto Rican-American investigative journalist, who, at some risk, delved into the closed worlds of Miami and Santiago.
- Saul Landau, Orlando Letelier's colleague and friend, is a recognized historian and artist whose crucial research, made public through the Institute for Policy Studies, was available for this study, as indeed it has been to anyone concerned with the unprecedented political crime and events of September 21, 1976, and after.
- Kirk Scott Vinson, James Cookson, and Fran Oberkamp, of the Citizens Research and Investigation Committee (CRIC), constituted an editorial and research team of commitment and diligence. Their motivation overcame a series of frustrating blocks that were put in the way of this murder case. Patty Ezor, for CRIC, edited the manuscript under difficult conditions, besides her many other contributions. Mo Klein and a list of citizen-researchers completed the volunteer team. Elizabeth Grady, Gail Singer, Larry Modell, Alan L. Gainberg, Halina Charwat, Jackie Stehr, Alain Gainsberg, and Fernando del Rio contributed considerable editorial and translation talents.

None of the researchers and investigators who worked on this study had the power to subpoena documents or witnesses. A book

*A list of research groups to which the reader may write for further information appears in the Appendix.

is not a legal arrest warrant. But it can be evidence, if not proof, of justice cheated. Free-lancers with no official power broke the cover-up of these murders. In many ways this work is part of their story.

A number of America's best investigative journalists have been invaluable in their cooperation and help.

Ernest Volkman and John Cummings of *Newsday* are the brilliant investigative writers without whom there never would have been any arrests or convictions. Without them and Saul Landau the trail would have grown cold, the cover-up would never have ended. Volkman and Cummings have continued to work on the case and selflessly shared their insights with the CRIC team.

Dick Russell has shared his widely published studies concerning the assassination of John F. Kennedy. Again and again, his research in Dallas, Miami, Havana, Washington, has overlapped the Letelier assassination.

Researchers everywhere are indebted, and those involved in this work are no exception, to the continuing generosity of leading political-intelligence analysts such as Victor Marchetti, George O'Toole, Col. L. Fletcher Prouty, Peter Dale Scott, Rodney Larsen, Mark Lane, and Daniel Ellsberg.

A special role in the search for truth and justice in the Letelier-Moffitt case has been taken by the North American Congress on Latin America and the magazines *Inquiry* and *Counterspy*, and Jon Newhall of *Zodiak* news service.

Any number of people must remain nameless. These invaluable sources include present and former members of American and Chilean police and intelligence agencies; members of the anti-Castro Cuban exile brigades; refugees from the terror of the junta, in America and, most courageously, in Chile itself. There is one man whose name can be mentioned at last. Aldo Vera Serafin was murdered just after Ambassador Letelier in October of 1976 in Puerto Rico. Before his death, Mr. Serafin provided keys to independent investigators for this book, to the murder of Orlando Letelier.

Death in
Washington

*I have lived so much that someday
they will have to forget me forcibly,
rubbing me off the blackboard.
My heart was inexhaustible.*

*But because I ask for silence,
never think I am going to die.
The opposite is true.
It happens I am going to live—*

to be, and to go on being.

*I will not be, however, if, inside me,
the crop does not keep sprouting,
the shoots first, breaking through the earth
to reach the light;
but the mothering earth is dark,
and, deep inside me, I am dark.
I am a well in the water of which
the night leaves stars behind
and goes on alone across the fields.*

*It's a question of having lived so much
that I wish to live that much more.*

*I never felt my voice so clear,
never have been so rich in kisses.*

Pablo Neruda

1 The System Works!

I knew him, and nothing can erase the memory
The carriages fell apart
war destroyed doors and walls
cities turned into a handful of ashes
but for me, he still is
he survives
though at one time
everything seemed more permanent than he

Pablo Neruda

THE ASSASSINATIONS OF DR. ORLANDO LETELIER, the noted Chilean diplomatic figure, and Ronni Karpen Moffitt, a young American aide to Dr. Letelier, have been perceived as the basis for a Marxist detective story by the Left. The Establishment Center, and the Right have, respectively, interpreted the Letelier-Moffitt murders, cover-ups, and investigations—the entire affair —as a bourgeois tragedy or a "Castro provocation," to borrow a phrase from William F. Buckley's perverse party line.

The Embassy Row murders are the red corner of a huge canvas of destruction and corruption—of Chile and Washington. That is what bleeds through the screen of propaganda.

Pablo Neruda, Chilean winner of the Nobel Prize and Orlando Letelier's friend wrote:

The epoch is rotting away,
stalled at time's center
like the bones of a cow
with its predators gnawing within

He was both poet and prophet, the conscience of Latin America. The Letelier death in Washington came to stand for the death of an entire country—Chile—and the mortal illness of another, America.

There is a sense of rotten nostalgia, of compulsive *déjà vu*, of Cubans taking the fall for high crimes, and of the same Watergate prosecutors—who told us that those crimes went no higher "than the men from Miami"—once again cutting deals that would contain the investigation and trial of the American connection to the death in Washington. And once again, as the penitentiary door slammed behind exiled Cubans, a hollow chorus echoes, "The System Works."

Chile is a country falling into the ocean. Bottomless volcanic lakes course through the mountains as if seeking reunion with the sea. But the novelist Caroline Richards says that more than any other Latin American country, Chile is "made to human proportions," like the Mediterranean lands it so resembles. Chileans, like Europeans, are proud of their political and cultural sophistication. Like the British, they take tea in the afternoon.

In the north is the burning desert, in the south the frozen Antarctic. A wildly beautiful land, peopled by a civilized and life-loving population—that is one setting for the world historical tragedy of 1973. The other scene of the political volcano is the capital of the United States.

The chronology of the crime and its punishment is deceptively straightforward.*

1976. September 18, Washington, D.C. Orlando Letelier, Ronni Karpen Moffitt, and Michael Moffitt, Ronni's husband, are on their way to work at the Institute for Policy Studies. Letelier is driving his Chevelle, with Ronni beside him in the front seat. Michael sits in back. Leaving the Letelier home at about nine a.m., they approach Sheridan Circle, on Massachusetts Avenue. They do not notice a car parked a short distance away. Three men are inside it, and a fourth is standing on the sidewalk. "All are of Latin extraction and approximately thirty years old," according to an eye-witness. As Letelier and the Moffitts drive past the Chilean chancery—Letelier's official residence in years past—a bomb is ignited under the car, converting it into an inferno of twisted metal, smoke, and blood.

*For source notes on the text, see pages 213-218.

The official Justice Department report reads: "Michael Moffitt was thrown out through the right rear window by the explosion. Ronni Moffitt, her face covered with blood, left the car trembling. Moffitt attempted to remove Letelier, who still moved his head and arms, but [he] couldn't because the explosion had blown off [Letelier's] legs and he had fallen down to the pavement through the hole in the floor caused by the bomb."

Orlando Letelier and Ronni Moffitt die. Michael Moffitt survives.

1978. August 1, Washington, D.C. A federal grand jury hands up indictments in the Letelier-Moffitt murders. Accused are Juan Manuel Contreras Sepulveda, Pedro Espinoza Bravo, Armando Fernández Larios, Guillermo Novo Sampol, Alvin Ross Díaz, Virgilio Paz Romero, Jose Dionisio Suárez Esquivel, and Ignacio Novo Sampol. The accused belong either to the official Chilean secret police— DINA (Dirección de Inteligencia Nacional)—or to an organization of Cuban exile terrorists. Contreras, Espinoza, and Fernández are Chileans.

Not named in the indictment is Michael Vernon Townley, an American citizen who lived in Chile for many years. Townley, a mysterious figure known in clandestine circles as "The Jackal," will not be tried. He has struck a bargain with the prosecutors. In return for his co-operation, he will plead guilty to a single charge of conspiracy to commit murder. (If found guilty of murder at trial, he could receive a life sentence in prison.) As a part of the bargain, Townley will receive a ten-year sentence which will make him eligible for parole after forty months. His Chilean wife, Mariana Inés Callejas, will testify, but will not be prosecuted.

1979. January 9, Washington, D.C.. Trial begins. Present are defendants Guillermo Novo Sampol, Alvin Ross Díaz, and Ignacio Novo Sampol. Absent are the Chileans and Paz and Suárez. Though the United States has asked for the extradition of the DINA officers—in an extraordinary legal action—Chile has refused to deliver them up. Paz and Suárez cannot be found.

February 14. The defendants are found guilty.

March 23. The judge gives Guillermo Novo and Alvin Ross life sentences in prison. Ignacio Novo receives eighty years.

May 11. The judge sentences Michael Townley, in accordance with the plea-bargaining agreement, to ten years in prison.

Justice has been done.

The assassination of Orlando Letelier was the first of its kind in the United States. More than an unprecedented political crime involving a foreign diplomat, the murder of Dr. Letelier was an act set in motion by some dynamic inherent in American policy since World War II.

There was credit enough and praise for all. In 1977 the State Department had forced Chile to yield up crucial evidence and their secret agent Townley, on pain of suspension of relations with the United States. These dramatic events followed what the press referred to as an "unrelenting investigation" by the Department of Justice and the Federal Bureau of Investigation, with "quiet but considerable help" from the Central Intelligence Agency. The media gave a heroic recounting of justice done against formidable odds.

There is, however, another story. A story beneath the story. There is a much more problematical version of the Letelier affair to consider after the official version of the crime has been digested. The murders of Orlando Letelier and his aide, Ronni Karpen Moffit, on Washington's elegant Embassy Row in September 1976 turned out to be both a huge symbol of, and at the same time a pathetic footnote to, a much larger and darker American saga.

The picture of a hidden America begins to bleed through the consolatory myth of a crime solved and justice done, the mere murder mystery with exciting political overtones, provided by the official sources and outlets.

Michael Townley—constantly referred to by the media and the prosecution as, at the same time, a "Chilean agent" and a "self-taught electronics expert"—can be seen now as a double agent, a man with two masters.

The FBI, it becomes clear, was as much concerned with protecting its own interests as in solving the case. The Department of Justice, we discover, was involved in containing the conspiracy during the trial with all the stubbornness it displayed in that other trial of Cubans known as the Watergate case.

The State Department and the White House are revealed to be locked in mortal combat with the Central Intelligence Agency, or rather with elements of the covert action section of the agency, and with certain powerful former officers and their "assets" who were purged along with the Nixon regime.

The tragedy that is modern Chile even has a title, CENTAUR, and subtitle, "The Quartered Man," provided by the Department of Defense and the Central Intelligence Agency, the intellectual authors of much that is still concealed about what happened in Chile and in Washington.

The premier analyst of the 1973 coup is the American-Chilean political scientist Dr. Fred Simon Landis. It is his monumental research that allows us to understand, at last, how an entire nation can become disoriented, how the ultimate instrument of torture is psychological, and how the American media became both a knowing and an unwitting spring to the trap that has pinioned, hand and foot, one of the most civilized peoples in the world.

When Dr. Landis returned from Chile after the coup, he delivered a stinging historical judgment to those in America who were interested. Chile, he wrote, was a small country on the outermost borders of the American empire. Chile was known as the Switzerland of Latin America; its national anthem proclaimed it to be "an asylum against oppression." It had taken a neutral position during World Wars I and II, and again during the Cold War. Like Switzerland, it declared a separate peace with violence surrounding it.

Chile was a historical anomaly, a poor country that had nevertheless managed to develop a degree of civilization admired the world over, with the strongest constitutional and democratic traditions in the hemisphere, as well as a large and growing middle class. Again, like Switzerland, it was an asylum for refugees from Hitler, Czechoslovakia, and Latin American dictatorships. While sympathetic to the United States, over 50 per cent of all social classes wanted to stay out of the Cold War. This piece of information comes from a classified USIA opinion poll of "Chilean attitudes towards communism and the Cold War." The USIA analysts stated that the only other place in the world where the same pattern of attitudes existed was Southeast Asia, and they marveled at the perfidy of the Communists who had managed to instill "the soft spot of neutralism in such disparate cultures."

Speaking of Chile in June 1970, Henry Kissinger declared at a meeting of the National Security Council: "I don't see why we should allow a country to go Communist due to the irresponsibility of its own people." In the file on Chile that the CIA gave to *Time* magazine we read: "Fact is that perhaps Chile and Chileans never recognized the true character of the Communist snare."

The CIA tried to warn them. They spent millions in 1970 to warn Chileans what would happen if they voted for Dr. Salvador Allende: There would be tanks in front of the presidential palace, and foreign warships in the port of Valparaiso, their children would be machine-gunned, Congress would be closed, there would be no more free elections. All freedom of expression and press would be stifled, multitudes would starve in the economic crisis, concentration camps would be set up, there would be an end to all civil liberties.

The Chilean people would not listen. And on September 11, 1973, just as the CIA had warned, it all came true.

2 The Assassinations

He made the bread with his hands
he moved the trains
the distances were filled with people
new men grew up
aviaries were created
and because man creates, is fruitful and multiplies
spring came to the market
among the loaves of bread and the doves

Pablo Neruda

RAPHAEL OTERO ECHEVERRIA, within moments of the explosion, knew that he was finished as a diplomat in Washington. Otero (Latin Americans are referred to by their paternal name) and his aides ran to the balcony of the somber gray building that housed Chile's embassy in Washington, D.C. Down the block people were rushing toward the smoking wreckage of an automobile in front of the Romanian Embassy. A young woman stumbled out of the smoke and sank to the curb. A young man rose from where he had been thrown in the street to help her. Sirens wailed. The personnel of five surrounding embassies emptied out to join the thickening circle closing around the crumpled car.

Raphael Otero Echeverria was the public affairs counsel in Washington for the government of Chile. The title was a cover for his actual work for the Dirección de Investigacion Nacional (DINA), the Chilean junta's fearsome secret police. Otero was also a highly paid contract agent for the American Central Intelligence Agency, and had been since the 1960s. Otero had a lifetime of covert intrigue and violence behind him, but the explosion in front of the Chancery had shaken him. The assassination in clear daylight almost in *front* of the Chilean chancery was more than a violation of orders; it was a detonation that might destroy them all.

Orlando Letelier, in death, might bring down the government just as, in life, he had haunted the junta.

On the street the young man, Michael Moffitt, was screaming up at the Chancery, "Fascists! Chilean fascists have done this!" The shocked crowd was growing larger by the minute. The Washington Metropolitan police were attempting to move people back from the twisted steel shell of the Chevrolet so that the paramedics could extricate the driver, Orlando Letelier, from the blasted vehicle. Michael Moffitt helped his wife, Ronni, stumble away from the wreck, then pressed through the onlookers to try to free Letelier, the former foreign minister of Chile. It was then he saw that Letelier's legs had been blown away from his body. Moffitt turned back toward his wife of three months, Ronni Karpen, who was choking to death in her own blood.

In the crowd now were agents of DINA, the FBI, the CIA, along with operatives of all the secret services housed in adjacent embassies. Within minutes, as the ambulance went screaming off, colleagues of Letelier and the Moffitts at the Institute for Policy Studies, began to arrive. A police officer picked up Letelier's heavy briefcase from the gutter and handed it to an inspector.

> *I was born a Chilean*
> *I am a Chilean*
> *I will die a Chilean.*
> *They, the Fascists,*
> *were born traitors*
> *and will be*
> *remembered forever*
> *as Fascist traitors.*

The audience roars its solidarity as Orlando Letelier enunciates his credo to 7,500 people at the Felt Forum of Madison Square Garden. It is September 10, 1976, the eve of the third anniversary of the military coup d'état in Chile.

Standing on the stage of the Forum, Letelier is a symbol of resistance to tyranny. Tall, graceful, handsome, sandy-haired, his words are an eloquent response to General Augusto Pinochet and the junta in Santiago who have just stripped him of his citizenship. The *gorilas*—as they are called by their enemies around the hemisphere—had every reason to take his citizenship away, for he had been literally organizing the whole world against them.

At the age of forty-four, Dr. Letelier was "a man of respect" in Latin American circles. He had been a central figure in the government of Salvador Allende. That government had been democratically elected by the Chilean people in 1970, and it had broadcast its intention of attempting to move the nation "along the *constitutional* road to socialism." Letelier had served in several high posts in that government, including ambassador to the United States.

When the political situation in Chile had become unstable in 1973, the Allende government began to fear a coup or civil war, and Letelier was recalled from Washington in May to assume the post of foreign minister. Then, the morning of September 11, 1973, the leaders of the armed forces violated their constitutional oath and—in the name of "saving the nation from Marxism"—moved on the presidential palace.

Letelier, now minister of defense, was awakened that morning by a telephone call from President Allende asking him to investigate "unauthorized troop movements" across the country. It was as his friend Pablo Neruda had written:

> The long knives are here!
> Holy Mother of us all,
> they cut whatever they please. They fall
> in, to the hilt: everywhere, anywhere.

When Letelier arrived at the defense ministry, he was arrested by his own bodyguards. He was carted off to a concentration camp on Dawson Island, a desolate wilderness at the southern tip of the country, in the area of Tierra del Fuego. There, at world's end, on a rocky island torn by the preternatural winds of the Antarctic regions, the socialist and humanist gentleman from one of Chile's most respected families was starved and worked like a slave. He did not go mad or commit suicide as some others did; he held on to life. There is a passage in Dostoyevsky that answers Letelier's ordeal on that frozen island in the Strait of Magellan: "If I were condemned to live on a rock, chained to a rock in the lashing sea, and all around me was nothing but ice and gales and storm—I would still want to live. Oh, God, just to live, live, *live!*" On Dawson Island the sky freezes. Silently, he vowed justice.

Isabel Letelier was a woman as widely respected as her husband. Within a year she had organized a movement to free Orlando. The government of Venezuela brought constant pressure. American Senators were asked to intervene. And on September 10, 1974, on the eve of the first anniversary of the coup, the junta, attempting to still the worldwide denunciation, released Dr. Letelier.

The Leteliers began the long march home. They settle in Washington, D.C., and start working out of offices in the Institute for Policy Studies. IPS is a group of political scientists and analysts drawn from the universities and the left wing of the Democratic party. Some had held important positions in administrations of John F. Kennedy and Lyndon Johnson and director Morton Halperin had stayed on to work under Henry Kissinger until the war in Vietnam reached in to split even the Pentagon and State Department.

Letelier is a gifted speaker, and soon he is meeting with socialists, communists, guerrilla militant spokesmen, Catholic activists, Christian Democrats, Social Democrats, in short, everyone to the left of General Pinochet and the *gorilas*. He travels widely, all across Europe, organizing opposition to the generals. In February 1976 he speaks to the Dockworkers Federation in Holland. They vote to boycott the handling of any goods bound for Chile and to help raise financial aid for refugees from the terror. Then he convinces the Dutch to cancel a $60 million loan commitment that the generals have been counting on.

Back in Washington, Letelier's influence is growing; there is talk of forming a government in exile. He lunches with powerful men, such as Senators Edward Kennedy, Hubert Humphrey, Richard Clark, and George McGovern. As a former director of the Inter-American Development Bank, Letelier is invited to begin teaching at the School of International Services of American University.

At home there are quiet evenings with friends. The Leteliers prepare delicious continental meals for their colleagues and fellow workers. The Letelier home has become a distinctive experience for well-known American intellectuals like Saul Landau or unknown young aides like Michael Moffitt and Ronni Karpen. Landau sums it up later. "His face, his clothes, his *presencia*, as they say in Spanish. He was the graduate of a military school and held degrees in law and economics. He was, in the British sense of the word, a gentleman."

In May, Ronni Karpen marries Michael Moffitt; Letelier embraces them. At the wedding, a Neruda poem of love and struggle is read. Ronni and Michael believe that Chile will be liberated, that Orlando Letelier will lead that liberation, and that they will be part of the justice and the children of a free Chile. The May of their love and their work has been captured by the poem:

> *I made my contract with the truth*
> *to restore light to the earth.*
>
> *I wished to be like bread.*
> *The struggle never found me wanting.*
>
> *But here I am with what I loved,*
> *with the solitude I lost.*
> *In the shadow of the stone, I do not rest.*
>
> *The sea is working, working in my silence.*

It is Indian Summer in Washington. On September 15 Letelier's car will not start. On that day Isabel Letelier receives another threatening telephone call.

"Are you the wife of Orlando Letelier?"

"Yes."

"No, you are his widow."

On the sixteenth Letelier reports his automobile keys missing from his office.

September 18 is Chilean Independence Day. The Leteliers celebrate. In the large gathering are more than fifty Chilean exiles. Letelier sings and plays the guitar. The food is national and delicious. The "Military Communiques" of the Chilean poet Efraín Barquero make the rounds.

Military Communique No. 1570

It is absolutely forbidden for individuals to call each other "*compañero*," and "manual laborer" should be used instead of the subversive term "worker."

And a magazine article by a junta economist, a protégé of Milton Friedman's "Chicago Boys," is considered, "The Poverty Boom and How to Manage It."

The party ends late. The residential street is quiet. The neighbor on one side is an FBI special agent, on the other a State Department officer.

The plastic explosive has been installed in the Letelier Chevrolet.

Two Chilean friends of Letelier have warned him that they think they have seen someone following him. Letelier brushes the warning aside. Later, others will wonder why some men—Gandhi, the Kennedy brothers, Malcolm X, Martin Luther King, Jr., Letelier—seem to disregard danger and continue to appear in public. Perhaps the reason is that certain people consider it death already to expend their energies in escaping the nightmare world of conspiracy. They reason and gamble that protection and security are to be found, finally, "in public," among the people, that it is in the concealment and secrecy that the conspirators wait, and that if they have to choose between a public life in the shadow of violent death and withdrawal and nothingness, then they will choose life at that price, choosing to fight death in the daylight.

On September 21, the conspiracy moves into the final stage. At 8:45 A.M., a Letelier aide notices an unfamiliar vehicle with Latin men sitting inside it parked near the house. Ten minutes later, Ronni and Michael Moffitt arrive driving Letelier's blue Chevelle, which they had borrowed the evening before. At 9:15 Letelier and the Moffitts drive off into the wet day. Ronni Moffitt sits in the front seat, Michael in the back. The Ford containing the Latins follows.

Letelier takes the usual route: River Road into the District, south on 46th Street through suburban Washington, left on Massachusetts Avenue, and slowly through heavy traffic into Embassy Row. They approach the baroque building that houses the Chilean Chancery, where once Dr. Letelier had resided as his country's ambassador. In those days he had met with Richard Nixon, chatted over dinner with Henry Kissinger. Today it is drizzling; the flag of Chile hangs soaking in the gray morning. The gray Ford is following.

Orlando Letelier's eyes, as always, are on the flag of his country as he drives past the embassy. A hundred yards, a few seconds later, a blast of orange flame shakes Sheridan Circle. The reverberations can be heard blocks away at the White House.

Letelier is free at last.

> *Now they leave me in peace.*
> *Now they grow used to my absence.*
>
> *I am going to close my eyes.*

3 Investigation

Me, I am just someone who knew him
he became for me what he left behind:
streets that he barely knew
houses he would never live in

Pablo Neruda

UNBELIEVABLY, WHAT REMAINS OF ORLANDO LETELIER still displays signs of life. Technically, he is "alive" for a half hour at George Washington University Hospital. Twenty minutes later, Ronni Moffitt is pronounced dead. Michael Moffitt has only a slight head bruise. It was his fate to live to report that he had "heard the sound of water on a hot wire" and seen "a white flash" at the moment of blast.

Intimates of those who are violently destroyed or martyred often feel such fear and guilt that they walk away from the cause for which the loved one was sacrificed. Gratuitous, unearned suffering can simply be too much to bear, so that flesh and blood turns against itself in denial of such radical finitude, and this turning-in is perceived as guilt. But not Isabel Letelier or Michael Moffitt. Before the mangled abstraction of her husband, Isabel Letelier dedicated the rest of her life to justice and failing that, if the sparks of revolution were extinguished altogether, revenge. The revenge of history.

For history, too, Michael Moffitt began to compose out of his whirling thoughts and the scream of his intact viscera a statement of sanity, so that the unspeakable could be linked through his anguish to the record of history.

The Chilean experience was a unique experiment, or "model" as the academicians phrase it. One of the few Third World countries with any semblance of constitutional rule, Chile under President Allende tried to establish socialism by peaceful means . . . .

Under President Allende, Chile had perhaps the most tolerant political system in the world. Allende tolerated the most savage and libelous attacks in the media and elsewhere—far less drove Nixon to move on his enemies—almost to the point of being politically naive . . . .

But the entire Chilean political tradition has been systematically destroyed in the three years since the coup. Trade unions, unsympathetic newspapers and magazines, academic freedom and, most importantly, thousands of lives and hopes have been extinguished by the junta and its henchmen . . . .

My wife and I loved Orlando Letelier because, like him, we believed that the abominable conditions in which the majority of the human race lives (especially, but not exclusively, in the Third World) are morally outrageous and politically insane. The struggle against these conditions is the legacy President Allende bequeathed to the world. Orlando Letelier and my wife accepted this legacy, and now they are dead. Millions of people will never forget Allende or them.

Michael Moffitt,
September 22, 1976

Michael Moffitt feared a "quashed" political investigation, feared that he might never learn whether the order to kill came from Santiago or the embassy in Washington. He might have added Langley, Virginia, to the names of death and still not have exhausted the options.

The day after the murders, a rally was held in Dupont Circle, near the Institute for Policy Studies. At the gathering, rage and grief are the dominant tones. At the edges of the crowd, agents from major American and foreign intelligence agencies swap pictures and take notes; these services include SAVAK, DINA, KCIA, FBI, the Washington Police, Secret Service, CIA.

"The government of Chile repudiates this outrageous act of terrorism." Down the avenue, Chilean Ambassador Manuel Trucco is again denying, in the most aggrieved tones, that his country has any connection to the murders. Ambassador Trucco appears glassy-eyed to observers, as if he had been drinking.

But in a wooden addition deeper inside the embassy grounds, two Americans and three Chileans are sitting around a table. The walls, from floor to ceiling, are lined with shelves of propaganda.

In this room is an immense anti-Communist library—volumes and studies provided by American friends of the Chilean junta. The secret agents of the two countries are busy at work on a "fact sheet" on the death. Xerox copies of papers belonging to Dr. Letelier are shuffled and studied.

The funeral rites are held four days later, on September 26. In clear autumn weather several thousand people pour through Sheridan Circle to St. Matthew's Cathedral for the requiem mass. Many mourners carry large photographs of Dr. Letelier and Ronni Moffitt, her youth and vivacity frozen on the placards, his picture brooding, framed by the statement of two weeks before, "I was born a Chilean . . . I will die a Chilean." Large banners at the rear of the march denounce fascism. Working together along the line of march, with cameras, are a complement of Chilean secret agents supported by agents of the Reverend Sun Myung Moon, who has been closely tied to the Korean Central Intelligence Agency.

"Orlando Lives in the Heart of the People," the banner reads. Isabel Letelier and Michael Moffitt are each carrying a single red rose. People lay their flowers down at the curb where the Chevrolet exploded. Hortencia Allende, the widow of the slain president, walks at the front with Mrs. Letelier. The scene looks to be more Santiago than Washington.

Down the avenue, in the Chilean Embassy, Raphael Otero's meeting of South and North American agents goes on without letup.

The Federal Bureau of Investigation has taken over formal jurisdiction from the Washington police and descended on the Institute for Policy Studies. IPS is suing the FBI and others for a series of constitutional violations over the years (including wiretapping and planted informants, fifty-two of them over a six-year period), but Special Agent L. Carter Cornick assures the dissident intellectuals, "We're on the same side in this one." Cornick comes from a Virginia family that, he says, considered Eleanor Roosevelt a Communist.

The investigation begins. While the FBI is quizzing IPS fellows and staff—about a jealous husband or a rejected mistress—the press produces the first results of their investigative journalism.

"Leftists Being Considered in Murder" and "Martyr Theory Probed" banners the *Washington Star*. The *Washington Post* announces that the Central Intelligence Agency was "cooperating" with the investigation and that Director George Bush was meeting with J. Stanley Pottinger from the Department of Justice. *Newsweek's* Periscope column is quite specific, saying that the CIA "has concluded that the Chilean secret police were not involved in the death of Orlando Letelier....The Agency reached its decision because the bomb was too crude to be the work of experts and because the murder, coming while Chile's rulers were wooing U.S. support, could only damage the Santiago regime."

The FBI is avoiding the basic test of Occam's razor: to seek first the simplest sufficient explanation. Instead of exploring the murderers' possible connections to DINA, the Chilean secret police, the FBI relentlessly searches for a jealous mistress. But the bomb in Letelier's Chevrolet is as clear a sign of DINA, a Letelier colleague writes, as a canary in the mouth of a dead informer is a calling card of the Mafia.

Talk like this stings the Ford administration. An unnamed administration official tells the *Washington Post* that the statements of moral outrage made by Senator Kennedy and others are "pretty despicable really. Well, great, I wish they had proof—I wish to hell they'd come down here and show us."

By October 7, 1976, the Ford administration was beginning to sense a potential political nightmare. Seventy-three persons were killed when a Cubana DC-8 en route from Barbados to Cuba blew up. The wreckage plunged into the sea carrying Cuban athletes and Guyanese doctors as well as other passengers. For ten days there was silence. Then Fidel Castro charged CIA responsibility and threatened to cancel a 1973 anti-hijacking agreement with the United States. On the seventeenth, the *New York Times* published a fateful headline: "U.S. Ties Cuban Exiles to Jet Blasts."

Authorities in Trinidad and Venezuela had arrested seven men and were referring to them as "former" Cuban CIA operatives. One of those being detained in Caracas was Orlando Bosch, a notorious anti-Castro terrorist. No one from the major American media or the Department of Justice went near Bosch. Blake Fleet-wood, a free-lance journalist did, and Bosch told him, at once, the names of the Cuban men from New Jersey who, he said, were involved in the Letelier case.

By October 20, the Justice Department had hard evidence that Cuban exiles were implicated in the Washington murders as well as other terrorist actions "in the United States, Venezuela, Trini-dad, Barbados, Guyana, Panama, and Colombia," according to the *Times.* In the fourth paragraph of its story, the *Times* included the Letelier case in the inventory of a "vast" number of unspecified exile crimes.

Within a month of the Letelier murder Venezuelan authorities had passed on to Eugene Propper, the United States Attorney in charge of the investigation, the names of Guillermo and Ignacio Novo, of New Jersey, as two of the Letelier killers.

After the presidential inauguration in January 1977, a State De-partment file containing the photographs of the Chilean planners of the Letelier murder, which had been missing, suddenly reap-peared, and the final proof, the last missing evidence, was in, although completing the legal case would take another two and a half years.

In July 1976, two months before the Letelier-Moffit murders, the American ambassador to Paraguay, George Landau, received a message from a high Paraguayan official urging him to expedite United States visas for two Chileans bearing Paraguayan passports who were on their way to North America. Landau, made sus-picious by the urgency of the message, began to look into the matter only after first granting the visas. The visa applications contained the names *and* photos of two Chilean army officers: Juan Williams Rose and Alejandro Romeral Jara. For unexplained rea-sons, Landau decided to revoke the visas. Then he transmitted to Washington the pictures of Williams and Romeral, accompanied by a warning of some sort regarding the two Chileans.

The photographs and warning were fed in the government's "watch list." They were not seen again until the winter of 1977. By then the FBI had learned the names of the two men, or rather the aliases of the two DINA agents, and that they had come to the States in 1976 using a second set of fake passports.

By February 1978 official documents known as letters rogatory had been publicly handed to the junta. These documents represented a request, at the highest level, for Chilean co-operation in a matter of international import.

For ten days the junta remained silent. Then, on March 2, 1978, someone leaked the Williams and Romeral photographs to the *Washington Star*. On March 3, the photographs of the two Chileans were wired around the world as part of a major story. Two days later, the junta's wall of silence disintegrated.Chile's largest newspaper, *El Mercurio*, identified Williams as a North American named Michael Vernon Townley, a thirty five-year-old native of Iowa who had been living in Chile for the past twenty years. That same week Romeral was revealed to be Armando Fernández Larios, a captain of the Chilean Army. By March 10, General Pinochet was announcing that Chile was the victim of still another diabolical "Communist campaign."

In America, Propper and the FBI were accorded full credit for their tireless investigation, and in a number of stories and editorials the Central Intelligence Agency, too, was mentioned as having played a quiet but important role in the case. Once again, as in the time of Watergate, "the system was working."

El Mercurio, stressing that Michael V. Townley was a *North* American, stated that he had been a member of a right-wing extremist group known as *Patria y Libertad*, Fatherland and Freedom, before the 1973 coup.

On March 11 General Pinochet vowed co-operation with the investigation, and stated that the junta would soon appoint a special judge in the Letelier matter.

Then, on March 22, General Juan Manuel Contreras Sepulveda, the man who had headed DINA at the time of the Letelier murder, quit "voluntarily." On the same day, the junta's special investigator for the Letelier case resigned, stating that he had no jurisdiction over the armed forces. Two days later, Townley's wife, Mariana Callejas, was also indentified by *El Mercurio* as having been a member of the extremist *Patria y Libertad* and of

DINA; the newspaper went on to state that Townley had "links to the CIA."

On the streets of Santiago, where U.S. Attorney Propper and Special Agents Carter Cornick and Robert Scherrer have gone to press the issue, crowds surround them to offer information about Townley and support for the investigation.

Near the end of March, Special Agents Cornick and Scherrer were at breakfast when an emergency call from the American Embassy directed them to go immediately to the Santiago airport; they were told not to pack. On the landing field an unmarked automobile of the Chilean secret police sped up to disgorge Michael Vernon Townley in handcuffs, ready for extradition to stand trial in the United States. The lanky, mustached American's last words on Chilean soil were, "I have full confidence in Chilean justice."

During April it became clear that someone was talking. On the fourteenth, Guillermo Novo and Alvin Ross were arrested in Miami for violation of probation in other cases, such as a 1969 plot to destroy the Cuban consulate in Montreal. By the sixteenth, both men had been identified as members of the Cuban Nationalist Movement, an extremist Cuban exile group whose headquarters in New Jersey contained explosive devices similar to those used in the Letelier-Moffitt murders.

On May 5, 1978, the government charged three more Cuban exiles with conspiracy to murder Orlando Letelier: Ignacio Novo, José ("Pool of Blood") Suárez, and Virgilio Paz. Suárez and Paz could not be found.

The *New York Times* quoted sources as saying that Townley had turned state's evidence and implicated seven Cuban and three Chileans. The *Miami Herald* reported that the FBI had found, in Alvin Ross's car, the electronic beeper that had been used to detonate the bomb. From London, in June, *Reuters* quoted the visiting Mariana Callejas de Townley as saying over BBC that Townley had killed under orders.

A major break followed on June 19. Paraguay's chief of military intelligence provided American authorities with sworn documentary evidence of efforts by DINA chief Contreras to obtain false passports for Townley and his fellow agent Armando Fernandez Larios prior to the murder in 1976. Then on August 2, 1978, a Washington grand jury indicted General Juan Manual Contrera Sepulveda and two subordinates, Pedro Espinoza Bravo and Fernández Larios, for murdering Orlando Letelier on Embassy Row, "by blowing him up with a bomb."

On September 21 1978, the second anniversary of the murders, the United States formally requested the extradition of DINA men Contreras, Espinoza, and Fernández. Ambassador George Landau delivered a satchel of four hundred pages of supporting evidence to junta officials who, in turn, referred it to the Chilean Supreme Court for final disposition. In the interim, the three former DINA officers were placed under "house arrest" in a military hospital.

In the United States, the attorneys began to prepare for trial. In Chile, Contreras's line, or alibi, transmitted by journalists, was becoming quite firm: Michael Vernon Townley was an operative of the Central Intelligence Agency. There was not a scintilla of proof of CIA involvement, shot back Prosecutor Propper.

The Cubans said nothing.

4 Trial

I keep seeing him, and every day I wait for him,
I see him in his grave and resurrected

Pablo Neruda

ON JANUARY 9, 1979, trained police dogs were deployed throughout the District of Columbia federal courthouse to sniff out any
explosives that might have been planted. Security was the heaviest
in Washington's history. Prosecutor Eugene Propper and District
Judge Barrington Parker were surrounded by Secret Service
agents day and night, for both had received death threats. Jury
selection was the longest since the Watergate trials.

Of the five Cubans indicted, only three were in court: Alvin
Ross, Guillermo Novo, and Ignacio Novo. The latter faced lesser
charges of harboring and false swearing, so Ross and Guillermo
Novo would have to absorb the wrath of the government, standing
as symbols of all the other Cubans and Chileans who could not be
found.

Representing the Cubans were Paul Goldberger and Lawrence
Dubin. Their defense was straightforward and upsetting to almost
everyone: "It is a horrible and monstrous thought that the CIA was
responsible for a murder on the streets of Washington, D.C., but
it will be proved." The all-black jury of seven men and five women
listened soberly to charges that seemed to imply that the thieves
and the murderers had fallen out. They must have wondered why a
CIA involvment, if there was one, would somehow exculpate the
Cubans. The defense then demanded of the jury that they "keep
asking themselves why the government of Chile let Townley return to the U.S. That question is something the [U.S.] government will *never* be able to answer."

On January 11, the second day of trial, the covert operations
branch of the CIA stated that it had once "requested preliminary

security approval" to use the services of Michael Townley. Robert W. Gambino, the agency's director of security, testifying for the prosecution, swore in a series of affidavits that the records did not show whether the American's services had ever been employed.

On January 18 Michael Townley began his testimony for the government in an articulate monotone. "The mission was the elimination, the killing, the assassination of Orlando Letelier . . .I was to kill him, trying to make it look like an accidental death or suicide . . . ." In the summer of 1976, he testified, his voice low but clear, his DINA superior, Colonel Espinoza, had told him that his "next assignment was the assassination of Mr. Letelier." He said he had arrived in the United States on September 7, 1976, and made contact with the Cubans.

The next day was another setback for the defense. The judge ruled that Townley did not have to testify about other assassination plots against Chileans in Argentina and Rome. Chief defense counsel Paul Goldberger, "Don't we have the right to show that Mr. Townley was assassinating people all over the world?" Judge Parker replied, with a widely quoted retort, "Mr. Townley isn't the person you want to sit next to you at a Sunday worship services, but . . . ." Townley, for his part, swore that the plot did not reach up to Contreras's superior, General Pinochet. Did *not*, he repeated.

During his third day on the stand, Townley spoke softly about the target of the plot. "He was a soldier and I was a soldier. In his own way, with his own party, with his own actions, he was carrying on a battle against the government of Chile"—thus the "self-taught electronics expert," as he was now known in the press, as if the adjective had become formal and Homeric.

"Mr. Townley, do you have regrets about killing Mr. Letelier?"

"No sir. The person accompanying him, yes, very much so, sir."

Later in the day, Townley apologized to the judge for repeatedly contradicting his earlier statements at preliminary hearings.

The Cubans had not taken the stand in their own behalf to accuse the CIA of doing the deed. Richard Helms had been subpoenaed but had chosen not to appear. The defense pled with the judge to issue a bench warrant to delay the trial one day—their entire defense of CIA provocation might hang on Helms's appearance. It had been Judge Parker before whom Helms had previously appeared, to be given a suspended sentence for perjury (for lying about United States involvement in Chile). Surely the Judge recalled Helms posing for the press in front of the court house, crowing, "I wear this conviction as a badge of honor." In vain, Judge Parker agreed with the prosecutor: they could not wait for Mr. Helms. The case went to the jury the next day.

On February 14 the jury found the Cubans guilty as charged. Relatives and friends sobbed and cursed the black jurors. Twenty U.S. marshalls circulated through the tense courtroom. The defendants were deadpan, then as they walked out Ross shouted, "*Viva Cuba!*"

Subsequently, Ross and Guillermo Novo were meted out life sentences, and Ignacio Novo was given eight years for concealing evidence. "Nigger! Black son of a bitch!" the Cuban contingent erupted with imprecations and shouts at Judge Parker. Townley's sentence was temporarily held in abeyance.

On October 2, 1979, for the third time, the Chilean Supreme Court rejected the U.S. extradition requests for Contreras, Fernández, and Espinoza, the Chileans whom Townley had implicated in the plot. Thus on October 3, 1979, the United States recalled its ambassador from Santiago.

The prosecution and the FBI had exposed and brought to justice an international network of right-wing terrorists. Or at least some of them. Blood had been shed on the streets of America's capital city; and in the name of Human Rights, America had spoken through its judicial system.

And Orlando Letelier was now, partly, abstracted into the judicial process. But for his family and colleagues, as they spoke to the media, he was not forgotten. It was not over. As for his enemies, they would someday, "have to forget [him] forcibly," in Pablo Neruda's words.

Only two questions had been overlooked: Who was Michael Townley? And, finally, to whom did he answer for his murderous actions?

5 The Jackal: Michael Vernon Townley

I knew that man and while I could
while I still had eyes in my head
and voice in my mouth
I looked for him among the tombs, and told him
grabbing his arm before it became dust
"All will go, you alone will remain!"

Pablo Neruda

ANY DOSSIER ON THE JACKAL, Michael Vernon Townley, will contain columns of sanitized, official facts. Quite unremarkable, an historian might say—a typical Cold War political sociopath. But the truth about Michael Townley (also known as "Michael Townley Welch," "John Younger" or "Yeater" or "Cooper," "Kenneth William Enyart," "Andreas Wilson," "Juan Williams Rose," "Andres Brooks," "Hans P. Silva," and many others) makes of him an archetype of Cold War America. His wife called him "a cog in a gigantic wheel"; and after Townley was arrested, she visited him in an American prison to tell him that he was "a talking machine" who had to co-operate with the government. Finally, Americans were encouraged to think of him as a "self-taught electronics expert," according to the newspaper of record, the *New York Times*.

Somehow, linguistically, a "self-taught" assassin like Townley is generically descended from a "lone assassin" like Lee Harvey Oswald. Men of such profound nonentity that the media must always include their middle names or an adjectival identification such as "self-taught" is made to seem to be reflexive, self-generating aberrations, *sui generis*, and so none of our responsibility.

At the time of his arrest for arranging the Letelier-Moffitt murders, Michael Townley's rank in DINA, the Chilean secret police organization, was equivalent to that of a lieutenant colonel.

By 1976, he had carried out perhaps fifteen political executions. He was an assassin of "world class." Yet he was nothing. "A talking machine," his wife called him. To the CIA and DINA he was a killing machine.

Tall, fair-haired, and blue-eyed, with a John Wayne or James Bond movie for a mind, Townley's name was legion. He was one of a crop of secret warriors: planted in the fertilized fields of World War II, harvested in the 1950s, consumed in Vietnam and Chile.

The future assassin was born into a typical upper-middle-class family in the middle of World War II in Waterloo, Iowa. The father, Vernon Townley, was an aggressive, constantly moving businessman. The mother, from the Welch family of Waterloo, is said by those who know her to be warm and concerned.

By 1957 the family had been transferred to Chile, and the hard-driving Vernon Townley had become head of Ford Motor Company operations in Santiago. Michael, aged fourteen, was an active member of a Methodist youth group in the American community. During this period, the Reverend Larry Jackson reports, Michael "was an intense, idealistic, sensitive boy." The family of a Ford executive could live very well, indeed, in Chile in 1957. The Townleys had servants, and there was an exclusive school for Michael, St. George's High School, run by the Episcopal order of the Holy Cross. But the boy was a dreamer and had difficulty concentrating on the demanding curriculum and on Spanish.

Michael was, the minister remembers; "An awkward, appealing, alienated youth, yearning for affection and a meaningful place in the world. With a gentle nurturing he could have become a healer, a builder, a responsible citizen."

Mr. Jackson knew the young Mike Townley and, of equal importance, he thought he knew what America was becoming, what it might do to its children.

"The institutions of good government have traditionally nurtured and educated and served the people by promoting the rule of law. When governments ignore the rule of law, they foster violence and the corruption of the young."

The Townleys were socializing members of the relatively affluent American community of Santiago, and Michael's father was prominent in circles that included the international diplomatic set. One family friend was a deputy from the American Embassy;

another was an English-language journalist-publisher: both were covert operatives of the Central Intelligence Agency.

In the 1950s, while representing Ford in the Philippines, the senior Townley had worked with remnants of Edward Lansdale's CIA team, so the Townleys were an "intelligence family," as it is put in the trade.

The adolescent boy was increasingly at odds with his dominating father. By 1960 Michael had dropped out of school and was carrying on an affair with a woman ten years his senior. The Townley home was torn. Michael was "too young," according to his mother, and "crazy," according to his father. This woman, Mariana Callejas, was a left-winger, and a woman with a past. Besides being a divorcee and a mother and so much older than their son, Callejas was also associated with a mixed crowd that included many from the fringes of the left.

As this family crisis was building, Chilean politics was turning extremely volatile. The presidential contest of 1958 was among Jorge Alessandri, the candidate of the traditional Right; Dr. Salvador Allende, the leader of the Left coalition; and Eduardo Frei, the head of the new Christian Democratic party, which was struggling for control of the Center. When the veteran senator, Allende, came within a few points of winning the election from Alessandri, the United States, like the American community in Santiago, was stunned. The Townley family and their friends had been involved in raising funds for conservatives as well as for the Christian Democrats. The English language press was especially active, as was the Ford Motor Company. Both were co-operating with the Central Intelligence Agency. Vernon Townley's relationship with CIA was a natural expression or extension of a mutuality of deeply held financial, patriotic, and religious beliefs.

The family's personal problems seemed to center on the older woman, Mariana Callejas. Callejas was an occasionally published newpaper and magazine writer with two children, and two marriages behind her. Townley had met her through another writer and a photographer, both of whom were "stringers" or contract agents for the CIA station in Santiago.

Before he was twenty, Michael had broken with his father to marry the dark and vivacious Chilean. He looked so much the American adolescent, and perhaps that is why, to compensate, he began to adopt a serious and even austere air. To the family and some of their friends the youth had "gone native." However, Santiago is a great and cosmopolitan city, and the conservatively suited Michael and his chic wife were elegant members of the younger boulevard coterie of journalists and second-level management executives on the make.

Callejas was born in the small town of Ropel. As an adolescent, she, too, had broken with her father, a local justice of peace. She dropped out of college ("I am an Aries," she would say later, by way of mystification). In defiance of her father's militant anti-Communist sensibilities, she had associated herself with student socialist groups, for a brief interlude attending meetings and passing out literature on the streets. By the age seventeen, she was married.

Her second husband was a Jew, and for a while she had lived on a kibbutz in Israel with him. There had been two children by that marriage.

In the early fifties, Callejas returned to Chile. Bored and impatient with the socialists, she began a lifelong flirtation with the secret police. At first, as an *oreja*, an "ear," an informer, and later as an agent she was to become an important operative for several secret services. Whether her stay in Israel was a nonpolitical interlude is unclear, but by 1960 she was working for Chilean military intelligence. For the first time she was on friendly terms with her father, and soon young Michael came to admire the stern judge. Clearly, Callejas maintained her combined bourgeois-leftist political image both then and, indeed, until 1978 among a rather large number of people in several parts of the country.

As a presentable, bilingual American, Michael was able to find a salesman's position with Investors Overseas Services, the international swindle founded by Bernard Cornfeld that Robert Vesco was to bring to a criminal apotheosis during the Nixon years. There were many friends for such an interesting couple, including a few of the Americans Michael had first met in his father's house.

By 1964, Townley and Callejas (who retained her maiden name, as is the custom in Latin America) had two children and a comfortable life style. They also had a Swiss bank account and a double life. Michael Vernon Townley now called himself Michael Townley Welch, using his mother's maiden name in the Latin fashion. It was under this name, Welch, that Townley was first entered onto the "nonexistent" contract agent rolls of the Central Intelligence Agency.

In the election of 1964 the CIA made one of its great efforts in Chile. Senator Salvador Allende had come to the brink of power in 1958. To stop the Left, it was decided in Langley, the Christian Democrats under Eduardo Frei would have to co-opt, somehow, Chile's increasingly militant proletariat.

Although Chilean law prohibited electoral propaganda within forty-eight hours of an election, the night before the 1964 election a recorded message was broadcast from an unlikely CIA asset, Fidel Castro's sister, Juana. She warned Chileans of the dangers of voting for Allende: "Like Fidel Castro, Che Guevara, and Nikita Khrushchev, Allende only follows the line established by the Communist party. If the Reds win in Chile, no type of religious activity will be possible. The new Gods will be Marx, Lenin, and the Communist party."

Castro's sister had been brought into the campaign by the Central Intelligence Agency. The agency was operating through Agencia Orbe Latino-Americano news service, a hemisphere-wide propaganda center emanating from the CIA station in Santiago. Their subject matter featured Juana Castro and Isabel Siero Pérez of the International Federation of Women Lawyers, a CIA front. Meanwhile, the CIA was pouring millions of dollars into Chile in support of Frei and the Christian Democrats. This money, when exchanged on the black market, increased phenomenally, eventually reaching roughly $20 million. The same per capita investment in an American election would have amounted to some *$400 million!*

Years later, in 1973, the *Washington Post* would quote a high American intelligence source as saying that the United States intervention in the 1964 election "was blatant and almost obscene." The *Post* detailed how the CIA had funneled "$20 million into the country using both the Agency for International Development (AID) and State Department as conduits." The *Post* did not mention the Peace Corps, which, for a time, Michael Townley also used as cover.

The Peace Corps had entered Latin America as the "person-to-person" face of the Alliance for Progress. Working out of the U.S. Embassy in Santiago was Nathaniel Davis, the first head of the Peace Corps in Chile. (He would return as ambassador before the September 1973 coup.) Under the skillfull guidance of Davis, many of the youthful volunteers headed straight for the neighborhoods housing the poorest sectors of the Chilean working class and the unemployed.

Over all this, in 1965, presided Richard Helms, chief of the Clandestine Services of the Central Intelligence Agency. One of his important aides was a man who had met Townley as a youth, through the family.

Traditionally, certain universities and so-called think-tanks have performed research for different branches of the American intelligence community. For example, RAND for the Air Force, the political science department at MIT for the CIA, and American University for the Army.

Sometime during the sixties, the Army entered into another research contract with American University. It would be called Camelot. In the Kennedy era, the word had stood for bright and shining promise, but now Project Camelot would stand for a blueprint for mass manipulation unrivaled since the era of Goebbels's Germany. Not since the military and the academy combined to produce the atomic bomb had there been such a profound marriage of power and science.

In subsequent explanation of the project, Dr. Theodore Vallence, director of the Army's Special Operations Research office said: "In response to a series of urgent requests for rapidly produced information on which to base psychological operations in Vietnam, we have developed several products. These include . . . a method of using word associations to determine culture-specific meanings and values . . . and descriptive materials about the application of principles of persuasion in foreign cultures . . . . This research effort, which is shared by other government agencies, may be subdivided into psychological operations: this research studies methods of communicating with selected groups of foreign nationals through the use of propaganda and other actions in order to influence their opinions, attitudes and behavior in ways that favor the accomplishment of the Army's combat mission."

Dr. Vallence's words do not explain all the specifics, but the basic idea behind the project is clear. In the transition from underdevelopment to modernity there lies a dangerous collapse of traditional institutions and the spread of what Walt Rostow called "cancer communism." So the plan was to send American social scientists around the globe with questionnaires to discover the natives' attitudes toward communism: their tape recorders would act to detect the cancerous red menace.

In its early phase, Project Camelot involved an in-depth study of one country—Chile. In phase four an attempt would be made to validate the results of earlier stages by applying them to another, unspecified, country. However, the project did not get any further than Chile: its cover was blown by leftist Chilean newpapers. This exposure, by itself, would not have created an insuperable obstacle, but the attitude of the United States State Department did: it chose to support the allegations publicly. As subsequent congressional hearings revealed, the State Department regarded the project as an intrusion by the Army into the conduct of foreign policy. In the resulting furor, Project Camelot was officially cancelled; in fact, it simply went underground, supervision shifting directly to the CIA.

Then the Pentagon's cover was blown.

Only by chance had the origins of Camelot come to light. In 1965 Johan Galtung, a Norwegian professor who was teaching in Santiago at the time, refused to participate when he learned that Camelot was an Army, not an academic, project. When Galtung denounced the deception, the case became a *cause célèbre* in the Chilean press and Congress.

After Camelot was exposed, a period of discretion followed. The ranks of sociologists and students departed for the States. The pace of intrigue slowed. In the wake of the Pentagon debacle, the CIA had fallen back on the Christian Democratic parties of Chile and West Germany to fund its research projects.

The CIA uses two polling organizations for intelligence gathering abroad, both based in Princeton, N.J. The first, the Research Council, is a CIA "proprietary" (that is, a company receiving 100 per cent of its income from the CIA). The Council, founded by Hadley Cantril and directed by Lloyd Free, was a subcontractor for Gallup. The other organization used by CIA, specifically in Chile, was Gallup itself and its Chilean affiliate, the *Instituto de Opinion Publica*. From 1970 to the present this organization has issued a steady stream of fabricated polls.

In its intelligence-gathering aspect, Gallup conducted bimonthly public opinion polls in thirty towns across Chile. These polls were accurate and operated within 0.5 percent error. The CIA funded these polls to secure an early warning of the spread of "Communist and neutralist" attitudes and to test the effectiveness of CIA propaganda in specific localities. Most of this information was kept secret. In its public aspect, bogus polls have been issued by Gallup in Chile at the CIA's convenience during the Allende period and the junta's since.

In 1967, the Townleys were in trouble. Michael was restless and bored. Investors Overseas was having legal troubles, and Townley's commissions had dwindled to nothing. Except for the mechanical work of picking up and delivering polls, there was almost no income from the Americans. Mariana was worried by her husband's brooding withdrawal.

Three weeks later, Callejas was able to tell Michael about an exciting offer. The Townley family was to move to Miami. Michael was to study electronics and secret warfare skills with a Cuban exile group that would be in charge of their careers in Miami. Their sponsor, they were told, was the Secret Army Organization (SAO). Its chief was a flamboyant soldier of fortune named Frank Sturgis.

Frank Fiorini, alias Frank Sturgis, is first discovered in the revolutionary bands of Fidel Castro. Except that he is *not* a Cuban, he is not a revolutionary; he is a mercenary working for American intelligence. Later, in 1971, Sturgis would join Howard Hunt—with whom he shared the alias "Edward Hamilton"—in a plan to assassinate General Omar Torrijos of Panama, which was cancelled at the last moment by the White House. Later, the world came to know them as two of the Watergate "plumbers."

But in 1967 and 1968, when Sturgis was running Townley and Callejas, he impressed Michael as "a real man," in the phrase reported by Mariana.

In Miami, settled in the Cuban community, Townley began an intensive study of electronics and explosives under the tutelage of several former CIA men who were in the process of taking over an electronics operation in the Fort Lauderdale area. Townley had real aptitude, and life in Miami's little Havana was busy and gratifying. He especially enjoyed learning how to plant plastic explosives inside automobiles. Once he and a man named Aldo Vera Serafin and another SAO man rigged a car to explode using a small repair shop as their cover. He was never told to whom the fatal vehicle belonged.

The Townley children were securely in school by 1967, and Callejas was free for more challenging assignments than merely composing or translating intelligence propaganda handouts. Just after 1968 began, Sturgis informed the Townleys that they were to infiltrate dissident and antiwar groups.

By the time of the convention that summer, Callejas had infiltrated the McCarthy campaign and become very close to important Florida organizers in the "Movement." She was thus able to steal documents all during the presidential campaign. At the same time, she managed to infiltrate Cesar Chavez's Farm Workers Union.

Townley, posing as a militant on local Florida campuses, was instructed by Sturgis to "stay in place." The deception was invigorating to the now long-haired amateur spy, but there was no real action until Townley, as part of an SAO street cadre, "kicked some ass" during outbreaks of violence while the GOP was busy nominating the "new Richard Nixon."

Then, in 1969, Sturgis suddenly disappeared. The Townleys did not know the SAO had managed to get itself discovered, compromised, and disbanded. Callejas was still enjoying auditing classes at the University of Miami, but Townley was lost again, wandering, depressed.

On several occasions he wandered into the Miami station of the CIA to offer his services in Chile, where presidential electioneering was beginning to galvanize the country. It appears that the second time Townley walked into the Miami CIA office, a message was sent to Langley suggesting that he be taken on in an "operational capacity." The record indicates that the Latin American department instructed Miami to have no further contact with Townley. This seems to have stemmed from a decision made high up in the Western Hemisphere Division at Langley. One of the officers in charge of covert action for Latin America (who had met Townley and knew his family) is said to have argued that if the Townleys were needed in Chile for covert operations it would be far better to run them through a "deniable cut-out," or third party, as *contract* agents.

Using the alias "Kenneth W. Enyart," Townley presented a forged driver's license and birth certificate to a Florida passport window listing his destination as South America.

Michael Vernon Townley Welch was invisible to the powers that be in Washington (except for an old acquaintance of the family at CIA, and even he was only vaguely aware of the young American's existence at any given time that summer). Townley was now highly trained Cold War cannon fodder for those grand CIA designs of secret war known at Langley as Plan Centaur. Clandestine meetings, codes, drops, secrets—Mike had found his *métier* and his secret identity at last. His parents would hardly recognize him now, lean as a blue-eyed wolf.

Townley is a epiphenomenon of world war, his "psychology" a function of his cultural existence. The son of a Ford Motor Company executive and international banker and CIA "asset", his ideology, like his activism, was an inheritance.

The "awkward boy" whom Reverend Jackson had known had been a tiny blurred figure under the huge gray sky of Operation Camelot. Under the war clouds of the CIA's Plan Centaur his shadow would lengthen halfway across the world. He was, in Neruda's words, "a blue-eyed disaster."

Orlando Letelier was still in his twenties when the Townley family arrived in Chile in 1957. His career was perhaps the most brilliant of his generation. As a student leader he had been outstanding at sports and in amateur theatricals. Joining him in the theatre was his future wife Isabel. The handsome couple was admired, and a great future was predicted for them.

It came true. By the mid-1950s, Orlando was recognized a national expert in the economics and international law of copper extraction, ownership, and trade. By the 1958 election, the future leader was studying and attending meetings for the government of Chile in London, Paris, Berlin, Rome, Geneva. His star was ascendant. People said that if he wasn't a socialist he might even rise to the presidency. Then, when the Allende ticket barely missed coming to power in 1958, it became clear that Orlando Letelier would someday, in the seventies or eighties, stand for the presidency.

Letelier's father, a graphic artist and publisher, had exposed his son to literature and the world of journalism. This may have bolstered the youthful doctor of economy and law in the writing of "The Political Basis for Development of Copper," a classic monograph which would later become the flag of the Allende coalition in its 1970-73 negotiations with Anaconda and Kennecott and, by adaptation, with ITT Corporation.

During these years, into the 1960s, Orlando and Isabel and their young children traveled to New York and Washington. They were seldom in Santiago. They would not have known the Townley family. They probably never even glimpsed the lanky, wide-eyed boy who had been born and bred to destroy them.

6 David Atlee Phillips: "The Other Man"

But—we already paid for our passage in this world
so, why—why don't they leave us sit down and eat?
We want to look at the clouds,
we want to sun ourselves and smell the salt air
frankly, we are not trying to be a bother,
it is very simple: we too are passengers

Pablo Neruda

DAVID ATLEE PHILLIPS WAS A SUPERAGENT, a tough link in the Old Boy network of the Central Intelligence Agency's Clandestine Services. In September 1970 he was ordered by the Director of Central Intelligence (DCI) to take charge of a special Chile task force: Track I (which would later become Track II, Plan September, Centaur, Djakarta, and by 1973, Plan Z).

David Phillips, the rugged cold warrior, was considered by old hands at Langley to be a "deception" or false propaganda genius. But he was, he says, quite baffled to learn that the Chile task force was to be kept a secret not only from the embassy in Santiago and the State Department, and of course, the Congress, but from almost all of the agency's own Western Hemisphere Division! The orders to the CIA and Phillips were to "prevent Salvador Allende from assuming the presidency of Chile." The order, he was told, came directly from President Richard Nixon through National Security Advisor Henry Kissinger to DCI Richard Helms. Even Secretary of State William Rogers was to be excluded from the operation. Since Allende's election was to be ratified by the Chilean Congress on October 24, Phillips knew he had been asked to launch a coup.

He would now eat and sleep inside the massive spy sanctuary at Langley as the tension built. Phillips was a man at the fulcrum of a lever reaching from the Oval Office to Santiago. He was the conductor and conduit for political assassination and sabotage. A Frankenstein monster—the current of power passed, raw, through his nervous system to be translated into detailed and surgical illegal operations in Chile. He was destined to be burnt out by the unremitting voltage emanating from the White House for the next three years.

What kind of man is a David Phillips? Behind the rugged, urbane exterior of the World War II hero is a classic CIA clandestine operator. Listen to what he writes about himself:

The games were exciting for me, as so much of the substance of the scenario had mnemonic roots in my own CIA past. It was like playing political god. Imagine, Dean Rusk sent a message to the American ambassador in Guatemala seeking information, and I composed the reply, an estimate of the situation. Fidel Castro spoke for four hours at the dedication of an artificial insemination center in Cuba, and I wrote the UPI dispatch describing his reaction to developments in Guatemala City. The Editor of *Pravda* demanded the party line for his morning editorial, and one of my teammates drafted it. Student opinion, United Nations anxiety, OAS indifference, messages enciphered in guerrilla caves, the private and public musings of de Gaulle—we created them all. A game, but stimulating.

Phillips is referring to his membership in a CIA psychological warfare team taking part in "political military" games at Massachusetts Institute of Technology in 1968. Just games, and yet the scenarios in Guatemala and Santo Domingo, where Phillips had been stationed, and in Chile, where he was going, were the realization and embodiment of these games. *Langley did play God.*

David Phillips was the source of and conduit for massive power. But he, too, was a cog in a gigantic wheel. The wheel is the Central Intelligence Agency, and the wheel within that wheel is Covert Action, Western Hemisphere Division. During World War II, Phillips had led a daring escape from a German prisoner-of-war camp. He was brave and imaginative and intelligent, but he was broken on the wheel of Central Intelligence. He could never escape from Langley.

As of 1966 the Western Hemisphere Division had a hundred officers at Langley and two hundred in the field. The division had been organized by Colonel J. C. King, who staffed it with former agents of the Federal Bureau of Investigation. By 1966, this division was headed by William V. Broe, who continued in this position until 1972, when his cover was blown by the ITT scandal and the defection of a clandestine officer named Philip Agee. While Agee did not know the names of Chilean CIA agents, he did know many of their American handlers, except for Phillips—who had been in Lebanon and at Langley. Phillips continued as head of the ultra-secret Chile task force, until it achieved success in 1973. He was then formally made head of the Western Hemisphere Division.

While Phillips concentrated on Chile, Ted ("The Butcher") Schackley was brought in from Vietnam to replace all the operations and agents that former officer Phillip Agee was writing about. Track II and its important "cover," the Institute of General Studies, was not compromised, so the task force continued intact —and Schackley, who was running the CIA's pacification program in Laos and Vietnam. It was these assassination and torture experts, fresh from Phoenix, that Schackley brought into the Western Hemisphere Division in 1972.

Just as Phillips and the Western Hemisphere Division were preparing to lay psychological siege to the Southern Cone (the CIA's term for Argentina, Chile, Paraguay, and Uruguay), CIA assets in Southeast Asia were being employed in the dissemination of the "Madman Theory." This was a Nixon-Kissinger construct designed to terrify not only the Vietnamese but their big power supporters, China and the Soviet Union, as well. When the secret and illegal decision to bomb Cambodia was taken by Kissinger and Nixon in 1969, they ordered the CIA to let it be known in diplomatic circles that Nixon was a madman and that in his obsessional hatred for communism he would not hesitate to trigger nuclear weapons. The President and his National Security Adviser called their ploy the "Madman Theory."

By 1973, Phillips would be unreeling a Latin American version of the Madman Theory in Chile. By 1976, in Washington, the theory would be reality.

David Atlee Phillips was recruited, by his own account, in 1950, by William Caldwell for the Central Intelligence Agency in Santiago, Chile. He was twenty-eight years old, and looked like a young John Wayne, rangy and handsome. He came from Fort Worth, Texas.

In 1949, Phillips was attending occasional classes at the University of Chile and pursuing his moderately successful career as a playwright. He and his wife had just about run out of funds when the CIA asked him to go to work under cover for a weekly English-language gazette, *The South Pacific Mail*, which Phillips would run while carrying out his espionage assignments. These assignments included recruitment of Chilean nationals as informants on various Left political parties, and training in the rudiments of psychological warfare. An intense orientation period in New York followed, including the obligatory crash course in Marxism, communism, and the American policy of "containment."

During Phillips's deep-cover days in Chile, one of his informers met an untimely death. The CIA had been using an American student as a Communist party penetration. The young man fell in love with a young Communist woman, decided to marry her, and to change ideological sides. He was found dead on his wedding day. This interesting anecdote does not find its way into Phillips's warm autobiographical memories of the period.

Phillips's "deep cover" role in Chile (no contact with the American embassy) came to an end in 1954, and he was ordered to report to the Miami Station for a new assignment. There he was briefed by the legendary spy Tracey Barnes and his aide E. Howard Hunt on Operation Diablo. Diablo would destroy democracy in Guatemala.

Guatemala was the first Latin American country in modern times to challenge American hegemony. *In free elections* it had voted into power the government of Jacobo Arbenz Guzman. Long before anybody had heard of Fidel Castro, revolutionaries like Che Guevara came to Guatemala to support the mildly anti-American regime of Colonel Arbenz. According to Barnes and Hunt, Arbenz was leaning too far to the left and so had to be destroyed and replaced by a client of the CIA, General Carlos Castillo Armas. Castillo Armas had been liberated from a Guatemalan prison (where he had been incarcerated as a traitor) by a CIA contract team headed by two agents named Jack Youngblood and Frank Sturgis.

It was Phillips's task to set up a clandestine radio station to orchestrate, with disinformation propaganda, the overthrow of the legally elected government by the invading Castillo Armas, who had been trained in the United States.

Phillips found in Guatemala a population of about four million, more than half of them descendants of the great Mayan civilization that had been decimated by the Spanish *conquistadores*. In this feudal state, Phillips knew, 2 percent of the population owned more than 70 percent of the land. The most important entity in the country was the United Fruit Company. United Fruit's vast holdings were worked by peasants who were paid an average of forty cents a day. When President Arbenz confiscated 225,000 fallow acres from *la Frutera*, his fate was sealed.

In Nicaragua, the CIA's client, President Anastasio Somoza, was providing the training for the Castillo Armas coup forces, and American officers were already coaching sabotage teams by early 1954. When the Arbenz government learned a part of the plot and confronted the State Department, a spokesman retorted that the United States would not "give the story a dignity it doesn't deserve."

On June 18, Castillo Armas and his Army of Liberation crossed the border into Guatemala from Honduras (the Honduran client regime was also co-operating with the CIA in the coup). Unmarked CIA planes now began the bombing of government buildings in Guatemala City while Phillips's Liberation Radio sowed panic and confusion.

At the same time, at the United Nations, Ambassador Henry Cabot Lodge rejected every accusation: "The situation does not involve aggression but is a revolt of Guatemalans against Guatemalans," he intoned. In New York, a spokesman for United Fruit echoed, "It is classical in the revolutionary movements down there that they confine themselves to national versus national, and Americans who stand on the sidelines and keep out of the way should be in no great danger."

Guatemala, then was what Brazil would become later, a base of American influence from which the United States might control a cluster of smaller surrounding countries. Guatemala dominates the isthmus of Central America the way Brazil does the Southern Cone. The American plan was to build Guatemala into a rich, hard base of counterinsurgency control for the central area, including

Mexico. Cuba and Chile, each in its way, were reactions to Guatemala.

After several days of rumors, Phillips's radio operations began to feed false messages to the Guatemalan Army on its wave length, and a rout began. The bloodless war was over. Secretary of State John Foster Dulles announced to the American people that the "evil purposes of the Kremlin had been cured by Guatemalans themselves."

By August, the CIA's liberator, Castillo Armas (whose army of 150 mercenaries had not fired a shot in its American-managed "revolution") had suspended all civil liberties. Now the police state began to shed blood. Enemies of "liberty" or of the United Fruit Company were tortured and executed. Death squads roamed at will. They still do.

An integral component of the coup team, Phillips was congratulated personally by President Dwight D. Eisenhower and promoted by the CIA. He spent only a month in Guatemala after the coup. These were "quiet days," he later wrote, though the terror had begun. His Voice of Liberation had been a great success, as had been the planted press headlines "Chaos in Streets," "Government Collapsing." *Trabajo, Pan y Patria*—Work, Bread and Country—were the code words used by Phillips for his clandestine radio, a crude precursor to the *Patria y Libertad*, Freedom and Fatherland, used in Chile. Other ominous themes that were sounded included "Government Will Destroy Army" and "People's Militias Being Formed." Women's protest marches were everywhere. In Phillips's own words, "In five weeks what had been a placid country was in turmoil."

In the quiet after the coup, over 800,000 acres of land were seized back from the peasants. In the silence thousands were murdered; the goal was the round-up of 200,000 enemies of the state! In tranquility, Phillips tells us, he reflected on his involvement in the overthrow of a constitutional government, and found Operation Diablo, on balance, good.

David Atlee Phillips, now one of the heroes of Guatemala, went back under deep cover as a lecturer on Latin America. In 1955, the author-lecturer arrived in Havana, Cuba. In December of that year, Fidel Castro and Ernesto "Che" Guevara set sail from Mexico to make the Cuban Revolution. It was a crisis in the Middle East that required the young veteran spy to leave Cuba suddenly in 1957, and Phillips, posing as a business consultant, was posted to Beirut, Lebanon. He arrived in the ancient city at the same time as a CIA assassination squad whose target was the famed Soviet agent, Kim Philby. Phillips's cover in the area was provided by a close associate of John Connally, the rising Texas political power.

In his informal autobiography, *The Night Watch*, Phillips footnotes the chapter on Lebanon: "This description of my Lebanese interlude is more travelogue than an account of my CIA duties. A more detailed explanation would violate my secrecy oath. . . ."

Phillips's "interlude" in Lebanon was, in actuality, an emergency assignment to combat the tremendous propaganda campaign that Egypt's President Gamal Abdel Nasser had launched across the Middle East. Using the United States Information Service and other covers, Phillips and his psychological warfare team set about establishing a network of illegal radio outlets across the entire area. Calling itself the Voice of Justice, the operation was soon locked in a bitter propaganda war with Nasser's Voice of the Arabs. Working with Israeli intelligence and right-wing Christian elements, Phillips was this time fighting a losing battle.

In July 1958, Iraq "fell" to anti-American nationalist forces, and Phillips narrowly escaped death. The CIA's clients, King Faisal and his uncle, as well as their puppet Iraqi premier, were all murdered. The next day, Eisenhower sent the Marines, Operation Blue Bat, steaming into Lebanon in a last-minute effort to shore up the American client President Camille Chamoun. Simultaneously, thousands of British paratroops were landing in Jordan. The Mideast was in flames. Phillips had to depart on the last commercial flight out of Beirut.

Since his "retirement" in 1975, the covert veteran has insisted that when he returned to Cuba in 1958 he was no longer a CIA officer. Yet another clandestine officer, Joseph B. Smith, describes how William Caldwell, one of Phillips's original case officers, was once again running Phillips in Havana, this time under the deep cover of David A. Phillips Associates, a public relations firm. At any rate, Phillips admits that by 1959 he was busy again, full-time, working for the agency, fomenting an early coup against the new Castro government. It was not long before his cover was broken by Cuban counterintelligence, and Phillips, who would later manage covert propaganda for the Bay of Pigs operation, departed for Washington.

Phillips has described in *The Night Watch* his growing doubts and second thoughts about the invasion of Cuba in 1961. But in 1960 he was keen on the invasion and encouraged others to participate. He told his junior officer, "Little Joe" Smith, "It will be good for your career. You better join us before it's too late and you've missed the boat."

The Cuban invasion effort was to be world-wide. Radio station WRUL in New York City, was again in play, as it had been during the Guatemalan action, and corporate executives such as Vernon Townley and corporations such as Ford were reactivated as prime assets.

Phillips was in the vanguard of the massive covert operation, along with Howard Hunt and the team of Colonel J. C. King and his Western Hemisphere right-wing ultras. Phillips's project was the famous Swan Island preinvasion radio operation, which beamed propaganda into Cuba. His liaison to anti-Castro exile leaders was Frank Sturgis, an old friend from the fifties.

Again, time was against the invasion. President John F. Kennedy refused to agree to the most extreme of the agency schemes to wipe out the new government in Cuba. Phillips, Hunt, and the hard-liners had begun to agitate for the assassination of Fidel Castro as the equalizer to the increasingly dim prospects of victory. At the center of the assassination discussions was Frank Sturgis.

On the morning of April 17, 1961, the CIA's front, "The Cuban Revolutionary Council," issued a press bulletin prepared by David Phillips: "Before dawn Cuban patriots in the cities and in the hills began the battle to liberate our homeland . . . ." (Later, in a transparent attempt to explain away the spectacular American humiliation, Phillips's "shop" would invent "Soviet tanks and fighter planes.")

In the aftermath of defeat, President Kennedy raged that he would "smash the CIA into a thousand pieces," as much for their bankrupt strategy and outright lies to the chief executive as for the failure of the invasion. Nevertheless, Tracey Barnes, Howard Hunt, David Phillips, and others were promoted. The President, it turned out, did not have the power to purge the agency of its extremists.

Barnes was put in charge of the new, most secret, and unconstitutional Domestic Operations Division (DOD), and Howard Hunt became his operations officer, running totally illegal domestic fronts, including one in New Orleans disguised as the Fair Play for Cuba Committee. The Cuban exiles, of course, would go on to decades of mad violence. The anti-Castroists in Miami would be involved in continuing attacks on Cuba, in the Watergate scandal, and with Chile and Orlando Letelier—for whose murder some of these Bay of Pigs veterans would be indicted.

Orlando Letelier followed events in Cuba from Washington where he was working with the Export-Import Bank. Phillips was made chief of covert operations in the Agency's huge Mexico City station.

On November 23, one day after the assassination of John Kennedy, the Federal Bureau of Investigation drew up the first comprehensive report on the assassination, but the report was *never* made available to the Warren commission. Researchers for this book discovered that the FBI report reveals that (1) the director of the CIA, John McCone, and (2) the CIA's deputy director of plans, Richard Helms, and (3) the agency's chief of covert action in Mexico City, David A. Phillips, had *all conspired to lie to the Warren Commission.** Each one of these men was to play a central role in the overthrow of democracy in Chile. We shall see how the themes of Dallas and Chile cross in the final report of the House Select Committee on Assassination. Leads were being supplied to the committee by a man named Antonio Veciana. Veciana had been a successful Cuban businessman when Castro came to power in 1959. Disgusted at the turn of events, he had been glad to talk to

---

*See Chapter 13 for details and documents of perjury.

an American gentleman, a businessman, living in Havana. The American who said his name was "Maurice Bishop," stood about 6'2", and was "expensively dressed with sun spots [sic] below his eyes." He proposed to train Veciana and others in sabotage and psychological warfare—"his specialty," he said. Another agent called "Melton' assisted Bishop; both worked for "American intelligence"; they would say no more.

The initial strategy was to spread rumors among the population about the economic instability of Castro's regime, a CIA tactic later used against Salvador Allende in Chile. When this failed to create a stir, Bishop used Veciana to co-ordinate assassination attempts. The first was scheduled as Castro prepared to introduce the Soviet cosmonaut Yuri Gagarin, but it was cancelled because Bishop feared a violent Soviet reaction. The next, planned for October 1961 during a Castro speech, involved firing a bazooka from a nearby rooftop.

Castro got wind of this plot, and Veciana was forced to flee Cuba. A month later, in Miami, Bishop contacted Veciana again. Together they laid plans to form the group Alpha 66. Then, after the Cuban missile crisis, Veciana says that Bishop organized a series of commando attacks on Soviet merchant ships in Cuban harbors. Bishop's plan, he adds, was to force another confrontation.

In 1963, Veciana testified that he saw Bishop in the Company of Lee Harvey Oswald in Dallas. Later according to the Cuban, Bishop urged Veciana to swear that Oswald was a Castro agent.

In 1968, Veciana was posted to Bolivia as a $30,000-a-year banking specialist for the State Department. His other job was to destroy the image of the recently murdered Cuban leader Che Guevara. (At this time, Phillips was assigned to the Guevara operation at Langley.) According to Veciana, three Cuban agents had been involved in Guevara's murder.

Veciana's next project centered on Castro's 1971 visit to the Allende government in Chile.

Once Allende was voted in, we knew Castro would go to Chile. A lot of the officers of the Chilean Army were very cooperative with me and Bishop. They knew everything, when Castro would arrive and where he was going to be. The plan was to have TV cameras with machine guns inside them. We had two agents ID'd as pressmen. All this was planned directly by Bishop.

Perhaps it was similar to the Kennedy assassination. Because the person that Bishop assigned to kill Castro was going to get planted with papers to make it appear that he was a Moscow Castro agent and then he would himself be killed. So he would have been seen to be a traitor to Castro.

It never got off the ground. One of the agents had an appendicitis attack, and had to be rushed to a hospital. The other said he wouldn't do it alone. We had all gone to Chile as diplomats, by car through Peru . . . a lot of differences began to come up. I was tired of waiting so long. So many lives being lost, and Castro still alive. On July 24, 1973, the DEA [Drug Enforcement Administration] arrested me and accused me of trafficking in cocaine. Two days after the accusation *I was given my money*. At the end of 15 years, they paid me. All Bishop had ever paid was traveling expenses; he said this was cumulative salary. Before I went to the Atlanta Prison, I told Bishop what my family needed. After that, Bishop never contacted me again. I do not know where he is now. But I am sure the trial was a set-up because of my previous activities. I was sentenced to seven years, paroled in 17 months—out very, very quickly. Then the Senate started investigating.

More important, was Phillips "Bishop"? The physical description is exact.* Veciana recalls that the first contact was made in Havana in 1959, for the purpose of assassination. What does Phillips say about his activities in Havana during this period?

I could approach and cultivate one of the conspirators using a falsxe identity . . . . After approaching and cultivating one of the conspirators, I attended a secret conclave in the house of another.

From Havana to Santiago, Veciana's timetable of "treffs" (secret meetings) with Bishop overlap and coincide with Phillips's espionage agenda and areas of control and influence.

The House Committee on Assassinations discusses in its final report whether "a former Chief of the CIA's Western Hemisphere Division" is Maurice Bishop. David Phillips's name is never mentioned by the Committee. Former CIA Director John McCone did

---

*Photograph and Senate composite may be compared by turning to page 254 of the Appendix.

recall the name Maurice Bishop but could not place the man. Another CIA officer said that he had seen Bishop at CIA headquarters in the early 1960s. And in late 1979, a close aide of Phillips in Guatemala told the author and witnesses, "Phillips always used the Bishop name."

The committee openly doubted the CIA position that it had never assigned Veciana a case officer—Bishop or anyone else—because Veciana was of great importance to the Bay of Pigs affair. Then, in a footnote, comes the confirming bombshell. Veciana and Phillips had been confronted to determine whether Veciana could indentity Phillips as Bishop. All Veciana would say was that there was a "physical similarity." But the committee suspected that Veciana was lying when he denied that the retired CIA officer was Bishop. The committee recognized that Veciana had an interest in renewing his anti-Castro operations that might have led him to protect the officer from exposure as Bishop so they could work together again. For his part, the retired officer aroused the committee's suspicion when he told the committee he did not recognize Veciana as the founder of Alpha 66, especially since the officer had once been deeply involved in Agency anti-Castro operations. Further, a former CIA case officer who was assigned from September 1960 to November 1962 to the CIA JM/WAVE station in Miami told the committee that the retired officer (David Phillips) had in fact used the alias, Maurice Bishop.

The trouble in the Dominican Republic began in May 1961 when the dictator Rafael Trujillo was assassinated. Trujillo had been the United States' man, but he had grown so vicious that Washington feared a Dominican Castro might arise. Hence Trujillo had to die.

Later, documents would indicate that President Kennedy learned of the plan to kill Trujillo only after the debacle of the Cuban invasion, in April 1961. Richard Goodwin, the President's adviser, ordered the CIA *not* to supply weapons for the dictator's assassination. Nevertheless, on May 30, 1961, Trujillo was ambushed and cut down with carbines furnished by Langley, in apparent violation of Kennedy's express directions. Some of those of interest from the CIA who worked on the death squad were Howard Hunt and Frank Sturgis; the team was run out of Mexico City during Phillips's period there.

The Dominican Republic, referred to by Phillips's friend at Langley, Ray Cline, as "a lousy little country," shocked Washington by electing, to replace Trujillo, a man with socialist aspirations, the poet Juan Bosch. Bosch lasted till 1963, when a CIA-backed junta took over until elections could be held. In 1965, Juan Bosch and his followers were determined to regain at the polls what had been illegally taken from them. Instead of elections, there was civil war.

April 1965 in Santo Domingo meant fierce, cruel street fighting. And Phillips was there. Promoted to a supergrade status by the agency, he was posted, under cover as a journalist, to Santo Domingo as part of the vanguard for Lyndon Johnson's expeditionary force of Marines and elite troops of the 82nd Airborne Division. As in 1906 and 1916, American gunboats stood at the approaches to the isthmus of Central America. Working closely with Ambassador Ellsworth Bunker, Phillips, as chief of station, was in over-all charge; his aide, under State Department cover, was an agent named Harry Schlaudeman.

In what was considered a masterstroke, Phillips was successful in infiltrating what Langley called "agents of influence" into all the factions involved in the civil war taking place in the capital city of Santo Domingo. Important "assets" Phillips had at play during the crisis were journalists like Jules DuBois of the *Chicago Tribune* and, especially, Jeremiah O'Leary of the *Washington Star*.

With all sides penetrated by Phillips's agents, the CIA could compose and call the political tune. By 1966 their candidate Joaquin Balaguer (who had been president under Trujillo) was ready to challenge Juan Bosch at the polls. Phillips, by using local media assets and foreign minions like O'Leary, was able to reach upper-middle-class layers of the small voting population. As in Guatemala, the women marched. The news media was tipped heavily toward the CIA's recycled myth of direct, massive "Cuban Russian Support." As in Guatemala, Phillips's rumor mills ground out such character assassination as that Bosch was a drug addict. And Balaguer was elected.

When the Dominican chief of station left the island in 1967, it was to receive personal praise from Lyndon Johnson. Phillips was riding high toward promotion—and the terror to come.

Michael Vernon Townley: Track II, 7 1970-1971

So, what is the matter?
Why are they so furious?
Who are they looking for with a revolver?

BEFORE SALVADOR ALLENDE'S RATIFICATION as president in October 1970, Michael Townley, Aldo Vera Serafin, and a third man had, as instructed, departed Miami for Santiago. There they made contact with a small neofascist group calling itself Fatherland and Freedom, or in Spanish, *Patria y Libertad* (P y L). Townley reported to Frederick Purdy at the American Embassy. Purdy hid his CIA duties under diplomatic cover. Townley was seen by any number of observers going in and out of the Embassy. He became friendly with several of the Marines assigned to guard the American facilities, and with the daughter of Edward M. Korry his relationship was more than friendly. Korry would later denounce the massive CIA intervention in Chile. He would also suspect, correctly, that Langley had maneuvered him out of his position (he was a Kennedy appointee) in order that the hawk, Nathaniel Davis, could come in for the coup.

In 1969, a handful of disgruntled generals of the extreme Right had begun to conspire against Eduardo Frei's Christian Democrat party. When Frei learned of the plot, he retired the extremists and appointed as Chief of Staff a strict constitutionalist, General René Schneider. But when Allende narrowly won the popular election in September 1970, Washington's response was to infiltrate the extremists and reorganize them as the *Patria y Libertad* under the direction of Pablo Rodriguez. Part of the strengthening and reorganization was the introduction of American double agents like Townley.

Phillips, from the commanding heights of the fortress-like facility at Langley, and Townley, in Santiago, in the streets and back

alleys, were both deeply enmeshed in attempting to bring about a
state of siege so that Allende could be blocked from power. This
Nixon-Kissinger-Helms plan for covert violence was first code-
named Track I, then, later Track II. Track II was a Pandora's box of
evil. Clustered around the gory sun of Track II were such satellite
conspiracies as Plan September, the "Quartered Man", Plan
Djakarta, and Plan Z. Track II, according to Thomas Karamessines, the CIA's Director of Plans in 1970, "never stopped."

In 1970, Track I called for militant rightists and renegade military officers to stage mutinies and riots in Concepción, to be
co-ordinated with the "kidnapping," or as it turned out, assassination, of loyal "constitutionalist" generals—René Schneider,
Carlos Prats, *Augusto Pinochet*, and Schaffhauser. (Pinochet's
actual sentiments in September 1970 require a separate discussion
in a subsequent chapter).

Joining Townley and home-grown Chilean fascists militants
were Cuban exiles fresh from Operation Eagle. Eagle was the
Cubans' name for one of the world's largest heroin rings. In 1970
this crime organization had been broken up, and arrests had been
made across Florida. Then, in the summer of 1970, Attorney
General John Mitchell managed to make a series of "technical
errors" and the militants were suddenly free. Free to travel to
Chile to join the killers stalking General Schneider and President-
elect Allende.

On October 22, 1970, two days before the special congressional
vote needed to ratify Allende's victory, Schneider, who was well
known for his commitment to military nonintervention in political
affairs, was shot and killed as he resisted his kidnappers. An
immense amount of confusion surrounded this incident initially,
but it is now known that the assailants had planned to kidnap
Schneider and attribute the action to a leftist group, thereby
encouraging the military to intervene before Congress could confirm Allende as President. The assassination created an extremely
tense situation in Chile, for no national leader had been assassinated there in over one hundred years.

Fortunately the MIR (Movimiento Izquierdista Revolucionario)
had tipped off the authorities, and the police quickly rounded up a
group of rightists as suspects. The press claimed the assassination

was a rightist conspiracy against Chile's electoral process, and the image of Allende and the Left as being committed to constitutional procedure was strengthened. The Right had blundered, and Allende and his Popular Unity party (*Unidad Popular*, UP) were able to turn the tragedy to their own advantage.

Track I had been a miserable failure. At Langley, Phillips's coup team officially closed it down and began the much more profound and secret Plan Centaur. Phillips left Washington for the huge CIA base in Brazil.

Track II was in many ways a logical extension of Track I, and it was to be associated with September 15, 1970, by the later Senate investigation chaired by Senator Frank Church:

On September 15, 1970, President Nixon met with his Assistant for National Security Affairs, Henry Kissinger, CIA Director Richard Helms, and Attorney General John Mitchell at the White House. The topic was Chile. Handwritten notes taken by Director Helms at that meeting reflect both its tenor and the President's instructions:

— One in 10 chance perhaps, but save Chile!
— worth spending
— not concerned risks involved
— no involvement of Embassy
— $10,000,000 available, more if necessary
— full-time job—best men we have
— game plan
— make the economy scream
— 48 hours for plan of action

In his testimony before the Select Committee, Helms recalled coming away from the meeting on September 15 with:

[the] impression...that the President came down very hard that he wanted something done, and he didn't much care how and that he was prepared to make money available....This was a pretty all-inclusive order....If I ever carried a marshall's baton in my knapsack out of the Oval Office, it was that day.

Director Helms also testified that the meeting with Nixon—at which the President screamed and cursed—may have been triggered by the presence in Washington of Agustín Edwards, the publisher of the Santiago daily *El Mercurio*. That morning, at the request of Donald Kendall, president of Pepsi Cola, Henry Kissinger and John Mitchell had met for breakfast with Kendall and Edwards. The topic of conversation was the political situation in Chile and the plight of *El Mercurio* and other anti-Allende forces.

The following day, September 16, DCI Helms called a meeting at the CIA to discuss the Chilean situation. At this meeting, he related to his colleagues his understanding of the President's instructions:

The Director told the group that President Nixon had decided that an Allende regime in Chile was unacceptable to the United States. The President asked the Agency to prevent Allende from coming to power or to unseat him. The President authorized $10,000,000 for this purpose, if needed. Further, the Agency is to carry out this mission without coordination with the Departments of State or Defense.

Seven thousand miles away, a troop of fanatical anti-communists and right-wingers from the military and the upper class, the *momios* (as the Left called them), together with hired help from the underworld, were in constant motion between October 5 and October 20. The assassins were provided machine guns by the CIA station.

After the popular election of Allende in September 1970, sectors within the CIA in coordination with the giant multinational International Telephone and Telegraph Corporation, felt that Allende's assumption of the presidency still could be prevented. William Merriam, an ITT vice-president, wrote John McCone, (an ITT director and former Director of Central Intelligence), in October 1970 and referred to his last meeting with people from the agency. "Approaches continue to be made to select members of the Armed Forces," he wrote, "in an attempt to have them lead some sort of uprising—no success to date." One of the obstacles to this "success" was General René Schneider, Commander-in-Chief of the Armed Forces.

At about the same time that Merriam was writing to McCone, the main office of ITT received a communication from one of its

"PR men" in Chile. It said that the military would only intervene if the country's stability were sufficiently threatened and, stated the ITT man, "the threat must be provided one way or another through *provocation*."

ITT's "PR man" was, in reality, a CIA agent—Robert Berrellez, an old hand in David Phillips's shop. Assisting Berrellez was Juan Luis Ossa Bulnes, who later proved to be among those responsible for Schneider's death.

Patria y Libertad became the CIA's new army in Chile. Its philosophy was based on national syndicalism, preaching the creation of a corporative state under the control of an authoritarian government. It was, in a word, fascist. The political directorate of the group included the country's most powerful industrial and landed interests. *Patria y Libertad* worked both publicly and clandestinely. The public side concentrated primarily on propaganda, which was disseminated to a wide audience through a chain of radio stations headed by Radio Agricultura. Mariana Callejas was active at Radio Agricultura.

The clandestine side of *Patria y Libertad* was run similarly to early Nazi groups in Germany. To become a member, the individual underwent an elaborate battery of intelligence checks, indoctrination classes, training in arms and communications, and, for the proven cadre, classes on explosives and intelligence gathering, some of them taught by Townley. The military apparatus of *Patria y Libertad* was divided into cells: training squadrons, death squads, and shock troops. Former military officers, many of them graduates of the CIA's International Police Academy or the Army School of the Americas, gave the classes.

After the success of Allende's Popular Unity party in the 1970 elections, U.S. Ambassador Edward Korry was replaced by Nathaniel Davis, an expert in the use of paramilitary forces. The CIA's in-country team in the Santiago embassy maintained direct contact with Patria y Libertad. Ambassador Davis had frequent meetings with both Orlando Saenz and Pablo Rodriguez of P y L. The United States also had another contact close to the CIA who was a high-ranking member of *Patria y Libertad*, Sergio Miranda Carrington. Miranda, an attorney, would later represent General Juan Contreras Sepulveda in the Letelier affair. Miranda knew both Phillips and Townley well.

According to the CIA's plan, under Phillips's direction, *Patria y Libertad* began to set up an apparatus of support throughout Latin America. Brazil and Bolivia were particularly important, both countries having military dictatorships, installed after U.S.-supported coups d'état. Under Phillips's guidance, right-wing Brazilian groups offered $8 million to *Patria y Libertad* and a force of some 500 men.

While the Phillips's psychological warfare machine and P y L were warning of an impending "Cuban invasion," the CIA was smuggling weapons and explosives to Townley and the extreme Right in coffee boxes from Brazil. P y L leaders were regularly seen at the American Embassy meeting with Frederick Purdy and others of the CIA coup team. Besides Townley, a frequent visitor was P y L leader Pablo Rodriguez, whose instant-coffee company provided a central base for assembling the contraband from Brazil.

During this tense period, before the installation of Allende's Popular Unity government, Mariana Callejas had joined a propaganda campaign that had begun in mid-September 1970. Callejas played a reporter, one of many, to Phillips's "senior editor," a cog in his Langley disinformation machine. Callejas let it be known that she and Townley were no longer man and wife so that her Left-journalist cover, which she had never given up, could be maintained. In point of fact, she was at odds with her husband over the virulent anti-Semitism of the P y L people with whom Townley was involved in his adventures. Señora Townley's first two children were half Jewish, and now that their father had taken them away to the United States, she displayed signs of guilt and depression. It is said that Townley was somewhat frightened of his wife in those days and that he and his P y L friends refused to meet in her presence after several outbursts, at one of which she appeared wearing the yellow Star of David.

The modern history of International Telephone and Telegraph begins with its links to Hitler and the Axis powers before and during World War II. Congressional hearings after World War II established ITT's pro-Nazi activity, especially in Argentina, next door to Chile. More hearings, in the 1970s, chaired by Senator Frank Church, bring us to modern times and the multinational's criminal role in Chile.

It should be understood that ITT was in the vanguard of a group of corporations prepared to intervene in Chile. Though the idea does violence to the aesthetic sense of liberal political scientists and commentators, there did exist an active conspiracy of men who sat together in one room planning to ruin another country's freedoms in order to protect their own vast investments. The conspiracy—there *is* no other word—is not a Marxist daydream; it had a name, "The Ad Hoc Committee on Chile," and a membership of co-conspirators: Kimball C. Firestone (Firestone Tire & Rubber Co.); Francis D. Flanagan (W. R. Grace & Co.); William C. Foster (Ralston Purina Co.); Jack Gilbert (Charles Pfizer & Co.); Robert L. James (Bank of America); C. T. Mark (Dow Chemical Co.); Ralph Mecham (Anaconda Co.); Lyle Mercer (Kennecott Copper Corp.); Jack D. Neal (ITT Corp.); William R. Merriam (ITT Corp.) Ed Mollena (Ford Motor Co.); William Wickert (Bethlehem Steel Corp.).

By 1971, the corners of this conspiracy had begun to extrude. On March 21 and 22, Jack Anderson published two columns on secret ITT documents showing that the corporate giant had plotted in 1970 to stop Allende's election; that it had dealt regularly with the CIA to try to create economic chaos in Chile and encourage a military coup, and that ITT president Harold Geneen had offered to contribute "up to seven figures" to the White House to stop Allende. Anderson's accusations were based on eight pages of memoranda including correspondence with John McCone, that he subsequently made public.

These documents made clear that the United States was prepared to use its power to crush a government that, in its view, treated North American corporations improperly. There was no other "national security" issue in the Chile case, so the United States would destroy a small nation, *but it would no longer take public responsibility for doing so.* As CIA director William Colby stated, according to the *Washington Post*, during closed hearings of the House Subcommittee on Inter-American Affairs, on October 11, 1973, "The presumption under which we conduct this type of operation is that it is a covert operation and that the United States hand is not to show."

The Nixon Administration had passed the word to the Foreign Service to be more aggressively pro-American-business in representing the United States abroad. All diplomats received the following departmental directive: "Henceforth all officers will be evaluated on the basis of their concern for U.S. business." The Nixon shift was caused by a financial reality which necessitated what *Business Week* called "the death battle" to cut America's foreign trade deficit.

The paper trail unearthed by Jack Anderson and soon followed by the Church Committee reads like a penny-dreadful or a Brechtian living newspaper:

International Telephone and
Telegraph Corporation
International Headquarters

Date: September 17, 1970
TO: E. J. Gerrity
FROM: H. Hendrix, R. Berrellez
SUBJECT: Chile

W. R. Merriam—This should be tightly held, ...

The surface odds and foreign news media appear to indicate that Salvador Allende will be inaugurated as President November 4, but there is now a strong possibility that he will not make it . . .

On September 22, 1970, vice-president Gerrity sent this memo to Harold S. Geneen, president and chairman of the board of ITT. (References to the CIA are crudely camouflaged as "the man.")

This is ITT Washington
22 Sept 1970
CRYPTEL-240

Please forward following message to ITT
Europe Brussels

To: Mr. H. S. Geneen
From: E. J. Gerrity, ITTW
CC: F. J. Dunleavy, ITT Europe
  J. W. Guilfoyle, ITTNY
  E. R. Wallace, ITTNY

(No other distribuition(sic) of this Memo should be made)

The Hendrix and Berrellez memo which we discussed last Friday has been confirmed. Bill Merriam reviewed the actions being taken today with the man you introduced to him some months ago. It is clear that the strategy outlined in the Hendrix memorandum is the best course to be followed. Bill's contact suggested that all possible pressures be exerted. He reported that pressure is building on the scene.

Gerrity   End of Message

On October 9, 1970, W. R. Merriam, ITT vice-president in Washington, sent a memo to John McCone suggesting U.S. government involvement:

Today I had lunch with our contact at the McLean agency, and I summarize for you the results of our conversation. He is still very, very pessimistic about defeating Allende when the congressional vote takes place on October 24. Approaches continue to be made to select members of the Armed Forces in an attempt to have them lead some sort of uprising—no success to date.

On October 16, 1970, Hal Hendrix cabled his intelligence estimate to the home office.

Unless there is a move by dissident Chilean military elements by this time next mid-week, the consensus in Santiago is that Salvador Allende will win the October 24 Congressional run-off easily and be inaugurated as President November 4.

The chance of a military coup is slim but it continues to exist—at least to this date.

A key figure in this possibility is former Brigadier General Roberto Viaux . . . . .

It is a fact that word passed to Viaux from Washington to hold back last week. It was felt that he was not adequately prepared, his timing was off, and he should "cool it" for a later, unspecified date. Emissaries pointed out to him that if he moved prematurely and lost, his defeat would be tantamount to a "Bay of Pigs in Chile." . . .

As part of the persuasion to delay, Viaux was given oral assurances he would receive material assistance and support from the U.S. and others for a later maneuver.

On October 23, 1970, Merriam sent a letter accompanied by recommendations to National Security Advisor Henry Kissinger.

October 23, 1970

Dr. Henry A. Kissinger
Assistant to the President
The White House

Dear Dr. Kissinger:

As a result of recent events in Latin America, foreign private enterprise in that area is now facing its most serious exposure.

President Nixon, one year ago, in his speech before the Inter-American Press Association said, "We will not encourage private investment where it is not wanted, or where local political conditions face it with unwarranted risks."

ITT does not wish to go where it is not wanted, but we, too, have President Nixon's "strong belief that properly motivated private enterprise has a vital role to play in social as well as economic development."

Our company knows the peoples of the Americas deserve a better way of life and we believe we have a substantial interest in diminishing their problems.

I attach a paper containing our estimations plus specific references to the Chilean situation. This is respectfully submitted; I would appreciate your comments.

Sincerely,
William R. Merriam
Vice President

Dr. Kissinger apparently planned to take the recommendations into consideration.

THE WHITE HOUSE
WASHINGTON

November 9, 1970

Dear Mr. Merriam:

Thank you very much for your letter of October 23 and the enclosed paper on United States policy toward Latin America. I have read it carefully and I have passed it to those members of my staff who deal with Latin American matters. It is very helpful to have your thoughts and recommendations, and we shall certainly take them into account. I am grateful for you taking the time to give them to me.

With best regards,
(signed) Henry A. Kissinger ·

Mr. E.J. Gerrity:
Believe this is more than perfunctory. Things are brewing on the Chile matter and will be back to you later on that subject.

W. R. MERRIAM

John McCone, the former DCI, would later say that President Geneen had in mind "not chaos but what could be done constructively . . . to build housing and schools. . . ." That was a subject on which Mr. McCone was an expert. After his service at Central Intelligence, McCone had been appointed to head the commission that investigated the "Watts Riots."

To use Vice-President Merriam's words, things were brewing. David Phillips would begin the subversion from Brazil. Hendrix, Phillips's opposite number at ITT, would be liaison between Langley, Rio de Janeiro and Santiago.

Within months William Broe's cover had been blown in the ITT affair, and Ted Shackley took his place as chief of covert operations for the Western Hemisphere Division. Langley's basic script or strategy during the 1970 Presidential campaign had been a scenario of terror aimed at middle-class women. The images used were of "Marxist violence," "Marxist terror," and "the end of civil liberty" (in Communist states).

Among the records of the CIA-funded, anti-Allende Andalien ad agency, made public in 1970 by Chilean Chamber of Deputies, was a memo headed: "Youth of Chile: A Direct Campaign, Brutal, Essentially Negative." This was a synthetic image—one of many—designed by the CIA's psychological warfare experts, but it turned out to be too direct, brutal and negative to employ in its original form. The 1970 campaign of terror proved far too crude for Chile's highly sophisticated political culture. By the time of the March 1973 election and coup, there was a much more sustained and steady buildup toward the terrible composite climax known in Phillips's shop as "The Quartered Man."

After the Schneider assassination CIA agents in Chile had to go to ground. Even *El Mercurio* was temporarily silenced. Allende was inaugurated. Orlando Letelier returned to Washington as an official representative of a sovereign state. And David Phillips, in Brazil, and the Townleys, in Santiago and the countryside, soon came back to life, to climb ever downward into the pit that was Plan Centaur.

David Atlee Phillips, 1971-1972

8

We did not know
that everything was occupied
the cups, the seats,
the beds, the mirrors,
the sea, the wine, the sky

Pablo Neruda

IN THE YEAR AFTER ALLENDE TOOK OFFICE David Phillips shuttled between Brazil, Venezuela, and Langley as head of the secret Chile task force. He now controlled scores of agents in Santiago alone through a series of fronts and agent handlers. To the tall spymaster, Michael Townley and Mariana Callejas were merely two well-known names among many.

To create perspective for Track II, and for Phillips's and Townley's roles, it is useful to quote from the Senate Select Committee on Intelligence (Church Committee):

Throughout the Allende years, but especially after the first year of his government, the American Government's best intelligence—National Intelligence Estimates, prepared by the entire intelligence community—made clear that the more extreme fears about the effects of Allende's election were not well-founded. There was, for example, never a significant threat of a Soviet military presence in Chile, and Allende was little more hospitable to activist exiles from other Latin American countries than had been his predecessor, Eduardo Frei.

Between Washington and Robert McNamara at the World Bank, the Allende regime was completely cut off from major world support, credits or loans. Yet despite this, unemployment and inflation *fell* during 1971, and production was up! The pressure on Phillips also went up by the numbers.

Later, Phillips would tell the Church Committee that after the Chile affair, covert actions trailed off in South America because "Fidel Castro abandoned his concept of the export of violent revolution and there's no need [for them]." At which point Senator Church could contain himself no longer.

Do we live by a separate standard? Do we have a superior right?...That's the thing that never seems to get answered, because I think the question answers itself. We do live by a double standard and do we have certain rights against other people that we would not tolerate for a moment for them to assert against us?

The CIA's Institute of General Studies (IGS) was Philips's key front. IGS included no Christian Democrats.

The first major piece of disinformation planted through IGS was the "Kunakov Archive." The initial installment of this six-part "exposé" appeared in *El Mercurio* two weeks before the 1970 elections. This spy novel, subtitled, "The Adventures of a Communist Agent,' appeared under the name of Juraj Domic. Domic was a Sovietologist at *El Mercurio* and a researcher at the IGS. Episodes of the "Kunakov Archive," including a chart of the KGB, always appeared next to news photos of Allende. This might have seemed a coincidence were it not that for twenty years *El Mercurio* had had a firm policy of never carrying Allende's picture as straight news during an election. The "Kunakov Archive" was greeted with humor and derision; the boomerang effect was so great that U.S. Ambassador Edward Korry protested to the White House about its appearance.

The pressure for escalation was on Phillips, despite Fidel Castro's visit to Chile in December 1971 to proclaim the end of the dogma of guerrilla struggle in Latin America. Publicly he supported the UP style of electoral politics. Privately, he gave Allende an automatic weapon—in case.

From 1970 on, Henry Kissinger complained constantly that the Left was crushing press freedom in Chile. Phillips, through a maze of CIA-influenced media operations, harped incessantly on this same theme. Nowhere in the world have the media ever attacked a head of state the way Salvador Allende was pilloried by the IGS and *El Mercurio* empire, following Langley's script. So far from being suppressed, the Chilean media were Langley's secret weapon.

For instance, the party line of the CIA's American "media assets" is exemplified by the reporting of the "March of the Empty Pots." On December 1, 1971, five thousand women marched to protest Castro's impending visit and food shortages, raising antagonisms between the Allende government and its anti-Marxist opposition to a new level of violence. This was a David A. Phillips production, but the protest was never put into historical perspective. Comparisons were not made to other, similar marches, such as the March 1964 women's demonstration, the "Family March with God for Liberty" in São Paulo, Brazil (with which Phillips was also involved). There, right-wing movements had helped prepare the emotional climate for the coming military seizure of power by staging a march with the women reciting the rosary to implore God to save Brazil from the "Bolshevist peril."

The North American press did not give its readers any indication of the middle- and upper-class status of the marchers or that the march was spearheaded by thirty youths, under Michael Townley's control, wearing hard helmets and carrying wooden clubs and rocks. The *New York Times* represented the women as engaged in "a peaceful protest," though *Le Monde* of Paris and *Excelsior* of Mexico City correctly reported that it was a right-wing riot which the police were forced to break up when the President and his palace were stoned. And as a London Weekly newsletter, *Latin America*, reported it: "No one denies that there are food shortages, although it is difficult to imagine women being better fed that those who marched the streets last week. In fact, all that they were complaining about was a decreased beef supply—hardly starvation."

Phillips knew that his orders were to keep Chile a "silent Vietnam," as Allende put it. Langley knew, of course; Allende and Letelier knew; Castro knew; everyone knew. If only the American press had been able to function to alert the Americans to what was about to happen.

The logistical basis for psychological war in Chile was almost complete. With the Institute for General Studies and the *El Mercurio* group in place, Phillips needed only one more big gun to help cover the gap created when Hal Hendrix's ITT-CIA network had been blown. The answer was an old friend: Copley Press, Inc.

When Phillips turned over the *South Pacific Mail*, now an agency front, to CIA man David Hellyer in 1964, Copley News Service (CNS) became, in Ira Copley's confidential words to President Dwight D. Eisenhower, "the eyes and ears against the communist threat in Latin America for our intelligence services." In those days, the old OSS hand Robert Richards, together with Nixon's agent Lyn Nofzinger, had been Phillips's contacts at CNS.

CNS's man in Latin America in 1971 was an old psywar expert, William Giandoni, who had experience in David Phillips's shop during the Bay of Pigs operation. Copley was close to Agustín Edwards, the publisher of *El Mercurio*, as well as Donald Kendall of Pepsi-Cola, both of whom were providing Phillips with key elements of support for his logistical base and order of battle, as he prepared for total psychological war.

The Banco Agustín Edwards, controlled by the Edwards family, had always been close to Chase Manhattan, the Rockefeller family bank. Furthermore, when the International Basic Economy Corporation (IBEC)—another Rockefeller holding—entered Chile in the late sixties, Agustín Edwards became its president. Edwards was also on the board of the Deltec Corporation, a multinational corporation in which Rockefeller interests were well represented. But these corporate connections are really only the visible parts of a network which reaches deep into the extreme right-wing and the Cuban exile community and the CIA.

At Phillips's direction the United States government arranged for a series of representatives of the Edwards conglomerate to visit the States during the three years of the Popular Unity government. Pablo Rodriguez, for instance, had important connections to both *El Mercurio* and *Patria y Libertad*. In May of 1972 Rodriguez had just been released from a Santiago jail on $82 bail after being charged with conspiring to overthrow the government.

And on May 14, Rodriguez was sitting in his hotel room in the Watergate complex. Bernard Barker, Frank Sturgis, Virgilio Gonzales, and Eugenio Martinez were just across town—on the second floor of the Chilean Embassy, rummaging through the files of Popular Unity diplomats for secret communications between Santiago and Washington and lists of UP supporters in the United States. As they left the offices, they grabbed the embassy's mailing list off a desk and quickly disappeared into the night.

Orlando Letelier and his wife were out for the evening.

But Phillips's secret weapon was always *El Mercurio*, which was managed by René Silva Espejo, one of the founders of the Chilean Nazi party. Alvaro Puga, a CIA agent, was in charge of the propaganda campaigns of the paper. He was also a conduit for the placing of stories written by the CIA experts back at Langley. Puga eventually achieved such success at his job that he became General Pinochet's press secretary after the coup d'état in 1973.

Langley's psychological warfare usually reaches its propagandistic heights with the founding of a so-called Radio Liberation similar to those set up by David Phillips in Guatemala and Lebanon and on Swan Island for the Bay of Pigs. Michael Townley was the protagonist of this activity in Chile. The first attempt at founding an antigovernment Radio Liberación occurred during the CIA-funded transport strike of October 1972. Townley, with the aid of Manuel Fuentes, a fellow P y L member, began broadcasting, with the use of highly sophisticated equipment, a plan for the overthrow of the government. While the plan was not successful at the time, Townley gained valuable experience, which he would put to use later.

Phillips and his team of hard-liners took the Allende victory personally. Phillips had joined the agency in Chile; his children were Chilean citizens. Three times he had been part of successful efforts to stop Allende from winning the presidency. Phillips's circle of friends in Santiago over the years had included executives like Vernon Townley and the powerful Agustín Edwards (Phillips's *South Pacific Mail* was being printed on *El Mercurio* presses when he began his spy career in Santiago).

The Institute of General Studies has been described by one of its American contacts, ITT official Harold Hendrix, as "some propagandists working again on radio and television" and by its British contact, Robert Moss, as "the nerve center of political opposition to Marxism." The classified version of the Senate Intelligence Committee's report on the CIA in Chile echoes Moss's assessment: "The Institute of General Studies became the brain center of all groups opposed to Allende Government [sic]."

The IGS organization grew out of a co-ordinated media campaign against Allende's election in 1970. At the center of this effort were the top executives of Chile's leading newspaper, *El Mercurio*, and the magazines *Portada* and *Que Pasa*. This media campaign soon meshed with a CIA coup attempt code-named Track II, whose objective, according to a CIA cable, was to "[c]reate a coup climate by propaganda, disinformation, and terrorist activities intended to provoke the left to give a pretext for a coup."

But the campaign did not result in a coup in 1970, because the opposition groups did not have the will, the organization, or the technical know-how to pull one off. Allende won the election, and many IGS members left Chile, apparently taken in by their own scare campaign against the leader of the Popular Unity party. The director of IGS, Pablo Baraona Urzua, fled to Paraguay; Cristian Zegers, who headed the CIA-funded Andalien ad agency, left for Venezuela; Enrique Campos Menéndez settled in Madrid; Marcos Chamudes, editor of *PEC*, a political journal, ran across the border to Mendoza, Argentina; and Carlos Urenda Zegers, an attorney for *El Mercurio*, went all the way to Australia. As the Senate Intelligence Committee report observes, "When Allende took office, little was left of the CIA-funded propaganda apparatus."

But there were a few intransigents, including CIA superagent David Phillips, who refused to give up. In the wake of the dispersal of the CIA's media assets after Allende's victory, Phillips set up a relocation center in Mendoza, Argentina, and went about bringing back those journalists who had fled. Within three months the CIA had re-established control over *El Mercurio*. That control was assured by IGS member Hernán Cubillos, who was left in control of the paper by its owner, Agustín Edwards, when he moved to the United States following Allende's victory. Cubillos had been head of *Que Pasa*, whose headquarters originally doubled as the home of IGS. Cubillos published *El Mercurio* from 1970 to 1973 on a CIA subsidy of $1,665,000.

Thus Phillips encouraged CIA sponsorship of the journalists at IGS as part of a long-range plan to regroup the CIA's friends in Chile following the failure of the Track II coup attempt. That attempt had failed because the vast network of CIA assets established during the Kennedy administration consisted mostly of Christian Democrats; the CIA in Chile in the 1960s, was geared to winning elections, not to carrying out a putsch. It is significant, therefore, that the IGS included no Christian Democrats and that it worked outside the framework of the mass political parties, but with militant groups like the truckers and the right-wing *Patria y Libertad*. The IGS was thus the link between September 1970 and September 1973; it is the proof that Track II was never terminated.

CIA funding for IGS began in 1971 and continued after the coup—until 1974, at least. Members of the IGS were not simply CIA contacts: they were CIA agents, a counterelite that the CIA backed to replace the Allende government. After the coup, with the military primarily concerned with internal security, IGS members largely took over the administration of the country. (See tables.)

Day by day, Chile was dying from psychological poisoning. "Only a visitor would have marked the subtle but fatal deterioration."

I arrived like a traveller feeling a bit dizzy from the gas of propaganda and counter propaganda of psychological warfare, a little sea sick from the ideological gas. I thought I'd find a capital where there was a one-sided press—new magazines and newspapers had proliferated like mushrooms and read like science fiction.

Chile is a small country, and it had been relatively isolated from Madison-Avenue methods of hard-sell. As such, it was unusually vulnerable to foreign media penetration. The opposition political parties purchased newspapers and radio stations, with CIA funds,

CORPORATE INTELLIGENCE CONNECTIONS

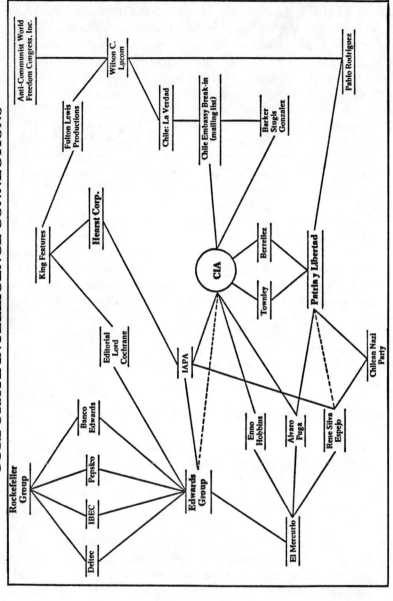

WHO'S WHO IN THE INSTITUTE OF GENERAL STUDIES

Allende Era		Military Junta Period
El Mercurio, editor	Pablo Baraona Urzua	Director, Banco Central; Minister of the Economy
El Mercurio, editor	Tomás P. MacHale (Freedom of Press Committee, IAPA)	Gabriela Mistral Publishing Co.
Portada, *Que Pasa*, editor	Jaime Guzmán Errazuriz	Assessor and adviser on rewriting Chilean Constitution; Council of State; Instructor, Academy of National Security
El Mercurio, Soviet expert; *Portada*, writer	Juraj Domic	Planning section, Ministry of Exterior; Chilean Mission to the United Nations
Portada, editor	Francisco Orrego Vicuña	Dean of Agrarian Economy, University of Chile
Portada, editor	José Garrido Rojas	Adviser to Ministry of Economy; legal adviser to U.S. corporations
Portada, founder	Ricardo Claro	
El Mercurio, *Portada*, *Que Pasa*, editor	Hermógenes Pérez de Arce	Director, *La Segunda*
El Mercurio, associate director; *Que Pasa*, columnist	Arturo Fontaine Aldunate (Winner of Freedom Award, IAPA)	Director *El Mercurio*
El Mercurio, *Portada*, *Que Pasa*, editor	Cristián Zegers Ariztía	Director, *Que Pasa*
El Mercurio, financial editor; *Portada*, *Que Pasa*, editor	Emilo Sanfuentes Vergara	Director, School of Economics, Catholic University
	Enrique Campos Menéndez (Director, IAPA)	Director of cultural affairs; Director of National Library
El Mercurio, director	Fernando Leniz Cerda	Minister of the Economy, 1973-1975
El Mercurio, owner and publisher	Agustin Edwards (IAPA president, 1969-1970)	
Portada, *Que Pasa*, editor	Jaime Martinez Williams	School of Journalism, Catholic University of Santiago
El Dario Illustrado, director	Fernando Zegers	Ambassador to Germany
El Mercurio, publisher 1970-1973; *Que Pasa*, founder	Hernán Cubillos (Director, IAPA)	Minister of Foreign Affairs
El Mercurio, Washington correspondent	Adolfo Yankelevic	Chilean Mission to the United Nations
El Mercurio, columnist	Alvaro Puga	Personal press secretary to President Pinochet
El Mercurio, chief attorney	Carlos Urenda Zegres	Retired

71

covering every town in Chile. Over half of the $12 million the CIA has admitted to spending between 1963 and 1974 went for propaganda. The purpose of setting up the IGS was to co-ordinate and synchronize the propaganda offensive. CIA psychologists selected themes which would serve to divide Chilean society into groups fighting against each other and against the government. According to the Senate report, *Covert Action in Chile*, during one six-week period (September-October 1970) the CIA had 26 agents in the media field in Santiago generating over 700 articles. When conducted at this level by a hostile intelligence agency—which is co-ordinating the propaganda with actual bombings and terrorist activities—this is no longer simply propaganda but a recognized form of warfare, psychological warfare.

Michael Townley: Code Name
9 "Centaur," 1971-1972

So now it comes out that
we don't even get a table
This can't be, we think
We can't believe it
And now they say that we can't
that there is no place for us on the boat

Pablo Neruda

ON NUMEROUS OCCASIONS DURING THE LAST TWENTY YEARS, the United States has used "coup teams" as a major weapon to combat anti-imperialist governments. Such teams are composed of CIA operatives with special skills in overthrowing governments. In Latin America alone, coup teams have been employed in Guatemala (1954), Brazil (1964), Bolivia (1971), Uruguay (1973), and Chile. In answer to Phillips's call for help, CIA operatives with past experience in "special operations" converged on Chile to work toward Allende's overthrow. Of the ten CIA operatives who have been identified, two participated in the 1954 Guatemala coup, two were in the Dominican Republic during the U.S. invasion in 1965, and three were active in the brutal pacification operation against the liberation movement in Guatemala in 1966-69; *all had worked closely with David Phillips*—in the days when the agency rode high and presidents personally shook hands with the he-men of Clandestine Services.

Former Chilean ambassador to Mexico, Hugo Vigorena Ramirez, actually saw documents outlining the CIA plan, code-named Centaur, devised to topple the Allende government. Centaur, he testified, involved economic and psychological warfare against Chile, including the introduction of counterfeit money, as in Cuba and Iran, disrupting the rhythm of crops and the spreading of a "swine flu" type of virus, also as in Cuba.

A *San Francisco Chronicle* news analysis by Waldo Thayer (September 1, 1971) reports, from "well-informed sources," that the CIA had developed a master plan for overthrowing six South American governments, with Bolivia first on the list. The coups, directed and financed with $14 million supplied by the CIA, were to be planned by an international "brain trust" which included four former presidents of the target countries, prominent leaders of the Catholic Church, and conservative military officers. According to this report, Chile's former president, Eduardo Frei, was a member of this conspiracy.

Such straws floated in the wind throughout 1971 and 1972. The names of the actual coup-makers were not yet known, but the American secret agents under the control of David Phillips included:

Nathaniel P. Davis, appointed ambassador to Chile in 1971, is a career foreign service officer whose specialty is anti-Communist affairs. Davis served in Prague (1947-49) and later was a political officer in Moscow (1954-56). He then became chief officer in charge of Soviet affairs in the State Department, which included the job of escort officer for Khrushchev's American tour in 1959. Davis next became first secretary of the Caracas embassy (1960-62), and then joined the Peace Corps (1962-65), rising to the position of deputy associate director. During this period, he was acting Peace Corps director in Chile.

In 1965 Davis became minister to Bulgaria with the purpose of establishing full diplomatic relations. From 1966 to 1968 he was a senior member of the National Security Council. In 1968 he became U.S. ambassador to Guatemala, replacing John Gordon Mein, who had been killed by guerrilla forces. There he headed an embassy staffed with veterans of Vietnam pacification programs. Under Davis's direction, they carried out a similar program in Guatemala: by 1971 20,000 Guatemalans were dead. Davis then replaced Edward M. Korry, a Kennedy-Johnson political appointee, as ambassador to Chile.

In December 1972, just before Allende visited the United Nations, Davis sent the following cable to Nixon:

Perhaps what is significant now is growing conviction in opposition parties, private sector and others that opposition is possible....Even more important is increasing realization that opposition is necessary. What government is doing goes beyond transactionalism. [Allende's] objectives are increasingly seen as incompatible and as going beyond what can be accepted. If opposition interests are to be protected, confrontation may not be avoidable.

Deane Roesch Hinton played a pivotal role in the campaign of economic chaos against Allende's Popular Unity government. Hinton had served with David Phillips in Guatemala under cover of the Agency for International Development (AID). Acting in conjunction with the local military and U.S. Green Berets, AID-CIA forces began a pacification program modeled after Vietnam programs. Hinton was still director of AID when Nathaniel Davis arrived as ambassador to Guatemala to lead a CIA terror campaign. Hinton preceded Davis to Chile as director of AID in November 1969. In 1971, he was recalled to the White House to serve under Henry Kissinger on the staff of the National Security Council.

Harry W. Shlaudeman joined the State Department in 1954, serving as a consular officer in Colombia until 1956. After language training, he moved in 1959 to Bulgaria. Shlaudeman is best known for the key role he played as Phillips's aide in the Dominican Republic in the mid-1960s. He was transferred to the position of second in command (Deputy Chief of Mission) in Santiago in June 1969.

Daniel N. Arzac, Jr., served in the Army (1943-46) and joined the State Department and the CIA in July 1953 as an intelligence research analyst. His first foreign experience was in Phnom Penh (October 1954-August 1956) following the French defeat in Indo-China. He next served in Montevideo (April 1957-February 1958), at the same time that E. Howard Hunt was CIA station chief for Uruguay. In 1971, one year after Allende's election, he joined the American Embassy in Santiago as a "political officer."

James E. Anderson served as foreign service Officer, with Phillips, in the Dominican Republic one month before the revolution and U.S. invasion of 1965. He next moved to Mexico City, again under Phillips, as a political officer. Anderson arrived in Santiago under the cover of "consular officer" (an unheard-of demotion for a "political officer" in the State Department) in January 1971, two months after Allende's inauguration.

John B. Tipton joined the State Department and the CIA in 1958 as an intelligence research specialist, and was a "labor officer" in Mexico City from May 1960 to September 1962 under Phillips. After a few months in Bolivia, he was trained in labor relations and served in that capacity in Guatemala with Phillips. After further training, he went to Santiago as a "political officer" in January 1972.

Raymond Alfred Warren worked for two years as a "labor union researcher." After college, he joined the State Department and the CIA in 1954, when he participated, with Phillips, in the CIA-sponsored coup against the Arbenz government in Guatemala. He then served as an economic officer in Caracas, under Phillips, for one year before shifting to Santiago. Warren arrived in Santiago as a "political officer" in October 1970, as Allende was being confirmed as president by the Chilean parliament.

Arnold M. Isaacs went to work for the CIA as an intelligence research specialist in 1959, one year after he joined the State Department. Isaacs was the political officer in Buenos Aires until he joined the embassy in Santiago in the same capacity in February 1970. At that time he became well known for his efforts to penetrate the North American Left community there. Sometime after June 1973 he returned to Washington to become the Chile desk officer at the State Department, and was in that key position when the coup took place.

Frederick W. Latrash gained his initial experience with the Office of Naval Intelligence. In 1954 he participated with David Phillips in the CIA-sponsored coup in Guatemala. He then went to Amman as a political officer, again working with Phillips in Lebanon. Latrash joined the embassy in Santiago as a "political officer" in May 1971.

Joseph F. McManus acted as liaison officer to the Pentagon, and had worked in Bangkok and Istanbul as the vice-consul. He arrived in Chile after September 1972 as a "political officer" at the embassy.

Keith W. Wheelock worked in the State Department and the CIA as an intelligence research analyst from October 1960 to March 1962. He appeared in the former Belgian Congo a year after the CIA-connected assassination of Patrice Lumumba in March

1962. This period was one of intense CIA activity in that country, aimed at wiping out the remaining guerrilla resistance. In March 1964 Wheelock returned to Washington as an intelligence research specialist in the State Department. In July 1966 he was transferred to Santiago, where he was listed as a political officer. He switched from a diplomatic to a civilian cover near the end of 1969. Communiques from North Americans in Chile, issued just prior to the coup, linked Wheelock to the right-wing, paramilitary terrorist group, *Patria y Libertad.*

Donald H. Winters was an analyst in the Air Force (1960-62), then served as a foreign service officer in Panama (1964-69), as well as in Washington at the State Department. Winters began serving as a political officer in Santiago in May 1969.

This was Langley's "first team."

In March 1971 leaders opposed to Allende's government began regular meetings under the direction of American agents to plot a calendar of sabotage and propaganda leading to a paralysis of the economy. When Townley demanded of his case officer that *Patria y Libertad* be unleashed, he was counseled to restrain himself until certain "problems" were solved. The problems included Jack Anderson's revelations of ITT-CIA ties to the Schneider assassination, and a leaked memo from Ambassador Davis to the State Department:

. . .prospects of military intervention for the foreseeable future are extremely small. It is held that military will turn blind eye to virtually any constitutional abuse . . . .Public not yet on brink of showdown . . . .Public opposition to Allende will have to become so overwhelming, and discontent so great, that military intervention is overwhelmingly invited . . . .

At last Langley had one of its own in Santiago—after years of bleeding hearts from "Foggy Bottom," like Dungan, who had pled with the White House in 1970 to "let [the Chileans] work things out for themselves."

In Washington, Ambassador Orlando Letelier denied that the Chilean Embassy was the source for any of the revelations about

ITT in the Jack Anderson columns. Chile's ambassador to France, Pablo Neruda, accused the United States directly of trying to overthrow the UP government. Neruda was quoted in *Le Monde* as stating, "The pivot of the [U.S.] conspiracy is former President Eduardo Frei Montalva."

President Allende appealed to world justice: "Small dependent countries such as ours have the right to be respected. Our laws are within the framework of our Constitution, written by a Congress more than 150 years old."

Everyone, the Townleys included, was hard at work on Plan September. Michael set about organizing two new paramilitary action groups, *Orden y Libertad* (Order and Freedom) and *Protección Comunal y Soberania* (Common Protection and Sovereignty).

At the same time, Callejas was a part of a journalistic team preparing a series for *El Mercurio* on the infiltration of the military by young Marxists toward the end of establishing a "Red Dictatorship." Callejas's name was not printed, thus protecting her cover, though she was associated publicly with a "Reds Invade Army" special on Radio Agricultura, another CIA asset.

During this period, Ambassador Letelier returned to Chile for urgent conferences with the Cabinet and to report from the economic firing line.

By August 1972 Plan September was underway. Townley, Vera Serafin, and their toughs were fighting police as the Pots and Pans marched again. A select Townley arson squad had been hard at work all through the spring. Townley's young freedom fighters were also active in middle- and upper-class residential districts organizing "security contingency" against the constantly predicted Marxist sacking to come.

By August 21, Allende had declared a temporary state of emergency in Santiago, primarily because of the street violence and burnings. In Concepción, the army took control of the city as P y L-staged violence provoked left-wing youth into street responses.

On September 2, President Allende charged that there was something called Plan September, a conspiracy to overthrow the government. A radio station in the provincial capital of Los Angeles was identified as a right-wing propaganda front and ordered closed by the government. The station was, in fact, one of Phillips's assets being fed violent disinformation, composed by Callejas and others. The next radio station to be closed for forty eight hours, as violence spread, was Radio Agricultura, another component in the Phillips network, for whom Callejas also worked. Townley led bloody street fighting to protest the closings.

On October 10, Plan September went into high gear. A nation-wide truckers' strike started on that day and grew into a general protest against the government. It did not end until November 5, three days after Allende had been forced to revise his cabinet.

In Langley and Rio, money and plans for the support and, in a number of instances, instigation of these strikes flowed through the fingers of David Phillips and Nathaniel Davis. By way of a dramatic compromise, President Allende shuffled his cabinet to bring a number of military officers into the government. Then he left to try to rally support outside of Chile.

On December 4, Allende, briefed by Ambassador Letelier, spoke in New York before the General Assembly of the United Nations. In a ninety-minute speech, he accused American interests of trying to prevent his government from taking power, and then of promoting an economic blockade that had severely limited Chile's ability to secure equipment, scarce parts, food, and medicine. This "financial strangulation" was "yet another manifestation of imperialism, one that is more subtle, more cunning and terrify-ingly effective in preventing us from exercising our rights as a sovereign state."

Because of pressure from American interests, Allende con-tinued, agencies such as the Export-Import Bank, the World Bank, the Inter-American Development Bank, private banking interests in the United States, and the Agency for International Development had cut off lines of credit to Chile. Such actions, he said were "legally and morally unacceptable," representing "the exertion of pressure on an economically weak country, the inflic-tion of punishment on a whole nation for its decision to recover its own basic resources, and a form of intervention in the interna-tional affairs of a sovereign state."

Allende centered his criticism on two American corporations, the International Telephone and Telegraph Corporation and Kennecott Copper Corporation, which, he said, had "dug their claws into my country" and proposed "to manage our political life." ITT, he charged, had "launched a sinister plan to prevent me from acceding to the presidency . . . . Before the conscience of the world, I accuse ITT of attempting to bring about civil war in my country." Allende included ITT and Kennecott among huge "transnational" corporations which he said were waging war against sovereign states and were "not accountable to or regulated by any parliament or institution representing the collective interest."

The President's return trip took him to Lima, Peru, and Mexico City, where huge throngs shouted support, and official statements denounced "the aggression of multinational interests" against Chile. The unequal fight to the finish had begun.

10 David Phillips & The Case of the "Quartered Man," 1973

Why so many advantages for you?
Who gave you the spoon before you were even born?

It bothers me during this voyage
to find, in corners, sadness
the eyes without love or a mouth without bread

Pablo Neruda

DAVID PHILLIPS, "THE GREAT OPERATIONS OFFICER" (in the words of DCI William Colby), was facing one of his sternest challenges. Private polls showed that Allende's Popular Unity government, (instead of losing support as *all* previous Chilean governments had), was gaining in popularity as the mid-term elections in March 1973 approached. The CIA-backed strike of the *gremios*, the "bosses" of the trucking industry, was making the economy "scream"—just as Kissinger had asked of Helms—but no one could predict whether the strikes plus the embargo by the United States and the World Bank would prevent Allende from completing his six-year term, which was slated to end in September of 1976. True, Townley and his neofascist extremists were tearing the country apart with every imaginable kind of violence and provocation, but their actions might also serve to split the military, under Chief of Staff General Carlos Prats, the strict constitutionalist, when the coup came.

Officers of the Chilean military, with their German training traditions, upon graduation from their military academy, swear on their swords an oath of allegiance not to the president or to the government, but to the *constitution*. Thus the Chilean armed forces like the Chilean political establishment presented the CIA and Phillips with special problems. Somehow, violence and black propaganda would have to be calibrated in such a way as to paralyze large parts of the populace and, at the same time, unleash the military in a blitzkrieg of blood; the military was the "target."

In spite of these obstacles Phillips could easily identify his assets. In Santiago, the American Embassy now boasted a crack coup team and, in Nathaniel Davis, an activist Ambassador. Davis liked to be thought of as an OSS-type World War II ambassador, and Frederick Purdy was a sturdy link to both the Central Intelligence Agency and the Defense Intelligence Agency. Phillips knew that at the decisive moment it would be the DIA and *not* the CIA that would act in concert with the *golpistas*, the military leaders of the coup.

Phillips knew, too, from long experience that the economy would have to be disrupted. That meant an increase in funds to the CIA's fifth column, the American Institute for Free Labor Development (AIFLD). AIFLD had been linked directly to the 1964 coup against Brazilian President João Goulart. In 1968 a colleague of David Phillips, William C. Doherty, Jr., of the AIFLD, told a Senate subcommittee:

What happened in Brazil on April 1 [1964] did not just happen—it was planned—and planned months in advance. Many of the trade union leaders—some of whom were actually trained in our institute—were involved in the revolution, and in the overthrow of the Goulart regime.

Despite the "union" label and the participation of George Meany, the AIFLD's main task is to protect American business interests. Sponsorship of AIFLD is tripartite: labor, business, and government. Among its corporate supporters are ITT, Kennecott Copper Company, Chase Manhattan Bank, United Fruit Company, Rockefeller Brothers Fund, Pan American World Airlines, First National City Bank, and W. R. Grace & Co.

After the election of the Popular Unity government in 1970, AIFLD sped up its data collection on Chilean workers. In 1971, AIFLD assisted in the creation of the Confederation of Chilean Professionals (CUPROCH), which was then used by Phillips to create widespread social and economic disruption. CUPROCH received funds from the CIA to support the truck owners' and merchants' strike in 1972. And when the rest of the country faced food shortages, the CUPROCH workers dined well.

AIFLD was also active in establishing the National Command of Gremial Defense. The National Command was made up of former Nazis and members of Patria y Libertad, but the American media did not notice.

With his propaganda flanks secure, at home and abroad, Phillips was ready for the final act in Centaur.

By March of 1973 a pornographic film purporting to represent President Allende and Ambassador Letelier was in circulation. This vile trick would be irrelevant in the great historical process emerging in Latin America were it not that Phillips was following pages from the CIA's book on Indonesia. There the film *Happy Days* had been concocted to destroy the character of President Sukarno. (In 1967 the FBI used similar tactics against Martin Luther King, Jr.)

Happy Days was an infantile (polymorphously perverse) prelude to Plan Djakarta in Indonesia, a bloodbath almost beyond imagination. Plan Djakarta was a generic antecedent of Chile's Centaur. Soon Djakarta would come to Santiago. *El Desquartizado* was coming.

El Desquartizado, "the Quartered Man," is a monstrous creation of the CIA. Using classical depth psychology and behavior modification techniques and theories developed by American psychological studies, Phillips and a team of behavioral scientists devised a secret agenda by which to program individual Chileans toward a destiny of victims or executioners. The CIA aim was to "serialize" and atomize the Chilean people by using psychological terror to fractionate what had been the growing popular unity behind the government. Chileans would be reduced to a new world-view of all against all.

Under the CIA program the middle classes had to be organized to "save freedom," the military to impose *temporary* controls, the workers to give up their drive for power. Phillips had at his disposal the fruits of the most statistically sophisticated social research in the world, for Centaur, in 1973, was the next lower order of abstraction from Camelot in the 1960's. Camelot's statistics became the basis for Centaur. The targets were the middle class, the largest in Latin America, and the military.

The Chilean reality thus forced Phillips to accomplish in secret what Joseph Goebbels in Nazi Germany had achieved in the glare of constant publicity and festivity. In place of the hypnotic wailing of Hitler's voice, beamed by radio to every corner of Germany, Phillips had to give birth *inside* individual Chileans to a private monster: *El Desquartizado*, "The Quartered Man." Hitler had been a public monster seducing the populace, calling out thwarted impulses of sado-masochistic love from the national psyche. But the Quartered Man was a monster of pure terror—without a voice or a name or a face.

The IGS fifth column at *El Mercurio* was given its orders after the stunning popular gain at the polls by the UP in the March 1973 elections. Allende, it was now clear, could not be stopped by votes, even after wholesale bribery and Townley-type terror. Langley flashed Phillips the Nixon-Kissinger message: *Smash the UP government by any means necessary so long as U.S. involvement is deniable at all times.* In other words, set the psyche of Chile ablaze with a secret fire.

No nation is immune to psychological warfare. Chile was a country with long, strong, vibrant democratic political traditions, yet she was a casualty in this secret war. Phillips and his mad doctors knew well the Freudian axiom that "the resources of the ego are not inexhaustible." The undermining of Chile's national sanity began with the invisible invasion of monstrous images; since there were no Marines or G.I.s, there was nothing for the Chilean people to resist.

Langley had studied the stated aim of depth psychology, as enunciated by Sigmund Freud—"Where id was there shall ego be"—and then reversed it. CIA's psychological warfare strategy is predicated on replacing the adult ego with the infantile id. In Latin *ego* means "I" and *id* means "it." Precisely the transformation from an "I" to an "it," from *person* to a *thing*, was the point of Centaur's *El Desquartizado*.

Freud once stated that the modest goal of psychoanalysis was to replace "hysterical misery with everyday unhappiness." Again, the Phillips plan was the reverse. Hysterical misery was about to be unleashed on the people of Chile like a fatal plague.

During the months preceding the March 1973 elections, *El Mercurio* built on the previously established theme of "Marxist violence." Minor traffic accidents and major crimes of violence were linked with "Marxism" (the UP government). Xenophobia began to spread like a communicable disease. "Clean up the Marxist filth!" became the compulsive litany of the coup-makers.

To substantiate the position of "Marxist violence," *El Mercurio* gave political meaning to the crash of a plane carrying an Uruguayan soccer team in the Chilean Andes, and then to a man who had been found with his arms, legs, and head cut off (the latter was to become known as the "Quartered Man"—*El Descuartizado*).

The plane crashed on the day of an abortive coup in October 1972. Rescue efforts were seriously hampered because of Air Force involvement in coup communications, and the plane and its passengers were soon given up for lost. Then, before the elections of March 1973, survivors came out of the Andes. The name of the mountain on which the plane had crashed was *El Descabezado*. This word would be integrated into a syntax including *descabezar* and *Descuartizado*, all of which connoted bloody mutilation.

During the 1970 elections the target had been women. Now *El Mercurio* brought international attention to the fact that the Andean survivors had eaten the flesh of a woman killed in the crash. The implication was that a barbarous monster, bloodthirsty, necrophilous, and sadistic, was loose in the country.

El Mercurio also claimed that a housewife had bought hot dogs made from the flesh of the Quartered Man. Death, painful and sadistic, was imminent. Compounding the terror was the threat that the slaughtered would become food for the survivors. The themes of cannibalism and castration were to be inextricably woven into the Chilean world-view.

El Mercurio and *La Prensa* both carried, as news stories, headlines "Marxists Slaughter Dog" at Liceo #12 (a girls' school). the slaughtered dog, henceforth referred to as Checkers #2, turned out to be alive and well—after the elections were safely won. "Dead Dog Lives."

Oscar Waiss, editor of *La Nación*, reacted with an editorial titled "Tropical Excesses":

The artificial crisis invented recently by the right-wing newspapers shows that the CIA has transferred past experiences in more tropical climates without any regard to the greater sophistication of Chileans. They ignore the tradition of serious debate of issues instead of tricks like the slaughtered dog at school #12.

Handicapped veterans marched in protest of a lack of parts for wheelchairs and other grievances. Headlines in *El Mercurio* read: "March of Handicapped Veterans, Marxist Government Orders Them Dispersed by Blows." Townley and his Patria y Libertad shock troops had knocked some marchers over, police had entered the crowd, and photos appeared showing only the handicapped on the ground and police officers standing over them. The protest and its coverage had been a David A. Phillips production.

The handicapped, the mutilated, symbolized the Quartered Man. The implication was that the UP police were degenerates who derived pleasure from the sadistic power they had over the mutilated. Langley's understanding of paranoia—that it is the result of a repressed nexus of polymorphously perverse and homosexual impulses—squares with that of classical depth psychology. The key is that the impulses are totally *repressed* and therefore can be manipulated and projected on to the "other" (Jew, Communist, etc.).

Unlike certain Latin American countries, Chile is not noted for an anti-Semitic tradition, and its Jewish population is small. Yet before the coup, vicious racist rumors about Salvador Allende's "semitic" background began to circulate, or rather, to be circulated by Rafael Otero Echeverria on Radio Agricultura. Orlando Letelier does appear to have had a Jewish maternal grandmother, and his name, too, was linked to the "Zionist Conspiracy."

On election day, March 4, *El Mercurio* and *La Segunda* ran full-page ads paid for by an aggregation of all opposition parties, CODE (Confederación de la Democracia), which read, "Case of the Suspicious Hot Dogs: It Wasn't Human Flesh but Just Dog Meat," and "Just Dog Meat!" The bottom of the ad reads, "Did You Ever Imagine We Would Reach Such a State! Vote CODE."

The combined circulation of the two newspapers was 500,000 (in a country of 9,000,000). It was the only ad officially sponsored by all five political parties opposing Allende. Lastly, this single ad summarized in one graphic image all the "news" stories about the *Descuartizado*, *El Mercurio* editorials, and political ads for the previous two months. With its appearance, it was no longer possible to believe that some lone neurotic at *El Mercurio* was slipping strange stories into the news columns. Whoever invented the *Descuartizado* was in a position to dictate the advertising of all five major political parties in Chile. That is when the great fear really hit. Suspicions and fears engendered by the earlier stories relating to *El Descuartizado* pressed the point: No child, no person, not even a little pet would be safe in Chile as long as the "Marxist government" was in control.

Another particularly ugly story well circulated by the IGS people was the practice of the military in digging up graves in "search of Cuban weapons." Yawning graves in the poor quarters were more of the *Descuartizado* shock treatment.

All five opposition parties cooperated in making the "*Descuartizado*/Marxist government" correlation. Horror brought the opposition to life; through the objectification of their sado-masochistic, pathological imaginings they felt alive. Not having the power to win at the polls, they had swallowed Phillips' word-salad of cannibalism, corpses, blood.

Alvaro Puga, the CIA's propaganda director at *El Mercurio*, was responsible for a number of subtle false news items from *Descuartizado* and for translating the monster into humorous terms, aware, as he was of the pointed wit for which the Chileans are famous.

THE CASE OF THE DESCUARTIZADO

"In the court there reigns a plague of fables"

I was sitting in the CIA's bar having my third daiquiri with Cuban rum while I waited the arrival of Dimitri Dimitrovich, KGB agent. "Look, my dear Dimitri," I told him, "the truth of the matter is that I can't sleep thinking about the case of DESCUARTIZADO."

"Alexis," Dimitri answered, "it is necessary to psychologically prepare people for what is to come and that is why our allies in parliament have been announcing for weeks now the anticipated coup; the same in all the newspapers. After a coup, which costs us a great deal of money, nobody would believe you people (CIA) were responsible unless he blamed you ahead of time."

Alexis, "Do you plan to continue the DESCUARTIZAMIENTOS?"

Dimitri, "According to the Brezhnev-Nixon convention, I only have to inform you of secret plans—and that is no secret."

Alexis, "I drank the rest of my Cuban rum while I thought of my future vengeance."

A Socialist party member suggested that, given the current artificial shortage of food produced by hoarding, maids should denounce gross cases of hoarding by rich people. The headlines "Government Studies System for Using Maids to Spy in Chilean Homes" and "Communism and Spies in the Home" caused panic and suspicion. Food is basic. Would hoarders be quartered and used for food? Worse than this, the male head of the household would be dominated by women—inferior women—and he would have to follow their rules. This is the overthrow of the *macho*: obedience and accommodation to women. The women of the middle and upper classes were made to feel fundamentally threatened by Langley's exotic comic book of lusty maids who would, in one way or another, devour their employer husbands— the *momios*.

Langley did not even scruple to spread, through IGS, an absolutely demented fantasy about the supposed propensity of Chilean women to bite their partners at the moment of erotic climax. This biting was advertised, in the rumor campaign, as having reached cannibilistic proportions in the repertoire of the nymphomaniacs of the Left. Always there was the implication that "Marxism" brings not only males but females into power. Leftist women are, to the fearful, symbols of the Amazons who would have strong young boys sacrificed to them.

Is it any wonder, then, that bourgeois women act as a frightened mob, for the CIA, across the world's stage? There was no comprehension by most of them, in Chile, for instance, that they were being threatened by and led in their attack by a corps of elite chauvinists in Langley under that urbane gentleman David Phillips.

There have been ranks of fanatical women all across the continent —from Guatemala City to Rio to Santiago— poured into tight expensive pants, or wearing silver foxes and flowered hats, who have stepped briskly to the call of the silent horn from Langley, brandishing pots and pans laboriously polished by their maids. They have smoked cigarettes, laughed, and talked with the Townleys and handsome young fascists who march alongside for their protection.

Paranoid images of penetration of a *passive* victim continued in constant variation. It was claimed that foreign extremists had *infiltrated* the government. The page following this "exposé" carried the headline, "Cuban Intromission in Chilean Politics." (Cubans who had visited the country were also referred to as "Two Sinister Foreign Agents.") Intromission carries the connotation of violent and criminal rape.

The implications of cannibalism and castration were enough to leave the men feeling impotent and the women terrorized. The hallucinatory power of these abstractions would eventually destroy, cut up, torture human flesh. Langley was waging a secret war of all-out terror, turning the screws tighter and tighter. Techniques devised to sell Americans deodorant, were now used in Chile to sell death and putrefaction.

Subliminal messages were transmitted by placing headlines near photographs that were unrelated. Of the themes that the CIA gave *El Mercurio*, the one which achieved world-wide currency was "Marxists Threaten Free Press," or its more specific version, *"Marxists Threaten El Mercurio."*

And so those who had never heard of Chile before read in newspapers around the world, "Allende Threatens El Mercurio." President Ford stood before the General Assembly of the United Nations, and without blushing, repeated this fabricated story as a pretext for the CIA's role in tearing apart the legitimate government of Chile.

Violence was now a daily diet for the ever-growing P y L shock troops. It was during this period that, in all probability, Townley, too, reached the psychological point of no return. In an environment of provoked, arbitrary violence it is understood that if a person kills enough, he too must one day be killed. Sadism, masochism, and necrophagia are not merely deviations from societal standards; they also become a way of life. Day by day, the "executioner" rehearses for the role of "victim" that will be his when one day soon the slave rebels, as he must, for the executioner will make sure that the slave is eventually driven to resistance. The Michael Townleys already, privately, think of themselves as dead men. That is why they need feel no guilt for their crimes against the innocent.

Chilean culture is oral, verbal, literary; and political debate concerns real issues. Since this had been true in the past, it might be presumed that the high-impact visual messages of Phillips's psychological warfare techniques, with their infantile logic, would not take in an educated Chilean of the middle class. This presumption would be incorrect. As Marshall McLuhan points out,

The unconscious depth-message of ads is never attacked by the literate because of their incapacity to notice or discuss non-verbal forms of arrangements and meanings.

For literary sophisticates who have had their sensibilities irredeemably skewed and locked into the fixed postures of mechanical writing and printing, the iconic forms of the electronic age are as opaque, or even as invisible, as hormones to the unaided eye.

The new *El Mercurio* had become a psycho-political montage, a subtly composed ideological poster with editorials on the front page. Over the years Phillips had worked closely with the author William Peter Blatty, a former CIA officer, and had been much influenced by the secret dialectic of Blatty's opus *The Exorcist*. Blatty, like Phillips and Hunt and generation of spies, was obsessed with communism and the Devil.

In *The Exorcist*, a young girl is confined to her room, possessed by the Devil. The girl's mother is at work on a film at a nearby college campus. There, we see mobs of students possessed by a rabid anti-Vietnam war passion. There are only glimpses of these insurgent young people, but enough to establish the figure-ground relation between the possessed girl and the possessed, *political* students.

Now Phillips drew on what he had learned from Howard Hunt about Devil cults, and from Blatty. The Quartered Man was actually the Devil. His footprints were pointed little words and signs.

At crucial times, at elections or in a coup, the CIA uses poisonous messages in the press which are not presented in coherent form until the critical day. *In the case of elections, the target of these messages is women; and, in the case of coups, the military.*

In order to hypnotize Chile's highly sophisticated political culture a gradual and subtle building-up toward a desired new world-view was required. There were at least five stages in the development of each image or component of this world-view. In the cases of POPULAR UNITY VS. ARMED FORCES; SOVIET SUBMARINE BASE IN CHILE; and RED PLANS TO BEHEAD ARMED FORCES, we find these stages in the development of each topic:

A. Ultraleft vs. Armed Forces
   MIR vs. Armed Forces
   Socialist Party vs. Armed Forces
   Popular Unity vs. Armed Forces, September 1973
B. Russian fishing boats in Chile
   Soviet ships in Chile
   Russian nuclear propelled submarines in Chile
   Soviet nuclear submarines in Chile
   Soviet nuclear submarine base in Chile, March 1973
C. Marxist infiltration of public education
   Marxist infiltration of Catholic education
   Marxist infiltration of military education
   Marxist infiltration of military
   Marxist plan to *descabezar* (retire) military leaders, September 1973

In Chile the verb *descabezar* has two meanings: "to retire" and "to decapitate." CIA played upon this ambiguity as they had with the image of the crocodile in Indonesia. There, military men had been pictured being chewed up by a crocodile. A huge crocodile with knifelike teeth, and prehensile jaws ajar, waited for the officer corps to fall into the black and cutting hole. A gigantic vagina with razor-sharp teeth could be seen in the gaping jaws of the crocodiles.

In Indonesia, as in Chile, officers received faked information of their imminent decapitation by Marxists. That is why over 750,000 were slaughtered in the CIA-backed coup, and countless "Communists" were *decapitated*. Later, CIA-connected anthropologists would speculate about the "darker recesses of the Indonesian mind."

From the recesses at Langley came the plans Djakarta and Centaur. It was American behavioral scientists, using scientific terms, who plotted the psywar attack on the "body armor" of the officer corps; Americans who calculated how to turn the inflated "masculine protest" of the military man into an ejaculation of cruelty; Americans who played upon the dialectic of "homosexual panic" and "male bonding," in Indonesia and Chile, until there was nervous breakdown and chaos.

Dr. Fred Landis, who spent weeks with the junta after the coup, reports on their continuing castration fear and *reactive* fury. Reactive to the Quartered Man and *descabezar* fictions because, in reality, there had been no threat to them at all under Allende. The *golpistas* (the military) were first the *target* of the CIA, after 1970; only later did they become the henchmen and puppets of 1973.

The Red plan to *descabezar* (behead) military leaders in September 1973 was the CIA climax to the case of the Quartered Man. The middle, educated class was paralyzed by masochism, and the military was tumescent with sadism. The public was warned night and day, as the coup approached, that invasion was imminent, that foreign forces were not far from striking (in fact were represented by the government), that mutilation was threatening, that human flesh and dog meat had been eaten by the people, that children were not safe (since maids were spying on their employers).

Descuartizado, the bloody castrated stump that haunted Chile and drove the officer corps mad, was not simply a creature of the media: in September each senior officer received from Phillips's shop a "personal" computerized letter. The letter spelled out how the officer and his children would be decapitated after the Marxists had imposed their totalitarian state. The correct names of the children were listed, and included was another list, of the "subversives" who would actually do the beheading, the *quartering*. This was Plan Djakarta.

Allende's government did not enjoy wide support among the Chilean middle class and almost none in the old ruling class. The aim of Centaur, September, "Quartered Man," etc., was *not* to change the political perceptions of the various anti-Allende political parties. The goal was to undermine their *moral* loyalties to the Chilean Constitution. The Center parties were always ready to *vote* UP out of office, but not to exterminate party members and the Constitution at the same time. That result had to be achieved.

Rafael Otero Echeverria, writing in his own magazine *SEPA* shortly before the coup, featured an article titled "Beria's Secret Diary." This purported to show that the former head of the Soviet secret police had left behind a diary outlining the ten Communist steps in the takeover of a country. One of the most important goals, according to the story, is to drive a country mad in order to facilitate the seizure of power. This is accomplished by infiltrating Communist agents into the fields of medicine and psychology.

The evident purpose of the article was to "explain" the by-then obvious social dislocations CIA psychological operations were causing and at the same time project the blame onto the future victims. This also explains the ruthlessness with which the military purged the Chilean National Health Service after the coup.

The centers of personal and public belief could not hold out against the Quartered Man. The beliefs that once gave direction to life had become hollow abstractions. A shrill new vocabulary of Langley gibberish had turned a proud small country into a lunatic asylum. When people have lost trust *completely*, then the personalities, the identities built on the original beliefs will disintegrate. The resources of the ego are not inexhaustible, far from it. The Chileans were destroyed first psychologically and then physically; they were made first mad and then blind.

There was no Quartered Man. The story had been invented at Langley. It was the people of Chile, finally, who were quartered. *El Descuartizado* had become the symbol of the Chilean people.

11 Coup!

You are our homeland, country, and people
sand, keel, school, house
resurrection, fist force
order, parade, march, wheat
struggle, greatness, resistance

Pablo Neruda

BY AUGUST 1973, THE CIA'S GOAL of modifying the military until it perceived itself as a class apart had been achieved.

General Augusto Pinochet was a paradox that can only now be partly explained. Pinochet, like Carlos Prats and René Schneider, was considered a moderate constitutionalist. He served under the new Minister of Defense Orlando Letelier and went to great lengths to ingratiate himself with the entire Letelier family. "He acted as if he wanted to hold my coat and shine my shoes," Letelier later said. Pinochet had *not* been involved in the Track II or Centaur coup plans, though he was aware of them. How, then did he become the butcher of September 11, 1973, and head of the junta after the coup?

From 1962 on, Pinochet's career had blossomed: "Special mission" in India, professorship at the War College, published works on geopolitics. His assignments included Washington, D.C., where he was military attaché to the Chilean Embassy. He was also seen at the United States Southern Command in the Panama Canal Zone in 1965, 1968, and 1972.

Pinochet had served with distinction, and Letelier trusted him to the end. If Letelier had not, he could have had Pinochet (or any of his associates) arrested at any time. Though it has been suggested that Letelier had damaging knowledge of something in Pinochet's past, this is unlikely. The most probable explanation, both for Pinochet's subservient demeanor toward Letelier and his ultimate participation in the coup, is that he had seen his superiors assassinated, isolated, humiliated, and he was not going to let that happen to him. He was not going to suffer the fate of Prats.

Especially critical to the success of failure of a coup in 1973 was whether General Prats would, at some point, go along with the traitors. Because each branch of the Chilean military is completely independent of the others, control of the Army, the largest and most influential, was critical if Centaur was to succeed. But General Prats was adamantly loyal to the elected government, so Phillips ran a psychological campaign against him (using Pots and Pans), and Prats suffered a temporary breakdown.

The tactics used against General Prats were based on a psychological profile of him prepared at Langley. On June 27, 1973, female agents, enlisted by *Patria y Libertad* to insult Prats, succeeded in provoking an ugly street incident.

Then, on August 21, several hundred women, including the wives of six Chilean generals and other officers, demonstrated in front of Prats's residence. These attempts to discredit the Chilean defense minister may seem petty, but in a society under the sway of *machismo*—particularly in the military—the organization of middle- and upper-class women by Phillips and the Right was an effective tactic. Prats resigned as minister of defense and commander in chief of the armed forces. His replacement as commander in chief: Augusto Pinochet. And in late August 1973, the code phrase, "Little Red Riding Hood is ready," signified that Pinochet was ready to take off his servile mask.

To recapitulate: By May, the code word "Djakarta," could be seen scrawled in red on walls everywhere, and Townley's thugs were provoking violence with frenzied compulsion.

Townley was running one of Phillips's tried and true operations, modeled on the CIA's Guatemala success, a clandestine mobile radio station. The powerful transmitter was mounted in the rear of the Townley Austin Mini automobile. Radio Liberación was incessant in its appeals to the military to act before the government could *decabezar* the elite officer corps. The corps began to panic.

Escalation: A wave of assassinations, including that of the President's naval aide, Commander Arturo Araya, on July 26, in his own home—Otero carried the usual stories in *SEPA* blaming the Left.

Even so, Allende's constitutional gamble—"I have sworn before history and my own conscience not to use violence"—almost succeeded. In the provinces, entire regiments mutinied against the *golpistas* and had to be rooted out and decimated as a lesson to cow the troops. The bodies of murdered loyalists were hurried away in garbage trucks and buried secretly. If it had not been for Pinochet, the noncommissioned army, under Prats, clearly would have remained loyal. And in a civil war, who could doubt that President Allende, at last, would have had to arm the still loyal working class.

That last night, Allende and his cabinet decided the President should submit to a plebiscite and let the people decide whether he should remain in office. Letelier and the others had been discussing this extraordinary step for days, *and Pinochet, who was present at most of the crisis meetings*, and informing the CIA, was ordered to move up the day of the coup from Independence Day, September 18, to September 11.

President Allende, on the morning of the *putsch*, telephoned Letelier, who had become minister of defense, with an urgent request for information of any troop movements. Letelier's chauffeur and bodyguard were junta agents, and it was they who arrested him and threw a black sack over his head. Minister Letelier's arrest at the Ministry of Defense spared him the terror and pity of the scene being played out at the presidential palace, the Moneda.

Earlier, Allende, with partial information of military plots, had warned a journalist, "You don't play with fire. If anyone thinks that a military coup in Chile will be like those in other countries of Latin America with a simple changing of the guard at Moneda legality here, there will be a bloodbath. It will be another Indonesia."

Allende was an historian of his country's institutions, and he knew well the fierce tradition of Chile's German-trained military. The great Latin American writer Gabriel Garcia Marquez, who has reconstructed Allende's last hours on September 11, had said that the myth of the legalism of the brutal military was "invented by the Chilean bourgeoisie in their own interest."

So Allende, in the end, relied on the *Carbineros*, the national police, popular and peasant in origin, and unlike the military, under the direct command of the President. Before the coup, the junta had to go six places down the seniority list of the national police to find a senior officer who would support the overthrow, one who had been trained at an American counterinsurgency school. The younger officers barricaded themselves in their school, shooting it out with the military, until aerial bombardment smashed down their resistance.

By September 18, people were being executed in the National Stadium where the Independence Day celebration was to have been held.

At the same time, Phillips, through Davis and Purdy at the embassy, had alerted secret police agencies from neighboring countries so that they could sneak operatives across the Bolivian border and lie in wait for the coup, and then seize their own citizens in exile from repression at home. Torture agents from Brazil coordinated this influx of political police.

Inside the somber, Italianate palace, Allende and his loyal aides prepared for the end. The President wore a miner's helmet and cradled a submachine gun given to him by Fidel Castro. Allende was calm, the lifelong revolutionary who would not depart from a constitution—drawn by the upper classes—to save his popular government, an exemplary figure who will finally be remembered as, perhaps, Chile's greatest patriot. However, he may have failed at a revolution that forced him to fight on two fronts at once: against the traitors in the military and the massive prongs of Centaur. Could anyone, even Castro, have won both a revolution and an American-provoked civil war at the same time?

Soon, Allende sent away his medical and secretarial aides. Around 10:30 A.M., the President was prepared both to fight and talk. A remarkable conversation between General Pinochet and Admiral Carvajal took place at this time, and was taped.

Pinochet: Patricio, Augusto speaking. they have just told me the President is thinking of attacking the Defense Ministry with Socialist brigades. Alert the troops and be ready with automatic weapons at the windows and attack the snipers on the roofs in front right away.

Carvajal: Yes, we are doing that. We have taken steps....

Pinochet: Right, another thing, Patricio. At exactly 11 o'clock we must attack the palace because this fellow is not going to give himself up.

Carvajal: It is already being attacked, we are surrounding it and attacking quite strongly. We will take it soon.

Pinochet: Right, and he will be taken straight to the plane and kicked out....

Carvajal: He refused the possibility of the plane....

Pinochet: He refused?

Carvajal: He asked the aide de camp for the commanders-in-chief to come to the palace.

Pinochet: No. He is to come to the Defense Ministry. Will he come?

Carvajal: No he refused.

Pinochet: I knew it, he wants us to go there and he'll put us in a cellar. So the answer is no. He is to go to the Defense Ministry and we will all go there. Now attack the palace—strongly.

Ten minutes later Admiral Carvajal called again.

Carvajal: Commander, Badiola is in contact with the palace. He is going to transmit the last offer of surrender. I have just been told they intend to parley.

Pinochet: Parleying means he has to go to the ministry with a small group of people

Carvajal: But he is offering to parley...

Pinochet: Unconditional surrender, no parleying.

Carvajal: Right, unconditional surrender and take him prisoner, offering to respect his life.

Pinochet: His life and physical well-being. He will be sent somewhere else immediately.

Carvajal: Right, so the offer to take him out of the country stands.

Pinochet: The offer stands.

Allende's last words were cut off as radio frequencies were jammed by the military's Pentagon advisors:

People of my country, I want to thank you for the loyalty which you have always shown, the trust you placed in a man who was only the interpreter of the great desires of justice, who gave his word that he would respect the constitution and the law . . . . I have faith in Chile and her destiny. Other men will overcome this gray and bitter moment . . . . The great avenues through which free men will pass to build a better society will open.

Long live Chile!

Shortly after two o'clock Colonel Javier Palacios managed to lead an attack group inside and up to the second floor. In the party was Armando Fernández Larios (later to be Michael Townley's fellow DINA agent). "Traitor!" Allende shouted as the raiding party reached the head of the stairs.

"There, in the midst of the fake Louis XV chairs, the Chinese dragon vases, and the Rugendas paintings in the red parlor, Salvador Allende was waiting for them," wrote the great novelist Gabriel Marquez. The storming party let loose a fusillade and Allende fell. Then all the other officers, in a caste-bound ritual, fired on the body. Finally, a noncomissioned officer smashed in the President's face with his rifle butt. Allende's epitaph belongs to Marquez, who follows Neruda as the authentic voice of Latin America.

He loved life, he loved flowers, he loved dogs . . . . Fate could grant him only that rare and tragic greatness of dying in armed defense of . . . . a Supreme Court of Justice which had repudiated him but would legitimize his murderers, defending a miserable Congress which had declared him illegitimate but which was to bend complacently before the will of the usurpers, defending the freedom of opposition parties which had sold their souls to fascism, defending the whole moth-eaten paraphernalia of a shitty system which he had proposed abolishing, but without a shot being fired. The drama took place in Chile, to the greater woe of the Chileans, but it will pass into history as something that has happened to us all, children of this age, and it will remain in our lives forever.

That winter before the coup Townley became involved with several of the women of the Pots and Pans, the wives of important men, and this infuriated Callejas. She hated the rich bitches in the marching force; she despised the anti-semites who were always lounging around her house; she was overworked and her husband was flagrantly unfaithful.

In June of 1973 Townley was identified as a CIA "contract agent" by the populist leftist newspaper *Puro Chile*. The story broke because, in March, a terrorist team led by Townley had bound a nightwatchman at a power station in Concepción, where the government had to set up an oscillator to jam a Catholic University television station, Channel 13, which had illegally extended its broadcast range. The jammer was blown up, but the watchman suffocated.

Phillips had ordered the sabotage as a part of the escalating communications-propaganda war, but Townley's gratuitous violence worried him. Callejas had dropped out of sight, and Townley had fled on a Canadian airliner to Buenos Aires, and from there to Florida. Townley's orders were to stand by for the *putsch*. This he did in Fort Lauderdale, at the National Intelligence Academy (NIA). Townley's parents now lived near Fort Lauderdale, and his father, Vernon, continued at Southeast First National Bank as a vice-president in the bank's international division.

During this summer exile Townley was reunited with his former Secret Army Organization friend Aldo Vera Serafin. It was common knowledge in exile circles that both Townley and Vera were CIA-connected. What the Cubans did not know was that Vera was an informant for the FBI as well. Documents obtained by the researchers for this book reveal that as of 1973 a *new* version of *Patria y Libertad* had been set up in Miami. In charge: Aldo Vera Serafin and Mike Townley. Then, on August 2, 1973, a Cuban exile, Juan Felipe de la Cruz, was killed in France, and Aldo Vera's fate was sealed. (See facing page for FBI document.) When it became known in 1976 that Vera may have been responsible for Cruz's death in France, Vera was murdered in San Juan. It was decided by the exiles not to kill Townley but, as we shall see, to use him to gain revenge on the FBI and the CIA.

As in the case of David Phillips, we have a footnote in Aldo Vera's life now added by the House Select Committee on Assassinations. Professor Peter Dale Scott in new research describes the existence, in 1963, of a Cuban group (the "Chicago junta") to which Vera belonged. According to Volume X (pages 90-100) of the Select committee's final report, the Chicago group was a terror cell boasting cash, arms, and influence with both CIA and the

UNITED STATES DEPARTMENT OF JUSTICE

FEDERAL BUREAU OF INVESTIGATION

Miami, Florida
November 26, 1976

In Reply, Please Refer to File No.   105-21705

RE: PATRIA Y LIBERTAD
       (FATHERLAND AND LIBERTY)
       NEUTRALITY MATTERS - CUBA
       (ANTI-CASTRO)

       It is noted and was previously reported that
the Directorio Revolucionario (DR) was a Cuban exile,
anti-CASTRO organization in Miami in 1972. It was mostly
involved in anti-communist propaganda activity. In 1973,
the DR sent three persons to Paris, France to bomb the
Cuban Embassy in Paris. On August 2, 1973, a bomb
accidentally exploded at Avrainvile, France, and killed
one of the participating terrorists.

       DR membership in Miami was immediately interviewed
by the Federal Bureau of Investigation (FBI). The membership all stated they were opposed to terrorism and resigned
from the organization in protest. The DR then disbanded
and was never reorganized. It no longer exists.

       A small group of former members of the DR decided
to form a new Cuban exile, anti-communist organization.
This group included the following persons:

mob. And until November 21, 1963—one day before the Dallas
murder—the "junta" was an operational hit team. Finally, names
connected to Aldo Vera and his junta were Orlando Bosch, Frank
Sturgis, Antonio Veciana: each one closely connected to either
Phillips or Townley or both.

Aldo Vera's career as a double agent ended in 1976 when
Bosch's men settled an old score.

As waves of violence cascaded against Chile during the days immediately after the coup, Phillips, from Langley, ordered his
secret team to shift into Plan Z. The Cold War rhetorical boiler
plate, instantly recognizable, appeared again in the junta's *White*

Book of events, a stale and predictable official rationale for the illegal overthrow, based on an imminent "Cuban invasion." The junta's code word for this immediate period of ruthless repression was Operation Djakarta, exactly as in Indonesia.

One urgent item in Plan Z was the *decabezar* bulletin to the media:

Extremists in Osorno distributed 400 metal files to the inhabitants of the Elmo-Catalan *población* so they could sharpen their shovels and use them as peoples' guillotines on Army officers, policemen and opposition leaders. the speedy intervention of the Army, however . . . .

Z was a bogus blueprint of decapitation and castration. It was *descuartizado* at a higher order of abstraction. Z was simply another of the bloody stereotypes in Phillips's merciless arsenal. Phillips and his teams had disoriented a whole country and driven its officer caste into a psychotic episode, labeled Djakarta.

There never was a *descuartizado*. The "Quartered Man" was a psywar construct, a creature of the Central Intelligence Agency. Some of the agents who orchestrated the Quartered Man Campaign would be reunited in Washington, D.C., in 1976 in the murder of Orlando Letelier.

Santiago had been the site of a great socialist and democratic experiment. Its epitaph, words Pablo Neruda had written years before about another city the victim of fascism, Madrid:

A dead city without kitchens
or outcries,
the somber enclave
of their purity . . . .
in a chaos beyond resurrection
a multitude lost to all vision . . . .
condemned to the truth of their godhead laid bare.

12 Michael Townley & David Phillips: Plan Z

The dark wheat of Cautin grows in me
I was born in the South. From this frontier
I brought with me the solitude and stride
of the last caudillo
But the Party knocked me off my horse
and revealed me to be a man
How could I exist if I did not march
with the flag that was passed
hand to hand down the line
in our long struggle
until it reached my hands?

Pablo Neruda

FRED SIMON LANDIS was a camera and a tape recorder after the coup. With remarkable resourcefulness Landis was able to camouflage his scientific presence and mingle with the new rulers of Chile. He was able to study their stress, reactions, and rationalizations. Documents supplied to the Senate Intelligence Committee show that the CIA station in Santiago was instructed to "author conclusive evidence Allende government planned to take country by force September 17, 1973." The CIA came up with Plan Z.

Plan Z and Plan Djakarta, before it, in Indonesia, attest to Langley's fear of a last-minute failure of nerve by client military forces. Guy Pauker, the Rand corporation specialist on Indonesia, had written that the Indonesia coup forces "would probably lack the ruthlessness that made it possible for the Nazis to suppress the Communist party of Germany . . . . ." However, a group no one had heard of—called the "September 30 Movement"—assassinated *six* Indonesian army generals and then, according to Pauker, "The assassinations elicited the ruthlessness" and 750,000 thousand Communists and their followers were slaughtered.

At the same time that the Institute of General Studies came out with its Indonesian model of a Communist putsch, in February

1973, *El Mercurio* carried a story by Teresa Donoso Loero on the Communist infiltration of shantytowns. The story was accompanied by an official-looking map of Santiago that purported to show how leftist camps were surrounding Providencia. The map played on the class fears of the residents of Providencia—many of them millionaires and leading officers—of surrounding shanty-towns, and made those feelings seem *respectable* by depicting those towns as a military threat. This map, a central clue to Plan Z, was the only illustration in the CIA-financed book by Robert Moss. Moss's map improved on *El Mercurio's* original: The small triangles representing the camps have grown huge, and deliberately point at Providencia. Next to the map Moss wrote, "They pointed, like long knives, at the heart of Santiago."

What did it feel like in those first coup days? Dr. Landis's diary is a rare insight into fascism:

"I went to a *quiosco* to buy some newspapers. Before the coup it was possible to get newspapers of every spectrum of political opinion. *Puro Chile*, *Clarín*, and *El Siglo* were workers' newspapers. *La Nación* always belonged to the government, which at the time had been socialist. None of those were available now. The only newspapers still existing were *El Mercurio*, *La Segunda*, and *Tribuna*, organ of the ultraright Partido Nacional. Magazines available were *Ercilla* and *Que Pasa*. *Ercilla* is a Chilean version of *Time* magazine . . . .they run the same photographs, same stories, same book reviews. *Que Pasa* is the organ of Opus Dei in Chile. *El Mercurio* headlined that General Pinochet had announced that all Marxist parties were now illegal. The article beneath the headline revealed that not only Marxist parties, but all those which had integrated the previous government, such as the *Izquierda Cristiana*, *Izquierda Radical*, and *MAPU*, which were not Marxist, were also illegal. Another story, Russia had broken relations with Chile.

"The front page of *Tribuna* was exactly the same. Inside, however, was a photograph of General Baeza (who led the assault on the Moneda and assassinated Allende) soberly holding up a card which read 'Djakarta is approaching.' The accompanying story is a classic of fascist cynicism. Baeza claimed that numerous members of the armed forces received cards before the coup. These cards were linked to a so-called 'Plan Z,' under which military officers were supposed to have been liquidated by the socialist party.

"It is a notorious fact that in the weeks before the coup a large number of *left-wing civilians* received cards saying 'Djakarta is approaching,' obviously an allusion to the massacre of Communists in Indonesia. This was exactly what happened to leftists in Chile following the coup. On July 31 a photograph of this same card had appeard on the front page of the Communist newspaper *El Siglo*. The newspaper reported receiving the card the day before, as did hundreds of leftist leaders. *El Siglo* printed in the July 31 issue photographs of articles threatening extermination of the left . . .the articles had appeared in right-wing newspapers.

"The next day *El Siglo* printed an editorial about Djakarta written by Communist leader Orlando Millas. Millas referred to an editorial in *La Tercera* titled 'A Communist Who Runs Won't Die.' He also referred to a letter to the editor in *La Segunda* to the effect that communists and Jews had tried to take over Germany but had been stopped by Hitler—why had we allowed them to be successful here? Another letter in *La Segunda* included a list of all the leftist leaders who were Jews. Still another suggested that Communists and Jews be strung up with barbed wire after the coup. In *El Mercurio* a letter suggested that people begin compiling lists of the leftists they like least.

"Looking over the newspapers the first day I arrived, I saw two clear patterns. First was the complete standardization of the news. The military was not just censoring the news, but substantially dictating it. Second was the projection of violent feelings and behavior by the military onto the Left. The killing of the workers was being blamed, by some perverse twist, on the Left. Allende was assassinated by General Baeza; Baeza says Allende committed suicide. The Left received cards warning of a Djakarta which *did* materialize; Baeza, holding a card, is pictured with a story blaming the Left for the cards and accusing them of a plot to assassinate the military.

"The 10 P.M. Channel 13 news, presented by a Catholic University television station, was in substance identical to the newspaper articles. After the news came American police programs, horror movies, and announcements by the Junta.

"...That same day appeared in the provincial newspaper *El Diario Austral* of Temuco (owned by the Christian Democratic party) what is probably my all-time-favorite news item: on the front page, 'According to *Time* magazine, there will be no elections in Chile for the next three to five years.'

"What we have here is the absurd situation that the only way Chileans can find out when they might have the right to vote again is by reading it in *Time* magazine in an exclusive interview given by General Pinochet to Charles Eisendrath. Of course, the average Chilean would have trouble finding a copy of *Time*, since it and all other foreign magazines and newspapers were prohibited from circulation in Chile at the time."

Thus the young political scientist read the papers and watched his country die from day to day.

Senator Symington: Did you try in the Central Intelligence Agency to overthrow the Government of Chile?

Mr. Helms: No, sir.

Senator Symington: Did you have any money passed to the opponents of Allende?

Mr. Helms: No, sir.

Senator Symington: So the stories you were involved in that war was wrong?

Mr. Helms: Yes, sir. I said to Senator Fulbright many months ago that if the agency had really gotten behind the other candidates and spent a lot of money and so forth the election might have come out differently.

Testimony of Richard Helms, former director of the CIA, in executive session before the Senate Foreign Relations Committee on February 7, 1973. On October 31, 1977, Richard Helms pleaded no contest to misdemeanor charges that he "failed to answer questions fully, completely and accurately" (in other words, he lied) when questioned by the Senate Foreign Relations Committee in February and March 1973. Helms postured for the media front of the courthouse after the sentencing, then left to address a cheering, stomping audience of the Association of Former Intelligence Officers, in convention assembled.

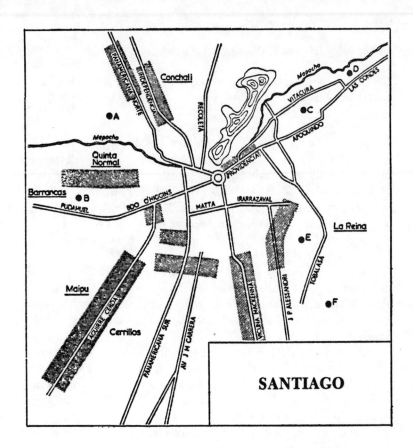

KEY EXTREMIST ENCAMPMENTS (Campamentos)
A Renca (Blanca Vergara, l' de Mayo, José Tohá)
B Pudahuel (O'Higgins)
C Av Kennedy (Ho Chi Minh)
D Las Condes (Fidel-Ernesto, Luciana Cruz)
E La Hermida
F La Florida (Nueva La Habana)

107

Officially, Henry Kissinger was stating:

The CIA had nothing to do with the coup, to the best of my knowledge and belief, and I only put in that qualification in case some madman down there....

Madmen Davis, Purdy, and Phillips had spent $12 million to tear apart a country of 11 million people, the equivalent of spending $200 million to sabotage an American government. *Every penny had been allocated by Kissinger's 40 Committee.*

Washington had become the City of Lies. Ambassador Edward Korry: "The United States did not seek to pressure or subvert...."

The State Department: "I wish to state...that we did not have advance knowledge of the coup...."

Harry Shlaudeman: "We had nothing to do with the political destabilizaton of Chile." Shlaudeman who was in Chile under cover as the deputy chief of mission in the U.S. Embassy had been Phillips's hard-line aide in Santo Domingo as he was now in Santiago.

"The United States Government, the Central Intelligence Agency, had no role in the overthrow of the regime in Chile," said James Schlesinger, Helms's successor as director of CIA and the man who is quoted as having written while at the Rand Corporation, "Politics is the art of lying without getting caught." The torrent continued, carrying President Gerald Ford along to the crest, "There is no doubt in my mind...."

Perhaps the most telling statements were made in an interview between William Colby and the Italian writer Oriana Fallaci.

Colby: CIA had no part in overthrowing Allende in 1973....
Fallaci: No? When Nixon called Richard Helms and ordered him to organize a coup to overthrow Allende who had just won the election.
Colby: It only lasted six weeks...and we did not succeed....We had no part later.
Fallaci: Really? Tell me about the financing of the strikes that ruined Allende's government, Mr. Colby. Tell me about the intervention through ITT.
Colby: Well, we gave a little bit of money, yes....We gave it to other people. I mean we gave it to a group who passed it to another....

In Chile, thermidor raged. Thousands were killed within the first hours of the coup. Phillips's false lists of those who could *descabezar* the officer corps were the first to go, of course, and as brutally as in Indonesia. The resistance in Santiago, as well as the countryside, was bitter, but the workers were poorly armed and the junta had U.S. tanks and planes with which to crush loyal citizens. The new *gorila* junta proclaimed a total curfew as they mopped up with heavy weapons and bombed the poor districts.

The scene is surreal. Chile is hemorrhaging. The Brazilian secret police, acting as third country cut-outs for the CIA, are leading torture squads at the National Soccer Stadium. Fifteen thousand foreign political refugees are rounded up. Bodies clog the river around the capital, mass graves lie open on the outskirts, the morgue is ankle deep in blood. At the stadium, the beloved folk singer Victor Jara tries to sing to the other prisoners. Torturers break his hands, then smash his head in. His last poem is smuggled out.

There are six of us lost in space
among the stars,
One dead
One beaten like I never believed a human could
be so beaten . . .
Slaughter is the badge of heroism

He is speaking for thousands in the stadium, in jails, the holds of ships, "hospitals," police stations, basements, "schools"—the torture is tipping Chile into the sea.

Allende's doctor, Enrique Paris, had been with the President at the end. He had seen his friend shot, then mutilated. He, Paris, had been tortured without letup after his capture. Four days later, he was mad, shouting, "I am Quinones the bull," over and over, then charging the guards, who clubbed him to death.

In this matter of torture, Americans do not know where to look when documentation pours in of CIA traning in Iran, South Korea, and Latin America. Vulgar comparisons with the Gestapo are not to the point. The point is Dan Mitrione paid for his deeds with his life in Uruguay. Upon his death at the hands of the Tupamaros, American notables, led by Vice President Agnew and that man of many causes Frank Sinatra, paid him tribute and eulogized him as an American patriot who had died for his beliefs. Those beliefs, as told to one of his agents, Manuel Hevia Cosculluela:

> When you receive a subject, the first thing to do is determine his physical state, his degree of resistance, through a medical examination. A premature death means a failure by the technician.
>
> Another important thing to know is exactly how far you can go given the political situation and the personality of the prisoner. It is very important to know beforehand whether we have the luxury of letting the subject die. . . .
>
> Before all else, you must be efficient. You must cause only the damage that is strictly necessary, not a bit more. We must control our tempers in any case. You have to act with the efficiency and cleanliness of a surgeon and with the perfection of an artist . . . .

According to Jesse Leaf, chief CIA analyst on Iran from 1968 to 1973:

> A senior CIA official was involved in instructing officials in SAVAK on torture techniques . . . based on German torture techniques from World War II.

And according to a former Mitrione aide:

> He [Mitrione] personally tortured beggars to death in demonstration sessions for Uruguayan trainees. . . .

When ABC referred to these matters in a documentary, "The Politics of Torture," the *New York Times* complained that the program had failed to take into account the problems posed by "security and economic interests."

Where was it all leading? Mounds of bodies, hills of corpses ("like in Nam," one of the DIA agents told Charles Horman, a filmmaker, who would be murdered, too). Headless corpses floated like logs clogging the Ñuble River. Fishermen at Talcahuano dragged in nets filled with pieces of human flesh. *El Descuartizado*, Djakarta: From the burning Atacama desert to the frozen Fastness at Dawson Island in Patagonia, Chile, the "England," the "Switzerland" of Latin America—Chile was one long torture chamber.

All foreigners are told to report to the nearest police stations. A young American filmmaker, Charles Horman, is murdered with Embassy connivance. This murder is almost unbelievable to some CIA contract agents in Santiago, but Horman had accidentally come upon evidence of Pentagon-DIA involvement in the coup, and there had been no choice. Deniability had to be maintained at all costs—those were, after all, their orders.

Charles Edmund Horman was born into a family of scholars and scientists in 1942. Charles graduated from Harvard *magna cum laude*, Phi Beta Kappa, before he served in the Air Force. In his brief career in communications, he had worked for *CBS*, *The Nation*, and the *Christian Science Monitor*. He had come to Chile with his wife, Joyce, to film the Allende experiment.

Near the port of Valparaiso, several days after the coup, he met several U.S. military advisors who had inside information on the overthrow. At first, the men assumed that Horman was one of them; they talked freely, boasted of the crimes against Chile. Then they realized that Charles "knew too much." Someone called the CIA at the American Embassy.

One intelligence officer who defected from DINA, because it had "become a Gestapo," told what he had seen and heard:

Charles Horman was brought from Valparaiso to Santiago. I saw the guys that brought him here. . . . I wouldn't say that the trigger was pulled by the CIA, but the CIA was mixed up in this. It was the Chileans who got rid of him, but the CIA was behind that.

The officer identified Frederick Purdy, John Tipton, and James Anderson as the CIA men at the embassy who were involved. In 1963 Anderson had been a part of Phillips's disinformation machinations in respect to Lee Harvey Oswald, and, again, had been an aide to Phillips in the election sabotage in the Dominican Republic in 1965.

Spring had come to Chile by the middle of September. Pablo Neruda was following the carnage, by wireless, and he was dying.

The *milicos* of the new junta had already destroyed his home, spreading excrement over priceless manuscripts.

Neruda's wife, Matilde Urrutia, describes the great artist's farewell to his beloved land. His last words were, "No one in living memory had been betrayed so cruelly as my people." Matilde Urrutia'a voice, as well, can be heard over the chatter of guns:

At the end of five days, I called a private ambulance to take him to a Santiago clinic. The vehicle was thoroughly searched. . . .There were other brutalities. They searched me and the ambulance. It was terrible for him. I kept telling them: "It's Pablo Neruda. He is very ill. Let us through." It was frightful. . . .Pablo died at 10:32 P.M.

When we arrived at the cemetery, people came from everywhere, all workers with hard, serious faces. Half of them kept shouting, "Pablo Neruda," and the other half replied: "Present!"

Fred Landis was at that funeral. He wrote that at "about 10:15 we saw the procession several blocks away. When it reached the cemetery, the procession had grown to a crowd of about 2,000. People along the streets had joined in. About three blocks from the cemetery we heard them chanting:
"Decente!
"Decente!
"As they came closer the chant changed to:
"Presente!
"Presente!
"Then:
"Pablo Neruda!
"Presente!
"Then:
"Compañero Pablo Neruda!
"Presente!
"Camarada Pablo Neruda!
"Presente!
"Camarada Pablo Neruda!
"Presente!
"Ahora y siempre!
"Neruda, Allende!

"Un solo combatiente!

"Then they began singing the *Internacional*. Absolutely incredible! The newsmen were just amazed. There were shouts against the Junta:

"*Que muera la Junta Fascista!*"

"It was obvious that most of the people were Communists. Their leaders had been killed, they were being searched for all over the country and shot. And here 2000 of them show up, not giving a damn. Telling the Junta to go fuck itself. Absolutely incredible and absolutely beautiful.

"The people in the procession were in two categories—either very young or very old. Either old beyond caring or too young to know any better. Nobody was crying, unlike most Chilean funerals. There was a stern, determined look on the people's faces. Immediately inside the gate of the general cemetery were four gravediggers who were drinking wine and making jokes. One of them broke away, moved outside of a little hut and scrawled on a blackboard that had been set up on an easel: '10:30 Neftali Reyes (Pablo Neruda).' "

At the Clinica Santa Maria the poet had been given an overdose of tranquilizers.

Neruda was gone. Night had come to the Southern Cone.

Following the coup, the reporting and commentary by correspondents, wire services, and editors of the six major American papers concerned with Latin American affairs (*Los Angeles Times*, *Miami Herald*, *Washington Post*, *Christian Science Monitor*, *Wall Street Journal*, and *New York Times*) shared perspectives which were in accord with what would become the junta's *White Book*. Perspectives which were never questioned or challenged by alternative or contrary viewpoints were presented in the pages of the major American newspapers.

The *New York Times* described General Pinochet as "tall and powerfully built," "quiet and businesslike," "disciplined and tough," and emphasized his "sense of humor." These reluctant, well-disciplined, witty, concerned, and virtuous men were returning the country to a "normal" and "businesslike" situation, said the *Times*.

The preferability of post-coup "normality" in Chile was empha-sized by veteran correspondent and CIA friend Lewis Dinguid in a report in the *Washington Post* as late as October 21.

The armed forces probably acted with majority support....It may turn out that the military intervention was a substitute for civil war, fore-stalling large-scale death and destruction by use of violence that was cruel and arbitrary, but *limited*.

Terming the massacres in Chile "limited" violence, used to "fore-stall" "large-scale death and destruction," is not syntactically unlike saying, "We had to destroy the village in order to save it."

Townley reported to General Contreras himself. Townley and Callejas were moved into a sprawling mansion by Contreras. The house was converted into a combination home and electronics station. From this location, Townley ran, by radio, teams of special operations or covert activists, many of whom had been bully boys of his *Patria y Libertad* terror teams. His starting rank was equivalent to that of a major in the army.

Townley was in charge of organizing former members of his various fronts into special interrogation units. Townley and Colonel Pedro Espinosa, together with members of the new DINA, were charged with liaison to a place called Colonia Dignidad.

The "Beneficient and Educational Society of Dignity" sprawls across thousands of acres in southern Chile. It is known as a "model farm" operated by West Germans. No visitors are allowed to see the acreage under cultivation, the hospital, the small factory buildings, the orphanage. The children are taught only German and English; Spanish is not used. The clothing of the adults is that worn in Germany in the early 1940s.

Townley and Espinosa took part in the reorganization of Colonia to handle the flood of new political prisoners. Later, the United Nations investigation of torture in Chile, as well as a report from Amnesty International, would say that the torture center is

in a specially equipped place underground: there are small, completely soundproof, hermetically sealed cells for prisoners.

Leather hoods are placed over the prisoners' heads and stuck to their faces with chemical adhesives. In these cells torturers allegedly carry out interrogations over a closed-circuit radio system, with the detainees naked and tied to their berths while electric shocks are applied.

To one of the prisoners, a torturer made the statement that in the Colonia Dignidad the "work" of the Nazi concentration camp is continued.

The implication is that this DINA center served as a grisly laboratory where experiments were conducted on prisoners, not only for the sake of gathering information, but to perfect the "science" of torture. The United Nations report from October, 1976, states:

In Colonia Dignidad prisoners have allegedly been subjected to different "experiments" without any interrogation: to dogs trained to commit sexual aggressions and destroy sexual organs of both sexes....Prisoners charge that torture is "personalized" through an initial interrogation which establishes the personal traits of the individual....This data is then used to program the torture sessions so that the result is a totally debilitated, exhausted person who will comply with any demand.

All this began in Germany with a home for boys. When the leader of the Colony, Paul Schaeffer, was accused of the criminal sexual abuse of children in 1960, the group moved to Chile.

In their new home, near the Argentine border, Colonia Dignidad soon enjoyed the support and protection of many of the country's most prominent business interests, many of whom had supported the Nazis, as well as both the West German and American embassies. Amnesty International states further of Colonia Dignidad that "this repressive apparatus counts on and receives direct support from abroad, in particular from West Germany."

By early 1974, DINA's Special Operations contingent, of which Townley was a member, had transformed the Colonia into "a torture and detention center," to use Amnesty International's language.

Finally, a DINA agent who worked with Townley at Colonia Dignidad's farm and in Dignidad's quarters in Santiago broke under the strain and defected.

My name is ————,* passport number 4.824.557-9 Santiago . . . .They
sent me to Colonia Dignidad, some 40 KM. inland from Parral. This is a
training center for the national secret police. My teachers were Chilean,
Brazilian and an American identified to me as a representative of the
Central Intelligence Agency named Welch.

"Welch" was Michael Townley Welch, as he called himself in
Chile.

There is a radio station in Dignidad which allows a wide range on contacts.
It is the center where all reports of DINA operations in foreign countries
are received, currently from Venezuela, Colombia, France, Sweden and
Italy. Fifty percent of the DINA agents—military personnel, not civilians
—work in these countries. I met Welch first at the radio station.

There is a death squad in this country, led by Captain Rolando Larena,
from the artillery, and a man named Puga.

The blood tide continued unabated. One international study
says

the body of Andreas Silva appeared without a head; the body of Daniel
Menendez had its arms torn off; that of Ruben Vargas was without ears; that
of Segundo Redrero without one arm; that of Orlando Baprizer without
hands and nose; that of Rosendo Rebolleda with one leg torn away at its
root. . . .

Everyday, hideously mutilated and disfigured corpses floated
down the canals and rivers and up onto the beaches. Now the
Quartered Men were everywhere.

Orlando Letelier was subjected to what the United Nations
Human Rights Comission described as "barbaric sadism." He
spent 364 days in eight concentration camps. The night before the
coup, he had passed in urgent conference with President Allende.
Before seven the next morning, he was on his way to the deepest
circle of hell, which the poet tells us is the cold beyond cold.

Dawson island lies on the fifty-fourth parallel south. The batter-
ing, freezing winds cut into the prisoners at eighty miles an hour.

*The name has been supplied to the U.S. Department of Justice.

Letelier's contingent of high official prisoners numbered thirty seven; and they were joined by other notables who had been held in Valparaiso on the tall torture ship *Esmeralda*. Fragments of Leteliers' own later oral record of his experience reveal not only the *ambiente* of the terror but the minister's deep insight into the dynamics of the boundary or limit situation—as a philosopher might call it—that was Dawson Island.

Suddenly, a jeep arrived at the beach, carrying Red Cross officials. This was theater, this was a show to demonstrate to the Red Cross that the prisoners practiced sports. However, Red Cross officials insisted on private conversations with individual prisoners. They could see that persons still had torture marks, including Carlos Gonzales, an ex-Congressman on whose back a huge letter Z had been slashed with a bayonet. Z was the alleged secret plan of the Allende government to murder the chiefs of the armed forces and the formal excuse for the coup. Curiously, however, I was never asked about Plan Z in interrogations during my year of incarceration, although I had been the defense minister and presumably would have known about such a plan. The junta used Plan Z to keep up the morale in the armed forces: there were posters in army barracks throughout Chile, saying "Remember—you were to die in September."

They accused me of having documents published in the United States in 1973 indicating that the International Telephone and Telegraph Company had been involved with the CIA in anti-Allende plots. They said they had proof that I had paid Jack Anderson, the columnist, $75,000, when I was ambassador in Washington, to publish these documents. But it happens that I have never met Anderson.

I thought that they were terrified human beings, the prisoners of a system. . . . I thought they were traitors. Traitors to the people of Chile. I felt rather superior to them. After all these things, one no longer has any fear. I felt that they were more scared than we were—and I'm not just talking about these two officers—because of all the terrible things they had done. The repression that is being applied in Chile is a demonstration of weakness.

Surely, there can be nobody more cruel than a coward, a scared man . . . even in Dawson, the same sergeant who had treated you brutally during forced labor would come to you and say, "Look, I'm against this sort of thing, I'm against those generals, but you know that I'm married. I can do nothing. I have a family. But the lieutenant is a fascist." Soon the lieutenant would come and say, "Look, Señor Letelier, you hate me, don't you?" Well, I wouldn't answer. So he would go on: "You hate me, but must realize that I'm a professional, that I have to obey orders. I have been trained to fight the enemy. I receive orders from Captain Zamora, who is in command here." Then, the captain would come, saying, "Well, Señor Letelier, surely you think that I do these things in a spirit of vengeance. I want you to know that personally I have nothing against you. I'm a professional. It is the major who gives me the orders. But I do fewer bad and cruel things than he would want me to do. But if I didn't obey orders, what do you think would happen to me? I would wind up in one of these cells as a prisoner. . . ."

There is great terror within the armed forces. There is an organization, the DINA, which is the Chilean Gestapo. Not all the officers belong to it. The captain doesn't know whether the lieutenant under him belongs to DINA and is watching him to denounce him if he is soft with the prisoners. Thus they live as prisoners of the system of terror that exists among them. . . .

I don't forgive them. I think that there's a level of moral cowardice among them and, collectively, I cannot forgive them. But I won't tell you that all the members of the Chilean armed forces are fascists, that all of them are torturers. Often, soldiers, when they were not being watched, tried to show us little gestures of humanity. For example, a soldier would say to me, "Look, rest a little bit while they aren't watching us." And sometimes a soldier would ask you for your autograph, so that later he could say that he had been at Dawson, guarding these terribly dangerous political prisoners, as the junta would put it.

Dr. Landis, who spent the first months after the coup near high junta leadership, reports that most Chilean military officers exhibited dramatic signs of reactive rage and panic, paranoid symptoms of fear of secret invasion, and what could be called "delusions of reference." That is, they were reacting *as if* the CIA scenarios had happened, were true; as if a Castro slave state had barely been avoided, as if Plan Z was *not* Langley science fiction.

The Quartered Man had done his work. The military chain of command had become a hangman's noose.

Michael Townley & David Phillips and 13 the "White Hand"

And that is when I ceased being a child
when I understood that my people
were being denied not only life, but even a decent burial

One can never abandon the sense of remorse at having
something when others have nothing. Man can not be a
happy island. This is not the whole of my philosophy, but it
is the most important part . . . We writers owe a debt to our
intellectual heritage and to what we have consumed of the
earth's resources. We should put something back.

Pablo Neruda, interview with Excelsior

THE REPORT OF THE UNITED STATES SENATE SELECT COMMITTEE
ON INTELLIGENCE *Covert Action in Chile*, finds that after the
coup, David Phillips's operations group assisted the junta "in
gaining a more positive image both at home and abroad . . . ." This
is a reference to Plan Z and the junta *White Book*, which the
agency, Phillips having written it, was good enough to distribute
widely in Washington and around the world.

In 1973 Phillips was rewarded handsomely for still another
successful task accomplished. He was promoted again, this time to
the rank of Chief, Western Hemisphere Division. The tall, rugged
Texan was a proper supergrade now, a GS-18, the equivalent of a
general in the army, the highest rank to which a CIA officer can
rise (the director and deputy director being appointed).

Chile was behind him. But within a year of the coup, the leaks
started. First, Phillips was faced with the problem of Victor
Marchetti. Marchetti had been a high-ranking officer from the
"white" or intelligence-gathering side of the CIA. He had left the
agency because of what he had seen. Marchetti was a terrible
problem for the Clandestine Services because, as a moderate, a
constitutionalist, and a recognized authority on the Soviet Union,

he could not be red-baited. And he could not be stopped from talking off the record with Seymour Hersh, of the *New York Times*, and other reporters.

Another former CIA officer, Philip Agee, was writing a book, and the agency had been able to acquire a copy of the manuscript in Paris after surrounding him with electronic and live (female) surveillance. Although Marchetti lived in the CIA's backyard, in Vienna, Virginia, and although Phillips tried, it was not possible to stop or steal the Marchetti manuscript, for he had a loyal and protective wife and family. It was Victor Marchetti—both before and after he was silenced by the United States government—who, through the *New York Times*, panicked the Old Boy network at Langley—forcing Colby "to go public" with a partial admission of Centaur, and Phillips to go under cover again.

A great chill had descended on Langley. Not since the exposure of Britain's Harold ("Kim") Philby as a high Soviet penetration agent in the Anglo-American intelligence community had there been such intimations of disaster. Two men with a wealth of knowledge of agency workings had decided, as an act of conscience, to "go public." Marchetti, from his commanding position as executive assistant to the Deputy Director had a clear overview of money, men, and the decision-making process of the CIA—he knew the facts. Agee, from deep cover, knew the details of operations in the field. Marchetti's revelations in his book had already done massive damage to Phillips's Chile cover story.

A whole generation of cold warriors, well symbolized by a man like Phillips, felt threatened. For years the ultras had believed that there were Soviet "moles" like Philby inside the agency. Their worst fantasies were now realized; knowledgeable former officers were preparing to lift the sacred curtain of secrecy, ready to expose their cult of intelligence.

The CIA and the Cult of Intelligence became the title of Marchetti's book when it was eventually published. "Eventually" because, for the first time in American history, the CIA was successful in initiating official United States censorship of a major published work. In order for Marchetti to publish at all, he had to take a collaborator, John Marks. (Marks, in his own right, was later to break a massive story of CIA drug experiments on unwitting Americans. Of course, censorship, and secrecy, must lead inevitably to revelations.)

The Marchetti-Marks book actually appeared in print with gaping white spaces left on the pages by an outraged publisher so that the public could see in dramatic terms the power of Power, reaching into every home and library in the country where the best-selling *CIA and the Cult of Intelligence* might be found.

Marchetti's magisterial overview had reached the public in censored form, but the author was enjoined from any further written or oral expression without permission from Langley. The former CIA officer continued to live in nearby Virginia, under a kind of First Amendment house arrest, and maintained the respect of many from the intelligence division of the CIA.

Then Philip Agee surfaced, and David Phillips was sent back under cover, and as of 1975, his *official* control of Michael Townley came to an end.

On September 8, 1974, Seymour Hersh began a series in the *New York Times*, and the Chile story began to emerge. It all began with Representative Michael Harrington, a determined Democrat from Massachusetts, who had learned of testimony DCI William Colby had given to the House Subcommittee on Inter-American affairs, chaired by Sam Nunn. Harrington asked to see the testimony, and was granted permission. He then wrote a letter to another Congressman, expressing his concern, and it was leaked to Hersh. Hersh is an excellent reporter:

CIA CHIEF TELLS HOUSE
OF $8-MILLION CAMPAIGN
AGAINST ALLENDE IN '70-73

Subsequent stories would explain how the $8 million was, in turn, parlayed into more than $40 million on the black market.

On September 9, the *Times* was announcing, "Hearings Urged." Suppressed portions of the Marchetti book, such as Henry Kissinger's quip, "I don't see why we need to stand by and watch a country go Communist due to the irresponsibility of its own people," now appeared in the *Times*. Such material was red meat to the lions of the media and the Congress. One day later Senator Frank Church announced that hearings would be held, and there was panic at Langley.

On September 15, Hersh named Kissinger as the prime mover in the overthrow of the legal Allende government. By the sixteenth, former Ambassador Edward Korry was beginning to talk off the record to the *Times*.

Starting on the twentieth of September, Hersh unloaded a new series of shocking charges on the agency:

CIA IS LINKED TO STRIKES
IN CHILE THAT BESET ALLENDE

KISSINGER CHILE BRIEFINGS SAID TO OMIT
MENTION OF CIA LINK TO LABOR UNREST

WASHINGTON SAID TO HAVE AUTHORIZED
A GET-ROUGHER POLICY IN CHILE IN '71

At Langley, Phillips, Colby, and the covert Old Boys knew that drastic action of some sort was called for. Demands for Helms's indictment for perjury were already abroad, and Phillips had perjured himself again and again since 1973. They all had. Hersh was taking aim. The Chile stories were devastating.

KISSINGER SAID TO REBUKE
U.S. AMBASSADOR TO CHILE

In recounting the incident, the sources said that Mr. Kissinger reacted angrily after having learned from a State Department cablegram that Mr. Popper had initiated a discussion of human rights during a meeting on military aid in Santiago . . .

"Tell Popper to cut out the political science lectures," the sources said Mr. Kissinger scrawled over the cablegram . . .

The agency's cover story was cracking under the pressure of the *Times*. The same thing had happened during the Watergate scandals. At month's end *Time* magazine decided, in the words of one editor, "to get out in front of it, before Sy Hersh makes a citizen's arrest of Henry Kissinger."

Time had learned that a CIA team was posted to Chile with orders from the National Security Council to keep the election "fair." The agents interpreted these instructions to mean: Stop Allende, and they asked for a whopping $20 million to do the job. . . .

In 1975, the great purges rocked Langley. Agency horrors in Southeast Asia, Africa, Cuba, and Latin America were under investigation, threatening to pour out. Former Director Helms swore that if he went down he would take the rest with him. The ultras, the hawks, and the hard-liners of Clandestine Services would have to disappear before the public and congressional wrath. Phillips would have to go to prepare the way, to build a propaganda "safe house," for the Old Boys, out in the cold post-Watergate world.

Covert operations, if they are anything, are actually a series of secret contingency plans in the pursuit of a goal. At Langley, the evidence indicates, the goal—power—did not change, only the image. David Phillips, the clever imagist of Santiago, Guatemala City, Havana, Mexico City, Santo Domingo, and again Santiago —one of the proud fathers of the Quartered Man—who better than David Phillips to lead the Agency's counterattack to regain the hearts and minds of the American people?

After all, the situation was not completely hopeless. Even as the ghastly saga of Chile was starting to reach American ears, a dinner party for Richard Helms was arrranged by such staunch friends as Henry Kissinger, Robert McNamara, Averell Harriman and Senator Stuart Symington (who was himself a member of the Church Committee that was supposed to be investigating Helms). The gala was held at the house of *Washington Post* columnist Tom Braden, a high-ranking CIA officer until the 1960s. An emotional toast was proposed by World Bank Director McNamara: "We will stand by Dick Helms to the end." This was all terribly heartening to Phillips and the Old Boy network, but rhetoric like McNamara's had a hollow ring: such famous last words had been heard too often during the Watergate years. Helms might be saved, but what about lesser lights like Colby and Phillips? Who was going to stand by them? They had been "burned," and they knew what to do.

In April 1975, Phillips, the chief of the Western Hemisphere Division, retired years early, foregoing honors and power in order to form the Association of Retired Intelligence Officers (ARIO).

The board of directors of the tax-exempt ARIO was composed of militant cold-war hawks. It contained men like General Raymond Piers, who found Lieutenant William Calley to be the lone psychopath responsible for the My Lai massacre. Then there was General Marshall S. Carter, former deputy director of the CIA, who brought with him the assets of the George C. Marshall Research Foundation and the American-Korean Foundation, two of a number of notorious Cold War fronts soon associated with ARIO under Phillips's direction.

Good old Dave Phillips—who passed among his liberal friends as a McGovern Democrat—was quickly involved in his new network, which included the American Security Council, the American Friends of Captive Nations, the Hawaii Foundation for American Freedoms, the Roman Catholic Club, the Stanford Research Institute, various Taiwanese anti-Communist components of the old China lobby, and a galaxy of fronts and dependencies. Clare Boothe Luce alone accounted for almost a dozen titles. Next, the ARIO board of directors had recruited a group of retired generals and admirals, a number of them borrowed from the extreme right-wing board of the American Security council. The Council, set up in 1955 to run security checks on prospective employees for member industries, is a key lobby and forum for what *Newsweek* magazine once called "the military Right."

Within a few months the ARIO had become the AFIO (Association of Former Intelligence Officers), and the 250 prospective members had become over 2,000 actual members (nineteen chapters) drawn from *all* American intelligence agencies. A new brochure promised, "In AFIO we have a unique pool of professional experience readily available to the public and government officials": thus the "completely independent" AFIO brochure, writ-

ten by the propaganda master himself. The bottom line of the new
and enlarged brochure bore the legend:

AFIO ACTS—JOIN THE ACTION.

The *New York Times* and the major newspapers duly announced
the formation of ARIO. Phillips began with an open letter to 250
former covert officers.

As chief of Latin American operations, I have been deeply concerned
about the decline of morale at Langley and abroad. Snowballing innuendo, gregarious stories and charges and even honest concerns have
presented us with the basic dilemma of issuing either a general statement
which reassures few but preserves security or a comprehensive accounting which satisfies some but at the expense of operations and agents.

Under the circumstances, there is little doubt that a thorough Congressional review is the best, if not only, solution even though some
leakage of sensitive details on foreign operations seems almost inevitable
. . .our capabilities abroad are being damaged. More of our agents and
friends . . .are saying thanks but no thanks. Friendly liaison services are
beginning to back away from us. The Marchettis and the Agees have the
stage and only a few challenge them.

Philip Agee, like so many of his fellows in Clandestine Services
who became his sworn enemies, was a loyal Catholic activist. The
Notre Dame graduate was a lithe, restless crusader who, in advance of publication of his book, named names of CIA officers and
secret operatives in Latin America and around the world. A series
of sensational Agee press conferences electrified left-wing parties
everywhere, and forced Langley to dismantle whole operations
and teams, from Mexico City to Athens.

An officer who served under Phillips at the time has said:

As a result of the defection of Philip Agee most of the operations of the
Western Hemisphere Division were ordered cancelled . . .A defensive
operation was started immediately and every activity, agent, and official
was scrutinized to determine if Agee had already blown them or would
write about them in his book.

Agee's book, the clandestine operators knew, would deal with the "great fear" in Latin America—Castro's Communist Cuba. With almost total recall, Agee, in *Inside the Company: CIA Diary*, would detail the obsessional quality of the day-by-day plotting against Cuba that had constituted the CIA's secret life after 1960.

In order to zero in on Philip Agee and stop him and any other aspiring Victor Marchettis, AFIO had to establish its *bona fides*. To this end, a *Washington Star* story of March 22, 1975, on the new organization began with an almost nostalgic montage of former cover stories in Santiago, Havana, and Beirut. Then:

Mr. Phillips said he was concerned that people might think he was still working for the agency when he gets started with the association's efforts. He said, "I wish to make it absolutely clear that the C.I.A. management has not had, and will not have, a hand officially, unofficially, or otherwise in this organization and its efforts."

Mr. Phillips said he would receive $15,000 a year as a retired employee compared with his present salary of $36,000. The association, he said, will be financed by $10 a year dues to be used for stamps, paper and similar expenses but not for salaries. He expects to provide for his own income through lecture fees.

The *New York Times* reported that "Mr. Phillips, who says his income dropped from $36,000 to $16,000 . . .has a couple of speeches in New York City. . . ."

Phillips began to let it be known in interviews that he had been offered $50 to $100,000 "if he would speak out against the agency."

U.S. PLOTTED AGAINST WARREN COMMISSION REPORT CRITICS. On May 8, 1977, a major newspaper, the *Baltimore News American*, ran this front-page headline. It was the only newspaper in the United States to do so.

The story beneath the banner reported that in 1964 the Central Intelligence Agency and the U.S. State Department had plotted a strategy "aimed at bolstering [public] confidence" in the findings of the Warren Commission. The findings in question were based, of course, in large part on "information" provided to the Commission by these very agencies in general and by David Phillips and the CIA in particular.

The targets of this conspiracy were authors, editors, reporters, researchers, and everyone else who, as the CIA put it, "played into the hands of the opposition." It is quite clear that the CIA thought the American people were the "opposition."

Against one early Warren Report critic, Joachem Joesten, the CIA passed on *raw Gestapo files* to liberal lawyers on the Commission whose role it was to assassinate the character of those who questioned the methods and conclusions of the official investigation. In 1977 *David Phillips admitted publicly to being a part of this illegal campaign.*

Similarly, in 1964, when *The Invisible Government* by David Wise and Thomas B. Ross appeared, the agency redoubled its disinformation efforts against even mildly critical works. Phillips's aide, Joseph B. Smith, reports that a series of false book reviews churned out at Langley was designed to prove that CIA acted only under presidential orders. According to Smith:

The line the book reviews took to explain such presidential authority contained a view of the President's office which would have forced James Madison to rewrite the "Federalist Papers." None of the Founding Fathers would have recognized either the Congress or the President the fake book reviews described.

Phillips and the AFIO found themselves, in 1975, in another world politically, for the America of 1963 had vanished. For AFIO to generate any credibility for the "new" and "reformed" CIA— the house that William Colby built—it was required of Phillips that he offer a series of partial admissions or "limited hangouts," to use Richard Nixon's dangling phraseology. The first category that had to be contained concerned assassinations in general.

After the assassination of John Kennedy, Phillips and Frank Sturgis had worked together to spread the Castro conspiracy story and to discredit critics of the "lone maniac" theory. But in May 1975 the relationship of years flew apart. The pressure was mounting on the CIA, as appalling Organized Crime-CIA stories began to dominate front pages. The plots to kill Castro were going to come out. Cuba again.

Phillips offered a partial admission that might contain the damage and place the responsibility for the CIA-mob combination against Castro on the Kennedy brothers. In Havana, Castro's deputy premier was giving the press documentation of over a hundred CIA-sponsored attempts to assassinate Fidel Castro. Then, under a London dateline, the AFIO founder was quoted as denying most of the Cuban allegations; in fact, he insisted, he only knew of *one* attempt against Fidel and that one did *not* involve the CIA. On the contrary,

" . . .the CIA arranged for Mr. Castro to be informed that an underground group was gunning for him.

"In late June of 1968 . . .I learned of a plot to assassinate Castro. It was a particularly vicious thing, made to look like it involved the United States government.

"I arranged for the Department of State, through the Swiss Embassy, to warn Castro. I'd be surprised though if Castro knows it was the CIA who helped him."

Phillips was actually referring to a betrayal, in 1968, of the Secret Army Organization. Hearing of Phillips's statement, one Miami man, Max Gorman Gonzales, told the Associated Press that he planned to sue the CIA for millions because he had been "thrown to the wolves" by Phillips's aborting of an assassination plot targeted at Castro. At this point, Sturgis interrupted to point out that the betrayed operation was Operation Sword, an SAO scheme that had included Gonzales.

In the Cuban community of Miami and throughout South and Central America feelings were inflamed. The Cubans, in their fury over *this betrayal would take their revenge on Phillips, and others, a year later*. Phillips did not know it, but as of the summer of 1975, he had fallen from grace in Miami.

Another man betrayed in Operation Sword was Rolando Otero. Otero's name has an abiding resonance in the Letelier affair. Otero was a Cuban exile hero and the youngest *Brigadista* at the Bay of Pigs. From the age of twelve years he had been a militant and totally committed "freedom fighter."

Otero's CIA connection, after the Bay of Pigs, kept him from serving any prolonged time in prison for his busy career of bombing and anti-Castro violence. Then, in 1976, the FBI found his hiding place in Chile. Otero's arrest in Chile by the FBI is central to a complete understanding of the Letelier case.

The arrest is not one piece in the puzzle, but several. Phillips's admission, in London, of the CIA's betrayal of Operation Sword is a key piece in the puzzle, but only one. In 1975, when Phillips learned of Otero's reaction, he denied that he had been referring to the Sturgis operation. Anyway, he wrote, "Sturgis never worked for the CIA." (If Sturgis, the notorious CIA gunman and *organizer* at the Bay of Pigs, could be sanitized from CIA records, what chance would there be to find the name of the faceless Michael Townley?)

In late spring of 1975 the director of the new ARIO was telling the *New York Times* that:

the agency had strong indications that the coup that deposed Dr. Allende, a Marxist elected in 1970, was about to take place in the fall of 1973.

We didn't warn him, we didn't prevent it, because we had no way of being sure.

By the end of May, old friends of Phillips at United Press International had been handed an astonishing letter.

The former head of Latin-American operations for the Central Intelligence Agency wrote the widow of President Salvador Allende Gossens of Chile, denying that the CIA was in any way responsible for the Marxist leader's overthrow and death in 1973.

David A. Phillips, who retired from the agency May 9th after 24 years, wrote Hortensia Bussi de Allende the next day:

"You have been led to believe that evidence exists which makes the CIA accountable for the circumstances which brought your husband to his untimely end. Because I supervised the component of CIA concerned with Chile and its neighbors, the accusation bothers me personally. The claim, I assure you, is untrue and the evidence tainted."

At month's end, the op-ed page of the *Times* featured a Phillips essay swearing CIA innocence in Chile. And so it went, until the incredible came to pass: On December 7, 1975, the *New York Times* reversed its post-coup position of outrage and adopted the agency party line on the death of Chile at the hands of Centaur.

Revolution and counter-revolution inevitably produce political myths. . . . The central fact that emerges is that . . . the United States still was not responsible for the overthrow of President Salvador Allende. Despite the left-wing myth that this country was the prime mover in that event, the coup was actually conceived and carried out by Chileans acting for reasons of their own . . . .

"Myth"?

Over that summer of 1975, a spate of Phillips stories moved on the wires. His was the moderate, responsible voice of measured self-criticism and perspective. Typically, readers learned:

The interior ministers of nearly all Latin American governments "collaborated" with the U.S. Central Intelligence Agency, according to David A. Phillips, former chief of CIA operations in Latin America.

Phillips told a press conference in New York, May 10th that although the Latin officials worked with the agency, they did not know "everything that the agency does" in their countries. The CIA's major preoccupation in Latin America was uncovering "the activities being prepared by the Soviet and Cuban intelligence services," he added.

Phillips denied that the agency had organized the overthrow of any Latin American head of state—notably, the late Chilean President Salvador Allende—but he conceded that "this type of operation might have been discussed as a possibility . . . ."

Slowly the agency, through Phillips and his AFIO network, was riding out the storm. The Church Committee had buckled on the crucial issues, and the House Select Committee on Intelligence would be destroyed, its report suppressed by the House itself.

Agee, from Europe, was working with a group of young American researchers, most of them former military intelligence officers who had been deeply radicalized by the terror of the Vietnam war. His Washington-based supporters called themselves the Fifth Estate and produced a heavily documented magazine called *CounterSpy*. The magazine had begun to produce lists of CIA men in deep cover in foreign countries. In December 1975, members of a Greek group took the name of CIA Station Chief Richard Welch from a newspaper story and traced him to what Welch himself called his "somewhat notorious house"—it had belonged to the former station chief in Athens—and killed him. Phillips and others responded with a full press of propaganda and blame against Agee and company, and the offices of *CounterSpy* were soon shuttered.

Word circulated that patriots would deal with the *CounterSpy* people for having published Richard Welch's name in their magazine and getting him killed, for that was the essence of the CIA's story. An enormous full-dress funeral was laid on at Arlington to complete the media circus staged by the agency.

In 1967, President Lyndon Johnson confided to aides that he wanted a new investigation into the murder of President Kennedy to focus on possible involvement of the Central Intelligence Agency. Johnson had apparently changed his long-held opinion that Castro was the planner of the assassination. At the same time, Johnson ordered that the CIA cancel any and all relationships or understandings with the militant exile Cuban community.

As usual, the CIA both did and did not follow orders. David Phillips was told to break the bad news to the veterans of Playa Giron and a thousand less dramatic agency escapades. However, he was instructed to let the men from Miami know that Clandestine Services was not made up of fickle politicians who sold their friends and agents down the river. "There would be help from Langley for certain ops"—that was the message, according to an exile source. Phillips had no trouble working out an *unofficial* arrangement among old comrades in arms.

Years later, an unidentified CIA official involved in 1967 in the dismantling of the Cuban network talked to two respected analysts of America's secret operations in the Caribbean, Ernest Volkman, and his collaborator John Cummings, of the influential Long Island, New York, daily *Newsday*.

It was not surprising in the slightest, that some of the exiles would get mixed up, much farther south in Latin America. In the first place, the agency had no idea, really, about what to do with these people. Here we had guys who were trained snipers, bomb experts, guerrilla warfare experts, and what not suddenly being told we no longer had any use for them. It was thanks very much and good-bye. And then what were they supposed to do? How many machine gunners do you know who can get a job, just like that? And a job doing what? They had spent their youth training for a specific job to which they had dedicated their lives: getting rid of Castro. That is all they thought about, all they dreamed about, all they lived for. Now we threw them out in the street. Some gave up at that point, but a lot of them said, 'Okay, you won't help me anymore; we'll just go out and get rid of that guy [Castro] ourselves. And if you won't help us anymore with arms and money, then we'll go someplace else.' White Hand was the someplace else."

If that is not Phillips talking, it is his double, for those are the words used by Clandestine to provide deniability in the years to come.

Some of these "independently operated and financed" Cuban militants now began to style themselves melodramatically as *Mano Blanca*, the "White Hand." The White Hand was actually a reorganization of various die-hard CIA elements.

As of 1967, then, Phillips had become the agency's cutout for the Bay of Pigs veterans. The exiles' trust of Phillips would be used by the CIA as a device to at once monitor, deny, control, and, on occasion, *use* the patriots from Miami. Phillips, using agents like Townley as penetrations and informers, was under pressure to control the new White Hand.

"It was certainly a tempting asset. Here you had a bunch of trained killers for hire, willing to shoot anybody. It's important to understand that the Cuban exiles were—and still are—very good. They are not only fanatics but also trained fanatics. Also, they were experienced in all sorts of operations. I'm afraid that some case officers in Latin America became a little too intrigued with those people and began broaching things with them that, shall we say, should never have been broached. As you know, the agency put a stop to that sort of thing later. But while it was going on, the damage was done; not only did you have a terror organization, but you had an organization that, at least to its members, would appear to have had an imprimatur of sorts from the agency."

The voice, again, of Volkman's protected source, speaking frankly
—about "*some* case officers". Another White Hand militant told
CBS that the group "had contacts" with their former CIA case
officers, that they were "talking privately," and receiving "very
good advice."

By 1968, the White Hand was flourishing in Venezuela, El
Salvador, Guatemala, Nicaragua, Costa Rica, and the Dominican
Republic. A lucrative occupation became, by the 1970s, the kidnapping of wealthy citizens, collecting high ransom, and then
taking credit in the name of organizations of the Left. Information
and contacts for White Hand flowed through informal channels to
the small army, as promised by Phillips back in 1967.

On the surface, the Phillips arrangement was working smoothly.
However, behind the scenes, the agency was keeping the exiles on
a leash by exposing just enough of their activities to keep them in
line. That is why, in 1968, Phillips betrayed Sturgis and Rolando
Otero's Secret Army Organization. The SAO was too aggressive
for Langley; its members would have to function on "their own."

By the 1970s, Otero and the Cuban mercenaries had graduated
to full-scale clandestine warfare. Under the leadership of El
Salvador's brutal secret police chief, Colonel José Francisco
René Chacon, the remnants of the CIA's army at the Bay of Pigs
had been welded into a ruthless hemispheric commando. The
ferocious Colonel Chacon, a long time CIA double agent, was
successful in placing Cuban militants in the secret police of a
number of right-wing regimes. After 1973, for instance, DINA
began an intimate relationship with the White Hand.

A former CIA official told the *New York Times*, "It worked out
well for everybody," referring to the unofficial and *deniable* relationship Phillips had worked out in 1967 for the agency and the
White Hand.

In June 1974, the five largest units of the White Hand met to
form a new umbrella organization to be called Co-ordination of
United Revolutionary Organizations, (Comando de Organizaciones
Revolucionaries Unidas, CORU). As chief of the Western Hemisphere Division, it was Phillips who dealt with the CIA informants
attending the meeting. One of Phillips's liaison men to the CORU

was Michael Townley, because Townley was DINA's liaison to CORU.

Townley had known many of the Cubans well since the 1960s. He was almost one of them, they felt, even if he was the "Company." They could trust him, just as they could trust Phillips. "It was almost as if," reports a CORU member of that period, "Mike was Phillips's son." It was true that Townley looked like Phillips; with his height and coloring he could have been the sypmaster's son.

By 1975, Langley was being convulsed by a struggle between hawks and doves. The great scandals had forced James Angleton, Richard Helms, William Broe, Phillips, and a small army of clandestine militants into retirement or silence. A caretaker executive, under George Bush, had been set up, and the unofficial, secret arrangement with the Cubans made by Phillips in 1967 would now have to be covered up. Bush was not as bad as Schlesinger had been (Schlesinger had been forced to have extra bodyguards for protection when he began to weed out the Clandestine Section). At least he was a Yale Old Boy who would help to cover for the White Hand if the Cubans could be separated once and for all from the agency.

The "new" CIA executives after the Watergate purge were shocked to learn that White Hand could claim credit for more than a thousand assassinations in the seventies alone and unnumbered bombings and kidnappings as well as vicious drug traffic industry.

The White Hand would have to rely, then, on its contacts with the hawks in Phillips's new AFIO and those still hidden in Clandestine Services at Langley. The agency had somehow to shackle this monster that it had created before the American election of 1976 and new catastrophic revelations. As a first step the White Hand had to be driven from the American mainland.

It is at this point in the Letelier tragedy that the name of Rolando Otero makes its penultimate entrance. Langley decided that the young terrorist had to be stopped. He and his complement were particularly active in Miami in the murderous war for control of the exile community. Dade County, Florida, authorities were threatening the CIA with exposure of the Florida-based illegal operations if the agency did not intervene to protect Miami from the mounting killings and bombings. Otero's fate was sealed when informers told Langley that the White Hand was responsible for the execution of six Cuban contract agents, Bay of Pigs veterans who still received a regular income from the CIA through commercial fronts. (Even as Phillips had been setting up the new unofficial conduits with the Cubans in 1967, the agency had budgeted $2 million dollars for a Miami informer network that employed nearly two hundred operatives).

It was decided by the CIA to somehow "neutralize" or put away for life the exile hero Rolando Otero. The man selected to put Otero on the spot was the Jackal, Michael Townley.

We had left DINA major Michael Townley rising through the ranks of the DINA officer corps. General Contreras had named him liaison to the Cuban CORU irregulars and similar mercenary groups all over the world. That and assassinations were his assignments.

General Carlos Prats, forcibly exiled after the coup, was working for Fiat in Argentina. The former defense minister was also writing his memoirs. According to a friend, he had learned that a plan to kill him would be made to look like the work of the Argentine Anti-Communist Alliance (AAA). Marchetti's censored book had slipped out, and Agee could not be conveniently stopped from publishing abroad; Prats's exposé would never see the light of day.

On September 30, 1974, shortly after the first anniversary of the violent overthrow of the Allende government, Townley and a team of assassins murdered Carlos Prats and his wife in Buenos Aires. Their auto was exploded by a bomb. The action was the work of DINA's "External Section." Major Townley's official alias in the External Section for the Prats assassination was "Juan Andreas Wilson Silva." Members of the AAA provided logistical support as well as generous hospitality for Townley and his Chilean-Cuban hit team.

In a related development, Marlise Simons, a Dutch journalist who reported on Chile for the *Washington Post*, said that General Prats had told her in correspondence before his death that various Christian Democratic parties in Europe had provided money to help overthrow the Popular Unity government and that Christian Democratic ex-President Eduardo Frei, the CIA's man since 1964, was mainly to blame for the military coup.

By October 7, a Mexico City newspaper, *Excelsior*, was identifying a long-time CIA asset, arch-conservative Juan Luis Ossa Bulnes, as implicated in the Prats assassination. Juan Ossa Bulnes was known as the "military chief" of the right-wing extremist National party in Chile, and Ossa's ties to Langley went way back. He had been indicted in the Schneider affair.

On the second anniversary of the coup, September 1975, the Townley death squad struck again. Former Chilean vice-president Bernardo Leighton and his wife were gunned down in Rome by local fascists (*Fronte della Gioventù*) working with DINA.

During 1975, Major Townley, DINA's liaison officer, crisscrossed the United States. His official obligations included a series of planning meetings with men like Rolando Otero and his White Hand militants. Townley was also busy purchasing electronic equipment in Florida from the National Intelligence Agency. At this "private nonprofit" business he rubbed shoulders with his counterparts from Iran's SAVAK and South Korea's KCIA. During 1975, Townley was given $25,000 by DINA to recruit assassins to murder junta critics in Mexico. The plan did not come off, but Townley's reputation as the Jackal was now secure. (Townley's recruits for the Mexican murders also happened to be CIA contract agents.)

Before his retirement from CIA, Phillips had been responsible for watching over the agency's creature, DINA, in order that some of the world-wide revulsion for the junta might be contained. The danger lay in the self-perpetuating dynamics of the Gestapo like apparatus that DINA had become. One way to control the secret police from within was to use men like Michael Townley. But if Townley retained his key role in assassinations and "special operations," and as liaison to terrorist units, he would have to participate in any important international acts of violence.

This is the vicious circle of information and provocation which emerges when one government, the United States, attempts to control another government, the Chilean junta, through the medium of double agents like Townley. DINA Chief Contreras, well aware of Townley's first loyalty to Langley, was alert to the need to involve the American in DINA's most violent acts outside of Chile. He did so in the belief that Townley's CIA contract connections would provide a secure insurance policy for the junta. This is why Contreras had cleverly named Townley liaison to the Cubans and other extremist groups.

In the war against Agee and his "traitors," the CIA hawks needed their old Cuban suicide squads. What it appears the Old Boys still at Langley, behind Phillips, had in mind was not to assassinate Agee—but instead to pick off the kind of Third World leaders for whose benefit, as they saw it, Agee was making his revelations. At the same time, Cord Meyer and other heavyweights would see to it that their assets in the Secret Services of the industrial countries made it impossible for Agee to live in peace anywhere in Western Europe. The Boys would force him to keep moving like a man without a country, force him—and this was the point of the plot in which Phillips was an important player—at last to go to a *socialist* country to live so that all his revelations could be discredited at one stroke as Communist propaganda, Cuban propaganda.

The "retired" Phillips, then, was to continue to work covert operations in Latin America just as he always had. Why not? He could use the same old cover, of lecturer and author, and the same old rationale, the good of the nation and "national security."

The ambivalence of CIA's relationship with the White Hand had become uncontrollable by 1976. The "new" CIA was threatened by the Cuban extremists; the "old" CIA was dependent on the men from Miami. They represented the potent narcotic of violence to the ever escalating habit of the agency cold warriors. The new CIA declared the Cubans *persona non grata*; the old CIA was organizing them to fight in Angola.

For David Phillips 1976 was a difficult year. The AFIO was growing rapidly, but as the date of the annual banquet, in September, approached, the past began to open up at Phillips's feet.

Hal Hendrix, the CIA-ITT man who had been a master player with Phillips during the coup attempt days of Track I and Track II, was going to be indicted for perjury, it appeared, for the lies he had offered the Senate Committee Investigation of ITT's activities in Chile. If Hendrix fell, could Richard Helms be far behind? And Phillips knew that Helms would take him down with him, if it came to jail. Phillips, along with Hendrix, Helms, Colby, and others, had committed perjury continuously in testimony before the Senate Committee Hearings: Multinational Corporations and U.S. Foreign Policy. Besides the lies about Chile, an earlier set of lies was beginning to haunt Phillips.

In 1976 the chief counsel for the House Select Committee on Assassinations, Richard A. Sprague, announced that both the FBI and CIA were potential suspects in the Kennedy and King murders, and he promptly called David Atlee Phillips to testify in executive session. At the time of the President's assassination in Dallas, Phillips had been the chief of covert action in the CIA's Mexico City station. Testifying before the committee, under oath, Phillips told general counsel Sprague that the CIA had monitored taped Oswald's conversations in the Soviet embassy. Sprague asked Phillips why the agency had not made these tapes available to the Warren Commission. Phillips stated that the tapes had been routinely destroyed on October 9, 1963, approximately one week after they were made. "Oswald was not considered an important character on October 8, 1963," according to Phillips. He could give no credible reason why the Warren Commission was never told that such evidence had existed.

But there is an FBI report to indicate that Phillips committed perjury before the Select Committee on Assassinations when he stated that evidence concerning Oswald's presence in Mexico City had been "routinely destroyed." The FBI document that destroyed Phillips's story was the Bureau's first "Comprehensive Report," dated November 23, 1963. Oswald was still alive when the photograph of a burly man of about thirty-five, identified as Lee H. Oswald—though it was clearly not the twenty-four-year-old stripling—and a tape of Oswald talking to a Soviet KGB officer arrived in Dallas. FBI special agents familiar with Oswald responded at once that the photo was not Lee Oswald. As for the tape, the Comprehensive Report states:

"These special agents are of the opinion that the above-referred to individual is not Lee Harvey Oswald."

In other words the tape had *not* been destroyed. As of November 23, 1963, a "second" Oswald—picture and voice—had passed from Phillips and the CIA to the FBI—but the Warren Commission never knew about the handover.

On Mexico City alone, Sprague had Phillips caught in a clear case of perjury, and Phillips knew it.

Just as dangerous, potentially, was the ugly insurgency taking place in Miami (there was no rest for the great veterans of Clandestine). A combination of cash and force would be needed to restore discipline.

One of the leaders of the exile insurgency was the young freedom fighter Rolando Otero. To recapitulate: In 1975, Otero learned for the first time that Phillips and the agency had betrayed him when, in 1968, Otero had been a member of Frank Sturgis's Operation Sword. Otero was a fiery believer in his cause, and a message was sent back to Langley in 1975 that the deal that Phillips had cut with the Bay of Pigs veteran in 1967 was "no longer operable." The *Brigadistas* wanted it known that the 1968 sellout had violated completely the 1967 understanding and that the exiles would now *do* and *say* what was in *their* best interests. When Langley reacted to this threat by feeding information about White Hand bombings to the FBI, Otero went into hiding in Chile.

Otero had to be stopped. Phillips's carrot had gone rotten. Langley handed the stick to Michael Townley.

14 The Cover-up, Part I

I had just been born when my parents took me to the extreme South of my country, to Temuco. In the surroundings there were forests where the Mapuche Indians lived. Temuco is my landscape, the essential part of my poetry.

I attended the city school in Temuco. My compañeros had German, English, Norwegian, and even some Chilean names. It was a society without castes, a world that had just been created. We were all equals.

Pablo Neruda, interview with *L'Express*

Chileans have always had a great inclination toward poetry. This may be related to the great geographical isolation of the country, which is both volcanic and maritime. During the entire period when I was a student I traveled the length of Chile reciting my poems, I felt that it was poetry that the masses most responded to. You could discuss politics or economics, but poetry is what they really came to hear.

JUST BEFORE THE COUP IN 1973, Townley had taken cover in Florida in the exile community and at the National Intelligence Academy (NIA) in Fort Lauderdale where his parents also now lived and where his father was listed as a vice-president of international corporate banking at the mammoth Southeat First National Bank of Miami. In order to understand Townley's support system for the assassination of Orlando Letelier and Ronni Moffitt, it is necessary to take a close look at both the NIA and the Southeast First National Bank.

NIA, also known as AID (Audio Intelligence Devices), is headed by a notorious CIA contract agent for Clandestine Services, John ("Jumpin' Jack") Holcomb. The NIA complex lists itself as a nonprofit private corporation whose only link to the United States government is the flow of money from the Law Enforcement

Assistance Agency (LEAA). Historically, however, NIA is a by-product of the CIA's huge JM/WAVE base of operations that proliferated across the state in preparation for the Bay of Pigs invasion. A subculture of fronts, proprietaries, suppliers, transfer agents, conduits, dummy corporations, blind drops, detective agencies, law firms, electronic firms, shopping centers, airlines, radio stations, the mob and the church and the banks: a false and secret nervous system twitching to stimuli supplied by the cortex in Clandestine Services at Langley. After defeat on the beach in Cuba, JM/WAVE became a continuing and extended Miami Station, CIA's largest in the continental United States. A large sign in front of the NIA building complex reads: U.S. GOVERNMENT REGULATIONS PROHIBIT DISCUSSION OF THIS ORGAN-IZATION OR FACILITY.

Jack Holcolmb had worked closely with David Phillips and Howard Hunt all through the 1950s and 1960s. The explosion that blew open the Letelier case—the downing of a Cuban airliner in October 1976—was carried out with electronic equipment pur-chased from NIA by Luis Posada Carrilles. Holcomb's name comes up whenever black operations in the Caribbean or Latin America are discussed.

The FBI, which is good at that sort of thing, refused to follow the footprints that lead from NIA to the Southeast First National Bank of Miami. Bloody footprints, since *Townley, the assassin, was in constant contact with both NIA and Southeast First from August 1976 through the day of Letelier's murder*. Townley actually received and made telephone calls in furtherance of the con-spiracy from NIA and Southeast First facilities.

We know that NIA and DINA had a financial arrangement, that NIA and CIA also had a long money history, and that Southeast First National, a banking giant, had a long and intriguing relation-ship with *both* NIA and CIA.

Southeast First is the largest of a subculture of banks in southern Florida. Interlocking directorates and major investors link such operations as the Bank of Miami Beach, Miami National Bank, International Bank of Miami, and the Key Biscayne Bank. South-east is the sun in the universe of Miami's financial institutions. In a monumental study, Jeff Gerth, now of the *New York Times*, hooked up these and subsidiary banks to organized crime leaders such as Meyer Lansky and Lucky Luciano as well as the Cleveland, Boston, Las Vegas, and Teamster-connected mobs. And at Miami National researchers discovered on the board of directors none other than James Angleton, the CIA's infamous chief of counter-intelligence, code named "Mother."

Southeast's ties to the CIA are long. The trail starts in Chicago with the Deering family who, in 1947, invested in the Ansan Group. Ansan, in turn, is connected to Keyes Realty, which was long used by Langley as one in its host of Florida fronts. Keyes Realty—who developed the Florida White House used by Richard Nixon—reaches deep into the organized crime culture of the Bahamas. Once again, the unholy alliance of crime and CIA can be followed from the banks to the casinos. Fidel Castro's revolution drove organized crime from Havana to Miami and into the arms of the Central Intelligence Agency.

One other example illustrates the connection between Langley and Southeast First. Southern Airlines, a wholly-owned CIA proprietary, was a long-time client of the bank. Townley, the Jackal, spent time at his father's bank and made telephone calls from a desk in its International Section. One of the calls was to the National Intelligence Academy. The Justice Department declined to investigate the calls made from the bank, *or* from the NIA, when Townley was making that private firm his headquarters. Townley spent time at the bank and NIA both before and after the Letelier murder.

The connections go further. In December 1974, after the Prats murder, Michael Townley and his father Vernon opened up a cover account named PROCIN at South East First. Michael used his alias Juan Andrés Williams. When this information threatened to come to light in 1978, prosecutor Propper withdrew the subpeona required to delve into Townley's activities in southern Florida. These activities included a sever of communications between the NIA and *both* Townleys.

During these NIA days of later summer 1973, Townley was in and out of the Miami area. There, in the old haunts of 1968, he spent many intense hours with the White Hand. Townley was well known for his *Patria y Libertad* exploits in Chile and a number of CORU men had also taken part in *Patria y Libertad* operations with him. Now they discussed the coming coup with relish. Townley bragged, according to witnesses, that he would have a high intelligence post in the new government.

At one of these 1973 White Hand meetings Townley told Rolando Otero that he would need CORU's support in order that he, a *gringo*, could receive support from other Latin American secret services. Otero pledged aid, including planes if needed, and made it clear to Townley that CORU, for its part, would also expect help in the coming escalation against Cuba.

There was only one problem, Otero told Townley, and that was "the Company." The Miami men had been appalled when their old case officer "Eduardo" (Howard Hunt)—whom they had trusted above anyone else—had betrayed the Miamians caught in the Watergate the summer before. Now there were only a handful left that had any balls, he said; David Phillips was one, of course, and Michael Townley another. One of the leaders that summer was the veteran Aldo Vera Serafin. He was chosen to head P y L in Miami.

Two years later, in 1975, Otero learned that Phillips had sold him out as long ago as 1968 during Operation Sword. After discovering Phillips's hand in the 1968 fiasco, Otero now was certain that Phillips or one of his people had informed the FBI of still another assassination attempt that Otero and CORU had planned for Fidel Castro during one of his South American trips. *Someone* had tipped off both the FBI *and* Cuban intelligence to that conspiracy. Otero vowed to Townley that CORU would pay back whoever had informed. Other exiles, in 1975, had begun to compile a list of traitors; by 1976 both Townley and Vera Serafin were on it.

It was against this background that the Letelier killing took place. An arrangement between General Contreras of DINA and CORU had made it possible for Otero to find asylum under the Junta in Chile. Townley himself, as liaison to CORU, had worked out the details of the understanding. Once in Chile, Otero had grown suspicious of Townley. This is why, when Townley was ordered to set Otero up for the FBI, he, Townley, had had to telephone Miami to learn Otero's whereabouts in Chile.

Using the pretext that Otero was in danger of being kidnapped by the FBI, Townley elicited the information from the unsuspecting Florida-based White Hand men. Then, on CIA orders, Townley informed the waiting FBI special agents, and Otero was arrested and hurried to the airport and out of Chile at gun point. In August 1976, Otero stood trial in a Florida state court in Jacksonville for the airport bombing. Forced to testify at the trial, by a grant of immunity, was Max Gonzales, who had been one of those betrayed by Phillips and the CIA in both 1968 and 1975. On March 18, 1977, Rolando Otero was sentenced to eighty-five years in prison.

The White Hand members in Chile with Otero were thunderstruck. Robert Caraballa's sentiments (here translated into English) are typical.

When he went to Chile in 1975 there was an agreement with DINA that he would not be handed over to the American police, which was looking for him for six bombs which exploded one night in Miami. Whether he was involved in that or not, the fact is that he was in exile, not because of drugs or any other kind of crime, but only because of a political problem. He was one of the younger members of the Brigade and he started fighting when he was thirteen years old.

We looked for an explanation and they only told us that the department responsible for turning him over did not know why Otero was there. Now out comrade is serving a long prison term.

Jose Dionisio Suárez—still at large and changed with actually igniting the explosives that destroyed Letelier and Moffitt—also remembers the Oter betrayal.

I believe that Townley was representing the CIA at all times. That is why Rolando Otero was handed over to the FBI

Mariana Callejas later tried to brush the incident aside.

Yes, and when we were in Miami in 1973 and the leaders [*jefes* of the Cubans] offered us airplanes and money to overthrow Allende, but all that wound up in nothing. Michael met and got to know the very high-level leaders of the anti-Castro forces. In 1976 he called them to ask them about Rolando Otero, who was in Chile, and he was considered dangerous for the security of Henry Kissinger. They [the Cubans] decided that Otero was crazy. DINA picked up Otero and handed him over to the FBI and the U.S. where he's now serving a very long term. But it was not Michael that gave him up, as they say. But in spite of that Guillermo Novo protested on the phone to Michael.

On the plane to Miami, after his arrest in Chile, Otero became involved in a violent struggle with his two FBI guards. He bit one agent's hand through to the bone. The injured special agent was Robert Scherrer.

Scherrer, Carter Cornick's partner, had led the FBI investigation into the Letelier-Moffitt assassinations, and was responsible for the arrest of Michael Townley in Santiago in 1978. Scherrer, to whom Townley had handed over Rolando Otero in 1976!

Based on this, it is worth looking at the FBI's official statement as to how it came to "capture" Otero in April 1976. According to the *Miami Herald* "the FBI wasn't telling...how Otero was tripped up." In an official FBI press release, Director Kelly gave credit to a "close coordination of investigative agencies. . . ."

A network of death squads that range across Argentina, Brazil, Chile, Paraguay, Uruguay, was organized, logistically, by the Pentagon and CIA. Scherrer monitored the leadership of terror in the Southern Cone.

It is known that Scherrer asked General Contreras to turn Otero over to the FBI and that Contreras, true to his arrangements with the Cubans, denied any knowledge of Otero. At this point, Scherrer confronted Contreras, telling the DINA director that he knew Otero was in Chile under official protection. Scherrer insisted that if the Cuban was not handed over to the FBI within twenty-four hours, there would be official American sanctions. Contreras had to bow to the demand. It was obvious that Scherrer had an informant. The informant was, Contreras verified, Michael Townley.

The FBI field office in Buenos Aires was composed of one full-time special agent, Robert Scherrer, and he monitored political activities of the Left and Right for all of SOCO, as the FBI calls the Southern Cone. Scherrer, as an expert and liaison to DINA, had a working relationship with Contreras and DINA. *Scherrer was well aware of the contract arrangements with such Cubans as the Novo brothers and Jose Suárez, later indicted for the Letelier-Moffitt murders.*

Scherrer's Buenos Aires station of the FBI has a singular history. David Phillips's first spymaster, Colonel J. C. King, had served in Argentina during World War II. There he developed extremely close relations with the FBI, which at that time was responsible for United States intelligence in Latin America. When the CIA was founded after the war, Colonel King became chief of the Western Hemisphere Division, and he recruited scores of FBI agents into the Central Intelligence Agency. These Latin America veterans, led by Colonel King, worked closely with both Latin and American business leaders.

After 1948 the FBI left Latin America to the jurisdiction of the CIA. The Bureau maintained one full-time liaison officer in the Southern Cone in 1975, and that was Robert Scherrer. The CIA station in Buenos Aires remained, through the 1970s, FBI oriented and enjoyed a uniquely close working relationship with the FBI office there. There, for once, the CIA and FBI shared assets and information and worked together with the police and intelligence forces of the Southern Cone countries. This is the context in which Scherrer came into contact with DINA and the White Hand, in Santiago, and Major Michael Townley—who was DINA's *liaison* officer to the various extremist groups that came under Scherrer's purview.

It was obvious in 1976 in Chile that Otero after being turned over to Scherrer, would get the maximum, with little chance of early parole, according to Suárez, Guillermo Novo, and others who confronted the Townleys after the Otero arrest. The Townleys swore that they were innocent, but Contreras knew better, and after a serious talk with Suárez and the others, the White Hand militants pretended to believe Townley's protestations. *But they did not.*

No one believed the fiction that Otero had been apprehended because he intended to assassinate Henry Kissinger when the Secretary of State next visited Chile. The Kissinger story, everybody in the Chilean intelligence community knew, was Langley's cover story for the Otero arrest.

According to the White Hand, an assassination list *was* shown to them by Townley. Kissinger's name was not on it, but those of Olaf Palme, prime minister of Sweden, and Senator Edward Kennedy, of the United States, were included, as was that of the former minister Orlando Letelier.

For the Agency, 1976 was the year of contract agent crisis. Langley was spread-eagled between Caracas and Santiago, between Orlando Bosch and Rolando Otero.

The man who was talking about the Letelier case in Venezuela, Orlando Bosch, was the chief of CORU. Bosch had contacts high up in secret police forces across Latin America. In Venezuela these included Orlando Garcia and Ricardo Morales. Both men had long American intelligence backgrounds. Morales had fought for the agency in the Congo; after 1967 he had become a double agent working for both the FBI and the CIA. Later, he would testify against Bosch.

Orlando Bosch had been the extremist's extremist since the 1960s. In 1968, the former pediatrician was detained for shelling a Polish freighter in Miami harbor. After serving a short sentence, Bosch redoubled his terror efforts, only to be arrested in Venezuela. But the United States authorities refused to ask for his return to face multiple murder and bombing charges. The Venezuelans, disgusted, released Bosch into the plump hands of DINA. By February 1976 Bosch was involved in Costa Rica in another "plot" against Kissinger. He was arrested again, then released, and it was after this that the meetings began to plan the Cubana airline sabotage and the Letelier murder. It is this man, Bosch, that the FBI and the Department of Justice refused to question in October 1976 until after investigators Cummings and Volkman had the names of the Cubans Bosch was fingering for the Letelier assassination. The man who had implicated Bosch in Costa Rica was Ricardo Morales, working with FBI Special Agent Joseph Leo.

Ricardo Morales Navarrete ("Mono," or "Monkey") damns the United States intelligence agencies utterly in their relationship to the Letelier-Moffit murders. Morales was and is a CIA executioner, according to the office of the U.S. attorney in Miami.

R. Jerome Sanford was a veteran United States attorney in the Southern District of Florida, and in 1978 a nominee for federal employee of the year. His first public statement on the Letelier case, below, should, by itself, compel the initiation of grand jury proceedings.

Ricardo Morales was a former Castro agent turned FBI informer and CIA executioner. Long before the Letelier murder on September 21, 1976, Morales was talking to the FBI. Within weeks after the murder, in the fall of 1976, the Justice Department was given the names of the men eventually charged *nearly two years later* with the Letelier murder. Secret documents related to the CIA informed the government that the Brigade 2506, the veterans of the ill-fated 1961 Bay of Pigs invasion, was involved in the killing up to its ears. And a federal prosecutor from Washington told me that the FBI had learned two months before the assassination that it was being planned. Yet Letelier was never told that his life was in imminent danger.

The information needed to indict these conspirators was in the hands of the FBI many months before the Justice Department even started to move against them in earnest.

When Letelier was killed...I asked to have my efforts dovetailed into those of assistant U.S. attorney Eugene Propper in Washington, I was told that information being given to Propper would go to others only "on a need to know" basis. Who more than I needed to know? Yet the stonewalling continued.

In the winter of 1979, the authorities in Washington, after repeated requests that had been met with silence, finally sent me the testimony of the government's chief witness in the Letelier case.

When I read it I was, to put it mildly, shocked and aghast because the very people I had been trying to investigate were involved in the Washington murder. It reinforced my decision to go public.

In carefully-orchestrated testimony, witness Michael Vernon Townley, a DINA agent who for years had been a CIA asset, very carefully responded to questions put to him. His testimony is revealing not only in what he says but more for what he *does not* say—and it carefully avoids tying Letelier's murder to the scores of others in Florida. Suffice to say I find the testimony beyond belief. I asked permission to question Townley. The request went unanswered. And the murders go on....

This U.S. attorney—who is preparing to "go public" because of what he has seen—describes volumes and crates of evidence in the Letelier or "CHILBOM" case in Miami that were never turned over to *either* the prosecution or the defense.

Morales had set up Bosch exactly as Townley had set up Otero, according to the source in the U.S. attorney's office in Florida. Slowly but surely, the CIA was mopping up CORU, through the use of double agents. Scherrer's role in the Townley matter is consistent with that of FBI Special Agent Joseph Leo in the Bosch case. Leo, in Caracas, knew Bosch and his White Hand gang. Leo and Bosch frequented a private detective office that had been a CIA front for years. Leo had sneaked Bosch's aide Fred Lugo into Puerto Rico under cover of *Vision* magazine. FBI agent Leo is also Interpol's man in Caracas, as Scherrer was in Buenos Aires. The point, again, is that the FBI and the CIA do have meaningful liaison in one area of the world—Latin America. One asset they used in common was Aldo Vera. Townley's old friend and fellow agent was, according to FBI documents received by the author, a member of Bosch's *Acción Cubana* (Cuban Action) until Bosch expelled him for spying in June 1976 and put out a contract on his life.

The Bosch and Otero cases have been tied together from their inception. It is important to remember that the Cubana airline sabotage and the Letelier murder were planned *at the same July 1976 Dominican Republic meeting*. Both operations were given the green light in August. One of the planners was Ricardo Morales who was working for both the FBI and the CIA. Besides Morales, the Justice Department told the *Miami Herald* that the FBI had infiltrated an informant into the highest levels of Bosch's inner circle. *That informant helped make up the murder list that featured the name of Orlando Letelier*. Morales also arranged for electronic surveillance of the meeting. There was also Aldo Vera Serafin.

The meeting at which both the Cubana and Letelier violence was plotted was organized by a notorious CIA operative named Sacha Volman. Thus the CIA had to know in advance what was being planned.

Morales, Lugo, Garcia, Volman, Vera, Townley: these men all had links with American intelligence, the DINA, and the White Hand. *Thus it can be stated that the FBI and CIA had to know, based on reports from their agents in place, that (1) the meeting took place in the Dominican Republic in the mountains of Bonao at the executive lodge of an American-based multinational corpora-*

tion; (2) The Bonao conference consisted of two planning groups, one focused on the Cuban airline sabotage, the other on the execution of Orlando Letelier.

Townley, now holding a rank equivalent to lieutenant colonel in the DINA, flew into New York City on September 9, 1976. According to the prosecutor at the trial, he brought ten "electric matches," or blasting caps, with him, but there is strong evidence that the caps came from a *former* CIA man, Edwin Wilson, a man who deals in the shipment of explosive devices. This information would plague the FBI during its murder investigation.

The prosecutor and the FBI posited that Townley constructed and attached the bomb under the front seat of the Letelier car while it was parked near his Bethesda home. A number of meetings in New Jersey and Washington are described by the government as the prelude and setting for the construction of the explosive device. The prosecution's version of events is strictly tailored to tie up the Novo brothers and Ross and to exclude Pinochet, Otero Echeverria, and the CIA.

What actually happened was somewhat different. The Cubans (but as we shall see, not necessarily those convicted) had been waiting for the CIA to call on them for a covert operation. The White Hand men who met with Townley never doubted for a moment that he was the CIA's agent *in* DINA, and to add force to this belief, Townley never denied that he was representing "the Company".

Without betraying that CORU was still seeking vengeance on the CIA for the Otero sellout, the Cubans presented their conditions to Townley. First, he would be responsible for making *and* planting the bomb (this because the Cubans feared another provocation, as in the Otero affair); second, a large sum of money would have to be deposited, at once, in a bank outside of the United States; third, Townley would not leave the country until after the assassination.

At a meeting, on September 14, Townley told the Cubans that the money would be "no problem." He also advanced conditions of his own: (1) the murder was not to take place in Washington, D.C. (2) the killing had to be made to look like a suicide or an accident.

It is now known that Contreras and DINA never at any time promised *any* money to the Cubans, much less the million dollars they were led to believe would be deposited for them in a notorious Caribbean asset, long an Organized Crime-CIA conduit. So either Townley was risking his life by leading the Cubans on or the million was coming from some source other than DINA.

Meanwhile, in the District of Columbia, Armando Fernández of DINA was stalking Letelier, keeping him under surveillance. Fernandez was in touch with Rafael Otero Echeverria at the Chilean Embassy.

Rafael Otero Echeverria of *SEPA* magazine had been Phillips's man right through the Quartered Man phase of Centaur, and after the coup a prime mover of Phillips's Plan Z. Now he was a junta diplomat in Washington.

Townley arrived in Washington around September 16, but he needed more parts for his bomb. When he was later questioned on the witness stand about his sources for the fatal components, he stunned the courtroom by taking the Fifth Amendment. The next day, he said that DINA had been his supplier, *before* his departure for the United States.

The government charged that Townley left the District after planting the bomb, traveling to New Jersey and then to Florida (there is no mention of either NIA or Southeast First in the itinerary), and that Paz and Suárez stayed on to trigger the bomb in front of the Chilean Embassy. *Why* in front of the embassy? *Why* on the very day junta representatives were in Washington attempting to get extensions on loans that were absolutely vital to the regime's crumbling economy?

Phillips's AFIO had been set up as a media front, and now it was put into high gear. "Papers" from Letelier's briefcases began to circulate in Phillip's English-Language translations. These papers and letters were hotly spiced with a number of Otero Echeverria-Phillips forgeries.

The scenarios that the Phillips network were peddling were three: (1). Letelier and the Moffitts had been on their way to blow up the Chilean Embassy and had been destroyed in a moment of poetic justice by their *own* explosives; (2). Letelier was a Castro agent and as such eligible for martyrdom, that is to be murdered by the Left in order to produce a rallying point for a new, global offensive against Chile's junta, (3). the killings were a nonpolitical crime of passion committed by (a) Letelier's jealous mistress, (b) Ronni Moffitt's jealous lover, (c) Letelier's wife, Isabel, or (d) Michael Moffit, who did escape injury . . . .

There is a tradition of disinformation following important political crimes. After the murder of Martin Luther King, the FBI spread three false scenarios: (1) a jealous husband had pulled the trigger; (2) black militants on King's left were responsible; (3) King's own aides co-operated in the making of a martyr.

After the slaying of Malcolm X, the FBI sold the "Muslims did it" story until 1978 when one of the killers revealed that to be a mere cover. At any rate, the FBI and its FOB's (as the files list "Friends of the Bureau" in the media) and the CIA, Phillips, and their "elite assets" (to use *their* word magic) could and did function smoothly in the execution of the old Cold War song and dance.

With this new-old tissue of lies the Phillips team sought to infect the media and confuse what had been clear from the first moment, when Michael Moffitt screamed murder up at the Chilean Embassy. But Moffitt, who was correct in his accusation, as far as it went, was up against much more than the junta. He also faced David Phillips the grand master of character assassination through the media.

The network lit up. Some of the names are: Jeremiah O'Leary, *Washington Star*, George Lardner, *Washington Post*, syndicated columnists Rowland Evans and Robert Novak, Ralph de Toledano of the Copley syndicate, station WRUL in New York, the Fulton Lewis Communications group, and the extreme right-wing congressman from Georgia, Larry McDonald, whose staff works regularly with an entire spectrum of right-wing extremist newsletters and newspapers. But, above all, there was that asset of assets, William F. Buckley, Jr. Buckley had served under Howard Hunt in Mexico in the 1950s and worked actively with Phillips over the years behind the scenes in Latin America. Now, he set in motion a major multimedia attack. The polysyllabic propagandist's magazine *National Review* functioned as little more than an Old Boy *agitprop* broadside, a sort of a North American *El Mercurio*. In each succeeding number of *National Review*, virtually every reference to Letelier after the murder, for years to come, carried the adjectival epthet "Cuban agent." The source was always "Letelier's own briefcase."

Phillips and Buckley had a handful of playlets they spread like cards before the suckers in the media. The Phillips propaganda team after the murder included, besides the Buckley network, Rafael Otero Echeverria and Manuel Trucco, the Chilean press attaché and the Chilean ambassador in Washington, respectively. By October what could be called the Old Boy "anti-theory" was making the rounds. October 8, 1976, Jeremiah O'Leary in the *Washington Star*:

The right wing Chilean junta had nothing to gain and everything to lose by the assassination of a peaceful and popular socialist leader, at a time when Chile's financial problems were about to be reviewed in Washington.

October 11, 1976, *Newsweek*'s "Periscope" column:

The CIA has concluded that the Chilean secret police was not involved in the death of Orlando Letelier...The agency reached this conclusion because the work was too simple to have been done by experts and because the assassination, committed at the exact moment in which the Chilean government is seeking U.S. support, could only harm the Santiago regime.

October 12, 1976, David Binder in the *New York Times*:

But intelligence agents confirmed that they understood the DINA to be firmly controlled by General Augusto Pinochet's government, and that to kill Mr. Letelier could not serve the purposes of the junta.

October 25, 1976, Buckley's *American Chilean Council Report*:

U.S. investigators think it unlikely that Chile would risk with an action of this kind the respect it has won with great difficulty during the past year in many Western countries, which before were hostile to its policies.

Senator Jesse Helms referred to the killings as an "act of international suicide." He may have been more accurate than he intended.

The sources which the various publications cite to substantiate the stories are from a worn-out Cold War stencil:
1. "Intelligence agents," or "intelligence sources"
2. "FBI agents" or "Investigators made it known"

3. "Preliminary investigation indicates . . ."
4. "Various agents indicated that . . ."
5. "The CIA has concluded that . . ."
6. "Official agents considered it unlikely . . ."

What is euphemistically referred to as a "cover-up" in the press, is often, as in the Letelier assassination, an integral part of a covert military operation. The U.S. Army Field Manual, *Psychological Operations*, gives detailed instructions on false stories to be planted to cover kidnappings and abductions. It is significant that the Army does not have the legal authority to plant false stories, called "black propaganda", only the CIA does. But the Manual is intended to give Army personnel sufficient familiarity with covert operations so as to be able to co-ordinate their activities with the CIA. The key word here is "co-ordination."

When Otero Echeverria, Buckley, and Phillips began planting false information to cover up the Letelier assassination, they could do so in a productive manner only by having detailed intelligence on the actual facts. The so-called cover-up is merely the final, logical stage in a covert operation, and its perpetrators, if not familiar with all the facts, have at least to be agents who are trusted, agents who are trained in the methodology of covert propaganda, and agents who know enough about the real circumstances so as to be able to know what to reveal, what to hide, and, most important, *who to blame*.

At 9:30 A.M. on September 21, 1976, the bomb exploded. Ralph Stavins a co-worker of Dr. Letelier's who arrived at Sheridan Circle shortly after the explosion, could see several men in plainclothes removing from the automobile the briefcase and other belongings of Orlando Letelier.

Immediately afterwards, FBI agents entered and sealed off both Letelier's office in the Institute for Policy Studies and his home in Bethesda, Maryland. This denied access to his family, friends, and the public, and gave the FBI free access to Dr. Letelier's personal archives for approximately five hours at his home and an hour at his office.

In an affidavit dated April 6, 1977, two colleagues of Dr. Letelier's stated that on Thursday, September 16, 1976, five days before the assassination, Orlando Letelier was looking for his car keys, which he thought had been misplaced. During the search he opened his briefcase and emptied its contents onto the office floor. These two colleagues saw the contents of the briefcase and stated that they included no more than a half dozen papers. (When the briefcase was finally returned to Mrs. Letelier, it was stuffed with documents.) The affidavit also stated that, about twenty days before his death, Orlando Letelier told one of his colleagues that he had lost a letter addressed to him by Beatriz Allende, a daughter of the martyred president living in exile in Cuba.

Yet a letter from Beatriz Allende, dated May 8, 1975, was leaked to the press; specifically, it was published in Jack Anderson's column of December 20, 1976. This letter, because it informed Letelier he would be receiving a thousand dollars a month as the U.S. representative of the UP in the United States, has been the principal means used to portray Letelier as a Soviet or Cuban agent. *This letter was stolen before the assassination, placed in the briefcase, and later leaked to the press; it had been stolen, as the car keys were.*

In addition, the affidavit shows that a typewritten note which Isabel Letelier gave Orlando Letelier in his office around July 1976 *was not* in the briefcase when the FBI finally returned it. The FBI has said it has no record that this note was part of the briefcase's contents. Nevertheless, in Jeremiah O'Leary's article in the *Washington Star* of April 3, 1977, the complete text of the note is reproduced, and it is identified as one of the documents found in the briefcase.

The Washington Police detective who picked up the Letelier briefcase at the accident was named Stanley Wilson. Wilson gave the contents of the case, he said, to the FBI.

Who is Wilson? In 1978, two years after the murder, the detective appeared in a federal courtroom in Miami on behalf of a White Hand gunman who was fighting extradition to Guatemala on murder charges. Was Wilson the CIA's man? Did he pass the contents of the briefcase to Phillips? Or did the FBI pass them along? According to documents obtained through the Freedom of Information Act *scores* of employees at Institute for Policy Studies (more than fifty!) were on the payrolls of both the FBI and the Central Intelligence Agency over the years.

The answer to all questions about the use of the briefcase leads to the CIA. It was Langley's agent, Phillips, who, with Otero Echeverria and others, received, concealed, translated, and distributed selections from them, along with misinformation and blatant lies in order to cover up the truth about the murder.

Phillips's friend O'Leary went so far as to mention that he had in his possession cassettes with the voice of Orlando Letelier. These, O'Leary said, the government investigators had used "to make a psychological profile of Letelier." This statement shows that O'Leary had close contact with the official investigators, who never mentioned the use of these cassettes to Isabel Letelier or private investigators with the IPS. On May 12, 1977, the government was asked to turn over the tapes to Isabel Letelier. But the attorney in charge, Eugene Propper, said they could not turn over certain tapes which had by then been destroyed as a result of having been played or copied many times. They also refused to give transcriptions of these tapes to the widow.

The following is the transcription of part of a conversation between Isabel Letelier and Propper.

ISABEL LETELIER: Mr. Propper, I am astonished by the news that you have given my secretary. Is it possible that an inventory of the objects in the briefcase does not exist in the Justice Department?

PROPPER: You must understand, Mrs. Letelier, that many of the documents were in Spanish. That's why the Police Department could not classify them. You know how the Police Department is . . .

ISABEL: Well, I know that they're very inefficient.

PROPPER: Mrs. Letelier, we can't have a conversation with this tone.

ISABEL: And we haven't been able to get correct, responsible information. How can you know if a document is missing or if a document has been added later if there never was a list of the contents of the briefcase?

PROPPER: I assure you, Mrs. Letelier, that it is impossible that anything of the kind took place.

ISABEL: Tell me, would it be possible for something like that to happen?

PROPPER: Who are you trying to implicate as the author of such an act?

ISABEL: Let's just say a ghost or something like that. I'm not yet accusing anyone in particular. But I'm very upset about the situation in general. With the leaks to the press, and now I find out there is no inventory, I think I have good reason to be upset and angry. How can I be sure of what really was in the briefcase, if they refused to show me its contents on the day of the assassination?

PROPPER: They [the Washington Metropolitan Police] made photocopies. Actually, it's not impossible for someone to have removed or planted evidence among the copies, but it would be vey difficult since they copied things in a certain order. On the other hand, they [the police] were very angry with us [the Justice Department] for turning the briefcase over to you. In any case, you may be very sure that you have all the contents of the briefcase.

ISABEL: That's the same thing you told me some time ago. Nevertheless, several things have appeared since. Things which have been very efficiently distributed among right-wing journalists.

PROPPER: I have nothing to do with that. It's impossible to control the press. We regret it deeply, we did everything we could. . . .

Phillips, and Otero Echeverria and the AFIO, had woven a net of journalists, politicians, and organizations whose primary mission was to cover up the facts of the assassinations of Letelier and Ronni Moffitt. No other explanation fits the facts described. Worse than that, they had organized a sinister campaign attempting to justify the assassination to the North American people.

The instruments used in this campaign have been enumerated. William Buckley's circle was especially prominent. The CIA's Phillips-Buckley network included:

1. Georgia Congressman Larry McDonald.

2. Accuracy in the Media: An organization of right-wing propaganda, which is dedicated to attacking the mainstream press for not being sufficiently anti-Communist.

3. American-Chilean Council: A group of agents of the Chilean dictatorship, which has a budget of $100,000 yearly for propaganda, and is directed by Nena Ossa, a former journalist for the Chilean bi-weekly magazine *PEC*, (for *Politica Economia Cultura*), and spokesperson for the CIA in Chile.

4. "Reverend Sun Myung Moon: a self-proclaimed South Korean evangelical messiah, financed by the Park dictatorship with close ties to the Korean CIA (KCIA).

5. Young Americans for Freedom (YAF): An organization of right-wing youth. YAF was set up in the eraly 1960s by William Buckley and E. Howard Hunt.

Phillips and Buckley operatives circulated actual media kits all over the world in an attempt to destroy Orlando Letelier's memory.

After decades of dining out on neo-Platonist political cant, William Buckley's celebrated charm has begun to spring a few leaks. It seems that when Mr. Buckley found God at Yale he also found the Central Intelligence Agency. In 1978, he finally got caught out.

On December 18, 1978, the Justice Department filed suit against Buckley's American-Chilean Council (ACC) for violation of the Alien Registration Act. The Justice Department's claim was that the American-Chilean Council was a front and that the ACC's parent organization in Chile, the *Consejo-Chileno-NorteAmericano* (CCNA), was similarly a front, organized for the purpose of disguising aggressive public relations and political lobbying efforts in Washington by the Pinochet government.

The plot begins on October 29, 1974. Buckley arranged a working luncheon to bring together Chilean government officials with two of his close friends: Nena Ossa and Marvin Liebman. Ossa, Chilean corresponsdent for *National Review* from 1970 on, later became a prominent official in the junta's Cultural Department. Marvin Liebman, the veteran right-wing "public relations specialist," co-founded with Buckley numerous conservative propaganda organizations, such as Young Americans for Freedom, and raised funds for *National Review* at its inception. Buckley, according to Justice Department documents, had recommended Liebman to the Chilean junta as a public relations consultant and arranged the luncheon to permit Liebman to discuss ways in which he could serve the new military regime. Liebman, in turn, drafted a letter to Buckley outlining his proposals—a letter that Buckley passed on to Mario Arnello, a member of the Chilean mission to the United Nations.

In his letter Liebman thanked Buckley "very much for inviting me to meet with your Chilean friends yesterday at lunch. The coversation was stimulating and informative." Liebman proposed setting up a public committee instead of a registered lobbyist for "counteracting the current image of Chile as a right-wing, despotic dictatorship." To Buckley and Arnello he admitted that the organization would be independent of the junta only "insofar as its public posture is concerned," and that contributions to it could be laundered through U.S.-based corporations. He further noted that in order to act "as advisers to the Chilean government on all matters relating to American public opinion," he would have "to have access at all times to the Chilean Ambassador or his designated aides."

Marvin Liebman is at the center of the Buckley net: he is associated with the Committee of One Million Against the Admission of Communist China to the United Nations; the American Committee to Aid Katanga Freedom Fighters; Young Americans for Freedom; American Afro-Asian Educational Exchange, Inc., American Jewish League Against Communism Inc.; Emergency Committee for Chinese Refugees; Committee for the Monroe Doctrine; Christian Anti-Communism Crusade; National Committee of Correspondence of the Council Against Communist Aggression; the Alex de Tocqueville Society; and others. Most of these were co-founded with Buckley himself.

Liebman was a member of the U.S. Communist party from 1938 to 1945. Then, in 1951, he went to work for the *International Rescue Committee*, a CIA front, and soon his extremist support of right-wing and fascist causes began.

The founding members of the American-Chilean Council are prominent right-wing journalists, authors, intellectuals, and educators. Between them they have connections to practically every international rightist organization or government. The groups and personalities in the Buckley organization, the ACC, *are almost all indentified with the Phillips front, the AFIO*.

In May 1976 the ACC launched a lobbying effort on Capitol Hill against the Kennedy and Fraser amendments to cut off all military and economic aid to the Chilean junta. Among the lobbyists chosen were Manuel Santana, foreign affairs secretary of the Cuban exile youth movement ABDALA, and another Cuban, Dr. Nohemi Labrada and members of the Freedom Leadership Foundation. ABDALA has received money from DINA, and from the Unification Church of the Reverend Sun Myung Moon, which is, in turn, connected to the Korean CIA.

On November 13, 1975, the ACC sponsored a rally against the United Nations resolution condemning violations of human rights in Chile. The rally held at the St. Rocco Church in Union City, New Jersey, was titled "Cuba and Chile Against Communism."

160 *Death in Washington*

The two main speakers were Mario Arnello, the junta's ambassador to the Third Committee of the United Nations, a founder of the Chilean National party, and right-wing personality; and one of the Novo brothers, later charged in the murder of Orlando Letelier. The Novo connection is, as we shall see, a ticking bomb. Novo's cousin William Sampol was an aide to the Buckley brothers, William and James.

The mastermind behind all this deception was not Pinochet, or the DINA; it was William F. Buckley, Jr.

Liebman had prepared an annual propaganda budget of $260,000 and submitted this to the junta. The junta does, in fact, finance the ACC and the CCNA, but when Liebman filed with the Justice Department as a lobbyist, he listed as his foreign principal the CCNA, rather than the junta.

Although it was Marvin Liebman who was made the defendant before the Justice Department, it was actually William F. Buckley who

1. Picked Liebman and his Chilean correspondent, Ossa, as the appropriate vehicles for furthering the interests of the junta in the United States.

2. Came up with the idea of disguising the role of the junta.

3. Suggested to Liebman that he outline in a memo certain ideas that they had discussed.

4. Forwarded this memo to the Chilean government.

On May 5, 1977, Buckley had an hour-long discussion of Chile on his television program *Firing Line*. Joining him was Nena Ossa, who was visiting the United States on a speaking tour arranged by the CCNA. With tongue in cheek, Buckley stated that, as an advisor to Amnesty International (he has since resigned), he was concerned over the status of human rights in Chile. Nena Ossa replied that there might have been a *"paredon"* (firing squad-execution wall) in Cuba, but not in Chile. Nobody, she claimed, was executed in Chile, except for Commander Pepe.

Commander Pepe was a complete pre-coup hoax, invented by Raphael Otero Echeverria and David Phillips's other CIA media assets in Chile. No one gave greater prominence to this malicious hoax than Nena Ossa. In a March 23, 1971 article, "Chile's Che

Guevara? Anarchy in Chile," *National Review* claimed to have uncovered a Castroite guerrila training camp. This camp was supposedly run by a "Commander Pepe," who was described as the Che Guevara of Chile. CIA media assets at *El Mercurio* describe "Pepe" as an Uruguayan Tupamaro. Later "Pepe" was transformed into a Cuban guerrilla leader.

Fred Landis, who studied the affair, reports that after Allende and Orlando Millas, the minister of the interior, denounced the hoax, a reporter from *La Prensa* was sent from Santiago to produce a photo of any "Communist guerrillas" running loose in the area. What the reporter came back with was the picture of an agronomy student by the name of Jose Gregorio Liendo. He was not the commander of anything, and no one knew him as Pepe. He was neither Cuban nor Uruguayan; he was a Chilean. There was no guerrilla camp; just a bunch of workers at a sawmill in a remote area bordering the provinces between Cautín and Valdivia. After Liendo was seized and shot by the local police at the time of the coup, "Pepe" became an inside joke at Langley and among the *National Review* crowd.

In a March 1976 letter from Nena Ossa to Marvin Liebman, she discussed potential members of the ACC lobby, apparently suggested in a March 7 letter by Liebman. She raises questions about the desirability of enlisting Herbert A. Mueller, who happens to be her cousin, because of his known connection with the CIA and the junta. Another name proposed by Liebman was Enno Hobbing. Hobbing was the CIA's man at *Time-Life*. In 1954, working for David Phillips and Howard Hunt, he personally took a hand in the overthrow of the Arbenz government of Guatemala. In 1956 Hobbing concocted a diary which purported to record the last days of a teenage freedom fighter in Budapest. In 1970 he was in Chile assisting the CIA-IGS propaganda efforts at *El Mercurio*.

On May 31, 1979, the court ruled that the ACC was in fact an illegal, unregulated lobby for Chile's military dictatorship.

William F. Buckley is no mere diletante, for all his high Restoration style. When he served in Mexico City in 1952, under Howard Hunt, he worked closely with a "media asset" named Eudocio Ravines. As of 1970 Ravines was writing for a CIA-controlled magazine in Chile named *Servicios Periodisticos Aso-*

ciados (SEPA). This psywar organ was used to carry coded
messages to *Patria y Libertad* and other extremist groups. The
editor of *SEPA* was Rafael Otero Echeverria.

Since Otero Echeverria was a Phillips agent in Chile, his background is crucial to the charge that he and Phillips are, at least,
accessories after the fact, in the Letelier-Moffitt assassinations.

When the bomb exploded under Letelier, Otero Echeverria
had been an agent of DINA for two years. And five years before
that, Rafael Otero Echeverria was one of the most active agents of
the CIA in Chile. Otero Echeverria was a penetration agent in a
political party, the owner of record of a CIA-financed wire service,
the publisher of a CIA-funded magazine, a penetration agent in the
Cuban news agency Prensa Latina, a journalist who himself wrote
agency-directed propaganda, and the control for other CIA agents
in the media field.

In 1969 the Radical party, which in previous elections had
supported the Christian Democrats, decided to join the Popular
Unity slate of Salvador Allende. The CIA wrote up a project to
split the Radical party off from this coalition. Their agent in this
effort was Otero Echeverria. Otero Echeverria failed in the main
effort, but he was able to break off a minority faction which formed
a new Political party, the *Democracia Radical.*

Otero Echeverria was the owner of a domestic wire service
which distributed on a weekly basis CIA-prepared press packets to
hundreds of newspapers, radio stations, and magazines in Chile.
The name of this wire service, like that of the magazine, was
Servicios Periodisticos Asociados. *SEPA* reflected the personality
of its publisher; while wearing the mask of the clown, it performed
subversive functions for the CIA:

1. It carried coded messages to resistance groups.
2. It carried columns by such CIA agents as Eudocio Ravines
and Robert Moss.
3. It reprinted CIA press placements from other media outlets.
(Two pages of every issue were set aside for this purpose).
4. It devoted special sections to the CIA's principal target
groups—military officers and urban Catholic women.

5. It used almost half of the entire editorial space to print cartoons of a pornographic or sadistic nature denigrating Allende and his cabinet.

6. It distributed CIA fabrications to serve as a smokescreen to cover paramilitary sabotage, in particular that of Michael Townley.

Otero Echeverria began his services for the Company in 1969 by penetrating Cuba's Prensa Latina and stealing all its files. For the next several months he ran about Santiago dressed like a woman. For a short, dark, fat, hairy mesomorph, it was not a completely convincing disguise.

Otero Echeverria's specialty was diversionary propaganda surrounding political assassinations. Within hours of the Letelier killing, Otero Echeverria had planted three separate stories in the Washington media, all blaming leftists. Before that, in 1973, when Townley had blown up an electrical facility in Concepción, killing a guard, *SEPA* carried the headline "Police Falsify Crime in Concepción." Otero Echeverria wrote an article blaming "Marxist groups."

At one time or another Otero Echeverria has been investigated by the Chilean Chamber of Deputies, the Chilean Journalism Association, the civil police, and the U.S. Senate. In August 1970 the Chilean Chamber of Deputies issued a report on foreign intervention in Chile during the election campaign. An entire section was devoted to Otero Echeverria. The Chilean Journalism Association expelled Otero Echeverria for inventing not only fake polls but also fake polling organizations. The U.S. Senate investigation of CIA activities in Chile, prepared in draft form, reports on the splintering of the Radical party as well as on Otero Echeverria's wire service espionage.

In his native land the double agent had immunity as a Chilean congressman. In the United States, when the FBI tried to interrogate him on the Letelier death in 1976, he claimed diplomatic immunity, and fled back to Chile. But always he had the protection of the CIA.

In 1970, Chilean traitors linked with the CIA assassinated General René Schneider in the hopes of blocking Allende from the presidency. Immediately after that murder, Rafael Otero Echeverria spread the story that the Revolutionary Movement of the Left (MIR) had killed Schneider. Later, a synchronized media campaign blaming a nonexistent Left group called Brigada Obrera Campesina (BOC) was engineered by CIA agents at *El Mercurio*. Besides *El Mercurio*, most of the publicity given to the phantom BOC came from Otero over Radio Balmaceda.

Two days before the March 4, 1973, Chilean congressional elections, Otero declared in a nationwide radio broadcast that voting the Left out of office was an illusion; then he publicly urged a bloody massacre. Otero reprinted his radio address of March 2 in *SEPA* under the title, "In the Face of Communist Destruction, the Example of Indonesia." He wrote, "The Indonesians freed themselves violently from communism. . . . We will do the same as the Indonesians did, beginning with Djakarta."

On July 26, 1973, Allende's friend, bodyguard, and naval attaché, Commander Arturo Araya, was assassinated. The civil police arrested and obtained confessions from eight members of Patria y Libertad. Otero blamed the assassination on Allende and MIR.

The last two issues of *SEPA* before the September 11, 1973 coup are illuminating. Issue number 133 refers to a Plan Alba. (A year later, General Pinochet, in an interview with *Ercilla* magazine, revealed it was the actual plan for the coup.) The September 10, 1973, issue of *SEPA* (and the last) carried the story that the CIA thanked the director of *SEPA* for his co-operation over the past three years and for his having faithfully spread all the CIA's rumors. It promised to pay for these services in dollars.

Between September 1970 and September 1973 Otero Echeverria was arrested approximately 38 times for various crimes, and to gain immunity from criminal prosecution he ran for the Chilean Senate. He was elected after a campaign featuring posters with one graphic device—a mailed fist (later to become the symbol of DINA)—and the slogan "Vote Otero."

Townley and every Chilean or Cuban indicted in the Letelier-Moffitt murders met with Otero Echeverria at the Chilean Embassy in the weeks and days before the murder. The Cubans' cover for calling was the imprisonment of their militant, Rolando Otero. When the Letelier auto was blown up in front of the chancery, then Rafael Otero understood at last that the Cubans had been in dead earnest about "justice" for their comrade Rolando Otero.

Otero Echeverria's mistress was Lucia Piedrabuena, who, under the pseudonym Paz Alegría, produced anti-Letelier propaganda. She was the Washington correspondent for *SEPA*. In July 1973 Paz Alegría wrote from Washington: "But what has most enraged Chilean colony in Washington was *Orlando Letelier*! Making stupid declarations that make us look like a country of Nazis." After that report, and up until the coup, Allegria focused her attacks on Letelier. As of this writing she works for Buckley at *National Review*. Paz Alegría, like Nena Ossa, is a member of DINA (both "journalists" were close friends of Mariana Callejas de Townley). She was also the first wife of the current Chilean Ambassador, Manuel Trucco Gaete. And Trucco, evidence indicates, was close to DINA activities and, both in Washington in 1976 and in the Netherlands in 1975, had been privy to plans for the assassination of Orlando Letelier.

Buckley hires agents *posing* as writers. How much does he know in advance of these agents' activities? Buckley's writers Robert Moss, Nena Ossa, Reid Buckley, Eudocio Ravines, Paz Alegría, buzz around the corpse of Dr. Letelier like fat flies. These, and others on his *National Review* masthead, all have worked for Buckley or DINA.

For domestic consumption, Buckley poses as an urbane anachronism. Outside the United States, the Buckley family oil interests are merged with extreme right-wing Latin and Israeli business, crime, and intelligence circles.

Another line of Buckley-ACC-Phillips-AFIO fronts includes: the Heritage Foundation, the Freedom Leadership Foundation, the American Council for World Freedom, and, in England, the Institute for the Study of Conflict. These "freedom" fronts, together with an old CIA "think-tank," the Center for Strategic and International Studies (CSIS) at Georgetown University, represent a powerful array of propaganda assets and psychological warriors.

Curiously, men such as Moss, Liebman, et al. are considered—and call themselves—"advisors" to the junta. Advisors, not employees. Dig away at the cosmetic mask of the ACC and AFIO and you find, in place, much of the CIA hard core that Langley's Western Hemisphere Division used all along to make Chile and Latin America "scream."

The Georgetown Center for Strategic and International Studies (CSIS) is headed by David Phillips's long-time CIA associate, the superagent Ray S. Cline. Cline and Henry Kissinger have brought together a virtual galaxy of New Right stars: writers like Michael Ledeen, Edward Luttwak, Walter Laqueur, Robert Moss, Claire Sterling, who write for organs influenced by intelligence agencies —*National Review, Commentary, The New Republic, The Washington Quarterly, The South Africa Digest*. In addition there are pamphlets, books, films—all worth mentioning because this array of media is, in large measure, taking the place of what had been the CIA-media connection that was exposed during the Watergate-Chile scandals.

In the wake of recent congressional investigations, the CIA has been forced to back off from its regular practice of recruiting agents from within the working press. But its version of history is today as widely aired as ever, thanks in good measure to the Cold War intellectual elite at the Georgetown center. In a study of CIA reorganization sponsored by the CSIS Ray Cline wrote, "I think links between our best intelligence analysts and the academic research people with expertise on subjects under study in Washington should be built up far more than has been possible because of fears that exchanging information and views with CIA is somehow a corrupting process."

Daniel Schorr writes, in *Clearing the Air*, that when he was investigating illegal CIA activities, his first big break came when Cline started talking about Chile, blaming it all on Kissinger. Despite Cline's attempts to evade responsibility, nowhere was his ideal of academic-CIA collaboration better followed than in Chile, in which his own CSIS played a direct role.

In addition to the rumors and forged documents, the CIA's media campaign was reinforced by the planting in Chilean military journals and in *El Mercurio* of "studies" by James Theberge, director of Latin American studies at CSIS. For example, on February 27, 1973, *El Mercurio* headlined, "Chile Gives Haven to Extremist Network." The article from the UPI wire began, "The

Center for Strategic and International Studies of Georgetown University today pointed out..." followed by several standard propaganda themes favored by the CIA, quoted from a forthcoming book by Theberge. In particular, the article claimed to have uncovered a clandestine Korean Communist guerrilla training camp that had been moved from Havana to Santiago with the approval of President Allende. The article ended by asserting that the Chilean leftists trained at this phantom base "have intimidated the democratic opposition during the electoral campaign of March 1973."

Here was a preposterous situation: A Chilean newspaper was making sensational allegations concerning events supposedly taking place in Chile and attributing the story to an institute in Washington, D.C. But it served the CIA well to have such non-news circulated by a friendly "expert" and laundered through a reputable news organization like UPI. And the timing was ideal. Although the CSIS only got around to publishing Theberge's entire work, *Russia in the Caribbean*, toward the end of 1973, the paragraph on the March elections had been planted in Chile's leading newspaper before the elections even took place.

The Theberge incident was far from unique. That same year, for instance, the CSIS published another book of similar title and content, *The Stability of the Caribbean*, edited by the British journalist Robert Moss. Moss's book was published jointly with the London-based Institute for the Study of Conflict, with financial support from the Tinker Foundation. Contributors to the book included James Theberge; Brian Crozier, head of the institute; and Moss himself, who was indentified as the author of "the forthcoming book, *Chile's Marxist Experiment*."

In January 1977 the *Guardian* (London) and the *New York Times* identified *Chile's Marxist Experiment* as one of the propaganda books produced by the CIA. These articles also revealed that the entire second printing of Moss's book had been purchased by the Chilean military junta at a cost of £55,000, to be given away as part of a propaganda package.

Subagents of these propagandists-spymasters were involved, for instance, in the CIA's 1971 introduction into Cuba of African swine fever virus, which killed 500,000 pigs in an epidemic the

United Nations called "the most alarming event of 1971" in the field of health. It was swine flu epidemic for "the first and only time in the Western Hemisphere," according to the United Nations report. After the slaughter, Buckley, Cline, and the network pumped out stories about the lack of meat under communism in Cuba; they featured pictures of Cubans standing in line waiting for rations. This inventory of gangsters, "Freedom Fighters," and "strong men" (like Somoza, who was a *close* Buckley-ACC asset), of double agents and anti-democratic idealogues is immense. These are the Cold War leftovers that American intelligence and its fronts have collected since World War II.

William Buckley and his brother Reid and his sister Priscilla are known to be deeply involved in a Center for Documentation, located in Madrid, with ties to fascist fronts around the world and to the International League for Human Rights, a CIA-backed competitor to Amnesty International for the propaganda harvest of "human rights".

During Dan Mitrione's tour of duty in Brazil, William Buckley came down for a visit with friends. A group of Brazilians who had been tortured knew of Buckley's visit and his journalistic reputation, so as the columnist toured Rio he was presented with the information that the victims had heard English-speaking voices, in the next room, as they were being tortured. Buckley promised to investigate. Later, he informed his American readers that the prisoners had overheard a radio playing in the adjoining room, not American intelligence officers.

The most dramatic information about the Buckley network ever to become known emerged in July 1979. Independent researchers verified through the FBI and Department of Justice—that on September 14, 1976, one week before the Letelier assassination, Michael Townley and Guillermo Novo drove to the office of Senator James Buckley in New York City for a meeting. Buckley had helped finance trips to Chile for Novo and others close to the killing. One of these trips brought Novo and Townley together as part of the conspiracy to plan the Letelier murder. We are here approaching the question of accessories and of a cover-up at a very high level.

At the trial, William Sampol, the Novo's cousin and Buckley's aide, was called but did not testify. Prosecutors Earl Silbert and Eugene Propper said that they did not want to delay the proceedings to wait for Sampol.

The unanswered question of the Buckley-Townley relationship grows ever more pressing. Townley did meet with Frank Terpil, a former CIA agent and an indicted terrorist, in New York in September 1976. The Buckley brothers have been linked to Terpil by John Dutcher, who was arrested in 1979 by New York police for involvement in terrorist activities. (Mark the name Terpil as a heavy indication of who Townley was working with and for. Frank Terpil will soon be further identified.)

Historian Garry Wills reports that when Priscilla Buckley (currently managing editor of *National Review*), went to work for the European Desk at the CIA, she decided to look up her brother Bill's file. She was amazed to find that no such file existed. Even though William Buckley had operated at a very high level, he was an "illegal," a deniable entity operating outside of diplomatic cover, whose name could not appear in any CIA personnel files.

If the name of William Buckley—one of the CIA's most important "agents of influence" in the world—does not appear on the agency's rolls, is there any wonder that the CIA would be able to sanitize Michael Townley's official personnel files?

It is standard operating procedure at CIA that character assassination should precede and follow physical assassination. That is the practice Phillips and Buckley learned at the Agency and used automatically against Allende and Letelier. In the Justice Department case against Buckley's Chilean-American Council is included a document dated December 9, 1974, which reads "...to destroy the image of Salvador Allende."

It is almost uncanny how Buckley—like Phillips before him and Townley after him—began as a totally illegal, "black" operative. Before becoming officers and gentlemen, these men, including Colonel Townley, worked in the darkest, most violent strata of the agency.

The mechanism set up by Buckley in late 1974 to do PR for the junta (Nena Ossa, Mario Arnello, Enno Hobbing, Paz Alegria) had been used by the CIA to cover up assasinations in Chile from 1970 to 1973. The White House tapes show that the individuals Nixon felt could be best used to cover up Watergate were Buckley, Helms, and Vernon Walters.

Where does spying end and journalistic inquiry begin? With rare cycnicism Ray Cline has been quoted as stating, "The First Amendment is just an amendment." Even as Phillips was circulating the Letelier disinformation, Carl Bernstein, the prize-winning reporter of the Watergate saga, was collecting research in indicating that more than four hundred American journalists had worked with the CIA during the Cold War. Colby had told the Church Committee that the agency's penetration of the news media was "the highest, most sensitive cover program of all."

According to Bernstein, the CIA had a "relationship" with the *New York Times*, *Washington Post*, *Louisville Courier-Journal*, *Copley News Service*, *UPI*, ABC, NBC, Associated Press, Reuters, the Hearst chain of papers, *Time*, and *Newsweek* magazines, to name only the most prominent. Bernstein said the CIA's most valuable link, among newspapers, was the *New York Times*.

Newsweek, long an immensely important CIA asset, was chosen to play a key role in Phillips's propaganda chorus. By using the good offices of Richard Helms, Phillips was able to plant his all-important message of October 11: "...the CIA has concluded that the Chilean secret police were not involved in the death of Orlando Letelier." This bold assertion was obviously meant to pacify any DINA outrage or fear. Phillips is here actually using the name of the Central Intelligence Agency at the heart of the lie of the bogus briefcase. He was gambling, at enormous odds, the credibility of the agency in order to deny involvement *not* of the CIA, but of its offspring DINA.

For the Letelier briefcase seemed to be bottomless. Phillips was mining deep for the obligatory Castro connection. It can hardly be disputed that, but for a dramatic and unforeseen development—the Cubana Airline explosion—the Phillips-Buckley-Otero Echeverria misinformation propaganda would have confused and controlled the situation, drowned out the IPS demands and charges, and obfuscated the entire affair.

What this all means is that—stated in the most conservative way—David A. Phillips, William F. Buckley, and Rafael Otero Echeverria are guilty of being accessories after the fact in the murders of Orlando Letelier and Ronni Karpen Moffitt.

We have arrived at the sticking place: On September 21, 1976, and afterwards, Rafael Otero Echeverria of the government of Chile and a long-time contract agent of the CIA, with full fore-knowledge of the crime, began the cover-up phase of the homicides, in league with David Phillips, William F. Buckley, and others associated with both the Central Intelligence Agency, the Association of Former Intelligence Officers, and the American-Chilean Council. Through innuendo and distortion, the network, orchestrated by former intelligence officials, tried to turn the murders of a distinguished Chilean patriot and a young American woman into what Peter Weiss, Chairman of the board of the Institute for Policy Studies, called "another maudlin—and accept-able—incident in the Cold War game of spy and counterspy."

But in November 1976, because Bosch was talking—and not about jealous lovers—the Agency's line shifted to "the Cubans did it alone." But because the Cubans took revenge on Townley for the betrayal of Rolando Otero, Phillips's hand would be exposed.

Except for FBI questioning of Mrs. Letelier and her fellows at the Institute for Policy Studies there was no immediate investigation into the double assassination. None because George Bush, direc-tor of the Central Intelligence Agency, had informed the Depart-ment of Justice and the Federal Bureau of Investigation that there was no Chilean connection in this "unprofessional" act of passion. And the CIA would know, of course, because it had reliable sources in both the junta and DINA and to offer more than that by way of explanation would touch on most sensitive matters of "na-tional security."

According to Andrew Young, Jimmy Carter believed that a faithful investigation would determine that both President Kennedy and Dr. Martin Luther King had died at the hands of a conspiracy. Carter was dealing with a shattered rogue intelligence as he assumed office. The President-elect, according to Young, had complained, "If they can do this [kill Letelier] and get away with it under the nose of the CIA and the FBI, then no President can govern. These are armed federal employees, and either we control them or they control us." Thus, Carter is said to have ordered a serious far-reaching investigation. The problem was that Phillips, the AFIO, and the media pack were able to call in enough favors so that the new President was *not able* to appoint a man of his own choice, Theodore Sorenson, director of the CIA or, finally, impose actual sanctions on Chile.

Sorensen had known *Letelier*, and like others in the Kennedy circle, he saw in the Letelier case a golden opportunity to clean out the "antidemocratic" forces in both the Agency and the Bureau, according to an associate. But Carter was not able to appoint a Kennedy man to be Director of the Agency. *The Agency was more powerful than the President.*

At the Department of Justice, J. Stanley Pottinger and Michael Shaheen were working overtime to blunt the charge that the Federal Bureau of Investigation might have murdered Dr. King and certainly had not investigated the crime. Thus, until a handful of independent investigators forced them to act in the Letelier case, the Justice Department left the field free for the AFIO-led disinformation steamroller. In 1977, when the Justice Department was forced to move, Attorney General Griffin Bell was driven to protest CIA interference to the White House, according to a *Miami Herald* investigator.

At IPS, bitterness grew as 1976 ended. The *New York Times* had not assigned a reporter to the Letelier murder case and it disappeared from the news. Jack Anderson's aide, Les Whitten, aired the charge of "Letelier as a Castro agent." When Isabel Letelier and Michael Moffitt confronted Attorney General Bell, he complained that he "didn't want another Watergate."

When, in 1977, the IPS investigation came up with the name Edwin P. Wilson as a possible supplier of explosive devices to Townley and insisted that the FBI interview the former CIA clandestine maker of coups in the Caribbean and the Congo, the agency broke off relations with the stalled Justice Department probe.

The attempt to question Edwin Wilson ended abruptly. Wilson, one of the oldest of the boys in the AFIO network, currently runs a consulting firm whose business includes the sale and shipment of electronic explosive time devices to clients at home and abroad. Wilson had been deeply involved over the years with the Agency's fronts in Florida's twilight culture of official violence, with just such fronts as the National Intelligence Academy and with banks such as a Southwest First National.

In April 1980 former intelligence officer Wilson's other shoe dropped. A federal grand jury charged three Americans, including two former CIA agents, with running a terrorist training program for Libyan strongman Muammar el-Qaddafi.

The indictment, released Friday, April 25, said that in 1976-77 the three men supplied former U.S. Special Forces and former military explosive experts to train the terrorists to use explosives. The terrorists were not identified.

In addition, according to the Associated Press, the indictment alleged the three supplied explosives that could be used in such household items as ashtrays, lamps, clocks, vases, and boxes of tea.

The indictment charged also that the two former CIA agents paid $1 million to three persons to assassinate a former Libyan government official who led an abortive coup against el-Qaddafi in 1975. The assassination never took place because the "hit men" backed out, prosecutors said.

Indicted were: Francis E. Terpil, Edwin P. Wilson, and Jerome S. Brower. Terpil, 41, of McLean, Virginia, was described by the U.S. attorney's office as a major supplier of arms, sophisticated weaponry and assassination devices to terrorists world-wide. Terpil, who was held in lieu of $100,000 bond, has been indicted in New York for attempting to sell machine guns to undercover agents. Wilson, 52, with a post office box in Upperville, Virginia, worked with Terpil in allegedly arranging the Libyan terrorits training program. Brower, 60, was listed in the indictment as a former president of J. S. Brower & Associates, an explosives manufacturing and distributing company in Pomona, California.

Terpil and Wilson are former CIA agents. The U.S. attorney's office in New York said that Terpil was fired by the Agency. The circumstances under which Wilson left were not clear.

Terpil, Wilson, and Brower could face life terms if found guilty on various charges, including transportation of explosives in foreign commerce with the knowledge that the devices could be used to kill. According to the Los Angeles *Times*, the indictment said that on July 18, 1977, in Libya, some of the explosive devices went off, killing several Libyans and injuring three employees of Wilson. The indictment did not elaborate on the incident but the similarity to the Letelier assassination is striking.

Terpil and Wilson are charged with conspiracy to commit murder and solicitation to commit murder. The indictment said Terpil and Wilson tried to arrange for the murder of Umar Abdullah Muhayshi, a former Libyan government official whose coup against el-Qaddafi failed in 1975.

Townley met with Frank Terpil one week before the Letelier murder, on the same day that he met with Senator James Buckley and aides in New York City. The explosives sent into the United States on Chilean airlines were to replace explosives supplied by Edwin Wilson, according to a source close to the office of Assistant U.S. Attorney Lawrence Barcella, Jr. Barcella had worked with Eugene Propper on the Letelier-Moffitt case.

Each increment of American involvement in the crime leads to the threshold question: What did George Bush and the CIA know and when did they know it?

On October 4, 1976 DCI Bush met with Eugene Propper and J. Stanley Pottinger and promised cooperation in exchange for FBI caution in any National Security matters. Then on November 8, Bush flew to Miami on the pretext of a "walking tour of little Havana." Actually he met with the Miami FBI Special Agent in Charge Julius Matson and the chief of the anti-Castro terrorism squad. According to a source close to the meeting Bush warned the FBI against allowing the investigation to go any further than the lowest level Cubans. This was a secret meeting but publically Bush was selling headlines like "LEFT IS ALSO SUSPECT IN SLAYING OF LETELIER" to Jeremiah O'Leary and the *Washington Star*. And just the week before on November 1, the *Washington Post* had quoted both Bush and Kissinger to the effect that the junta was not involved. This is obstruction of justice and misprision of a felony at the least. Why would the Director of the American Central Intelligence Agency violate the law in the interests of the Chilean junta?

15 The Cover-up, Part II

Pablo was my compañero on many speaking tours we made, in the North, Central and South of Chile, and I will always remember with emotion how the people, who came to hear our political speeches, would wait in expectant silence, and then were moved as they listened to Pablo read his verses. It was good for me to see and confirm the sensibility of the people, to observe how the verses of the poet fell on the hearts and conscience of the multitudes of Chileans.

Salvador Allende

THE DEADLY SILENCE AND OBSTRUCTION OF JUSTICE that was the official Letelier investigation exploded on October 6, 1976. A Cubana airliner en route from Barbados to Cuba blew up, killing all 73 on board. Within a week, Orlando Bosch, the chief of CORU, started talking about the Letelier case.

At this point Ernest Volkman and John Cummings, two free-lance investigative journalists, walked into the Justice Department to say, "We told you so!" Volkman and Cummings, with the help of the Institute for Policy Studies, and some of the former members of the Fifth Estate and *CounterSpy* magazine, had put the case together before Bosch began to talk, but the FBI and prosecutor Eugene Propper would later take the credit all the same.

The Volkman-Cummings team had located a White Hand man who led them to another, who, the journalists told Propper, could "break the case!" There would have to be a deal that would allow the informant to "take a walk" on other major charges. Under continuous pressure from the journalists, Propper and the FBI agent in charge, Carter Cornick, agreed to go to a rendezvous in Miami. There the officials, having interviewed the first informant, proceeded to "blow the lead" as the two journalists gazed on in disbelief. Waiting in a motel for a telephone call that never came was the second informant, who was prepared to deal.

In the meantime the Venezuelan secret police had learned from Orlando Bosch the names that the Justice Department had refused to check out! Yet Propper and Cornick still refused to seize the opportunity to go to Venezuela and wrap up the case. While Propper was shunning any contact with Bosch, another free-lance journalist, Blake Fleetwood of *New Times*, was *talking to him* and Bosch was confirming the Volkman-Cummings breakthrough that had *also* been rejected by Propper and the FBI.

The free-lancers, led by Volkman, had confronted Propper and the FBI, but it took the Washington Metropolitan Police to force justice to move. When a detective from the police department flew to Venezuela to question Bosch, Cornick *followed* him! Then Propper tried to get the detective *fired*, and demanded that the local police get out of the case.

After the Pinochet coup in 1973, a new day had dawned for Bosch's White Hand. Pinochet's personal representative, Eduardo Sepulveda, had flown to Miami to meet with Bosch and others. Later Pedro Ernesto Díaz was there for DINA to set up a front group (Buckley's and Phillips' American-Chilean Council) to represent the junta's interest, undercover, in the United States. Under the new arrangement with the *gorilas*, Bosch and other CORU luminaries were able to travel throughout the hemisphere on Chilean Airlines, protected by DINA bodyguards, carrying Chilean money and passports bearing false names.

In 1977 supporters of the despised Philip Agee published these facts and a detailed breakdown of CORU in *CounterSpy* and indicated strongly that both the FBI and CIA had connections to the White Hand components and so must have known in advance about the Letelier-Moffitt killings.

Early that same year Volkman and Cummings contracted to tell their story in a *Penthouse* magazine article. Despite a series of stunning investigative articles by some of America's most notable investigative journalists (Tad Szulc, Harrison Salisbury, George O'Toole), *Penthouse* was considered merely a sex magazine by Propper and the FBI. For *Penthouse* to announce that it had broken the Letelier case *and* cover-up was intolerable to the

Justice department. But that is what the various free-lancers working with IPS had done. Without guns, subpoena power, expense accounts, or any kind of official power, these academics, writers, and political analysts had followed the spoor where the Justice Department had not dared to go.

By the spring of 1977, IPS and the independent investigators had learned:

A formal agreement between DINA and CORU was made in November 1975. Michael Townley was selected as liaison between the groups.

In July 1976 Cuban terrorists and Michael Townley met in Bonao in the Dominican Republic at the executive lodge of the Falcondo Mining Company to plan joint ventures: both the Cubana bombing and the Letelier killing. *Sacha Volman, the veteran CIA agent, and Cuban exile Frank Castro, another CIA man working with Gulf and Western, hosted the meeting. Volman had been a key CIA-labor operative in the Dominican Republic under David Phillips.*

In 1977, Ambassador George Landau entered the case as a principal and revealed the circumstances of the Paraguayan passports. The false names and photographs of the two men had been lost by the CIA. Now, after Landau remembered them, they reappeared. "Juan Williams Rose" would later be identified by Chileans as Michael Vernon Townley, and the Department of Justice had no choice but to call the Cuban exiles identified in *Penthouse* before a grand jury. But it was too late to call Aldo Vera.

Researchers working on this book have learned that, by October 1976, only days after Letelier was murdered, the FBI was pressing Aldo Vera for information and that Vera was co-operating. Vera had been expelled from Acción Cubana in June 1976—according to FBI documents newly discovered—because of his informant activity. On October 25, 1976, he was murdered in San Juan. He and Townley had started out together in the SAO and P y L. Then Vera had helped to set up Cruz in France. Now he was dead, and Townley and his wife feared for their lives.

A revealing document located by the authors puts the FBI investigation in perspective as of November 1976.

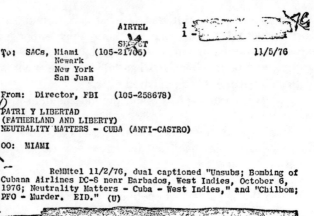

To: SACs, Miami   (105-21705)   11/5/76
Newark
New York
San Juan

From: Director, FBI   (105-258678)

PATRI Y LIBERTAD
(FATHERLAND AND LIBERTY)
NEUTRALITY MATTERS - CUBA (ANTI-CASTRO)

OO: MIAMI

        ReMMtel 11/2/76, dual captioned "Unsubs; Bombing of
Cubana Airlines DC-8 near Barbados, West Indies, October 6,
1976; Neutrality Matters - Cuba - West Indies," and "Chilbom;
PFO - Murder. EID." (U)

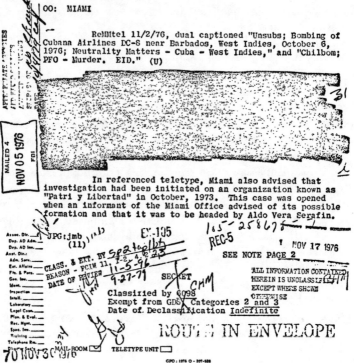

        In referenced teletype, Miami also advised that
investigation had been initiated on an organization known as
"Patri y Libertad" in October, 1973. This case was opened
when an informant of the Miami Office advised of its possible
formation and that it was to be headed by Aldo Vera Serafin.

SEE NOTE PAGE 2

Classified by 6098
Exempt from GDS Categories 2 and 3
Date of Declassification Indefinite

ALL INFORMATION CONTAINED
HEREIN IS UNCLASSIFIED
EXCEPT WHERE SHOWN
OTHERWISE

ROUTE IN ENVELOPE

Jose Suárez, given immunity and sent before the grand jury in 1977, refused to answer questions and went to jail for almost a year. When the life of the grand jury expired in 1978, Suárez was released, and disappeared. How could a main suspect in the murders just vanish? How could he not be under constant FBI surveillance, as he had been *before* incarceration?

As of 1977, then, the CIA line was "Get the Cubans," and Propper and his superior, Earl Silbert, had made it clear that the investigation was to focus exclusively on Cubans and the Chilean DINA. An embittered former FBI special agent spoke of the frustration anonymously. The Department of Justice, he said,

> Kept using "national security" every time one of the Cubans was willing to make a deal. I call these guys "Castro convertible".... They were ready to deal, Hell, two of them had been working for us, anyway—Suárez and Guillermo Novo, or at least we had worked together back in the '60s, so we owed them a fair shake, but they would have cooperated, but the Department was scared to death of the CIA....

The implications here are clear. A statement by Guillermo Novo's brother, Ignacio, only deepens the problem of FBI complicity:

> In 1969 the FBI invited my brother to plant a bomb in a Cuban ship which was docked in the port of New York. He wouldn't do it, so they set him up for an arrest anyway and fixed it so that he got one to five on probation. In other words he never served. The FBI kept him out, so he had to do what they told him.
>
> He was just about to finish his probation, working for them, when the Orlando Letelier killing took place and Orlando Bosch accused us of doing the killing. Then in May [1977] we got a tip from the FBI. They told us that Guillermo would lose his probation because he had traveled outside of the country—which they knew because they had paid him to travel to meetings and like that. That he would go to jail and die in a fight with a black prisoner....

Guillermo Novo, his brother goes on, was warned by the FBI to escape or take the full heat. He did run away, but was later arrested. Other special agents, who refuse to allow their names to be used, state that the FBI stuck so tightly to the Novo brothers and Suárez, normally, that all were on a "first name basis" in their *daily* meetings—which would begin when the Cubans walked into the street in the morning.

In 1979 independent investigators found and reprinted for the public two revealing letters:

REPUBLIC OF CHILE
PRESIDENCY OF THE REPUBLIC
DINA

CONFIDENTIAL

To Senor General of Division
Joao Baptista De Oliveira Figueiredo
Chief of the National Information Service
Brasilia, DE

SANTIAGO, August 28, 1975

Distinguished General:

I have received your shipment of 21 August, 1975 and along with thanking you for your timely and useful information, it is my pleasure to express to you my satisfaction with your collaboration, which we ought to firm up even further.

To this end, I comply by communicating the following to you:

1) I share your preoccupation over the possible triumph of the Democratic Party in the upcoming presidential elections in the United States. We are also aware of the repeated support the Democrats have lent to Kubichek and Letelier, which might, in the future, seriously influence the stability of the Southern Cone of our hemisphere.

2) Your proposed plan for coordinating our actions agains certain ecclesiastical authorities and well-known social democratic and christian democratic politicians in Latin America and Europe has our full support.

3) Your information about Guyana and Jamaica is of unquestionable importance to this Department.

It may interest you to know that the Chilean Government has decided to free a group of prisoners who will be expelled to European countries. We will pass along to you, as it becomes available to us, information relative to the political activities of these persons and their contacts with Brazilian emigrees.

Respectfully yours,
Manuel Contreras Sepulveda
Colonel
Director of National Intelligence

REPUBLIC OF CHILE
PRESIDENCY OF THE REPUBLIC
DINA

Copy No. 1 Page No. 1
DINA Ref. No. 1495/107
RE: Clarification regarding
requested increase in budget.

SANTIAGO, 16 Sep. 1975
FROM THE DIRECTOR OF NATIONAL INTELLIGENCE
TO HIS EXCELLENCY THE PRESIDENT OF THE REPUBLIC

As agreed with Your Excellency, I specify herein the reasons why I consider it essential to request an additional allocation of $600,000 for the budget of this Directorate for the current year.

1. An increase in DINA staff attached to the diplomatic missions of Chile. Ten persons in all: 2 in Peru, 2 in Brazil, 2 in Argentina, 1 in Venezuela, 1 in Costa Rica, 1 in Belgium, and 1 in Italy.

2. Additional expenses for the neutralization of the principal opponents of the Governing Junta outside Chile, especially in Mexico, Argentina, Costa Rica, U.S.A., France and Italy.

3. Expenses connected with operations in Peru: assistance to our supporters in the Peruvian Navy and press, particularly contributions to "Equis X" and "Opinion Libre" ("Free Opinion").

4. Allowances for staff of this Directorate who attend courses in the training of anti-guerrilla units in the Training Centre at Manaus in Brazil.

With my respects to Your Excellency.

Manuel Contreras Sepulveda
Colonel
Director of National Intelligence

Parenthetically, Contreras's lawyer, after Townley's extradition, became Sergio Miranda, a man who had volunteered to go to Nuremberg to defend the Nazis. Miranda let it be known in Santiago that if Contreras was indicted, then official DINA files—hidden in Germany—would be released.

Mariana Callejas is herself an assassin. In 1975 Townley and Callejas were sent to murder anti junta leaders meeting in Mexico City. Then General Contreras generously supported the killers with $25,000 and expenses. With help from the White Hand, in Florida, the Townleys gathered false identification ("Andrew" and "Anna Brooks") and explosives.

Contreras did not stint when a killing was *his* idea. But for the Letelier murder Townley actually had to borrow money during his few days in Washington and Miami; he had to keep a record, even, of bridge tolls between New Jersey and Washington. The money, as always, provides clues. According to Callejas, the Cubans pled for $25,000 from Contreras so that they could hide from the Letelier investigation. Contreras, acting like a man with nothing to fear, told the exiles, according to a witness, "Townley is Langley's 'shrimp man,' let them pay you poor *panzistas*." A shrimp man, in this context, is a police expert or technician, a *panzista* is a hungry belly (after Sancho Panza).

Callejas adds:

As regards Paz and Suárez, if Don Manuel Contreras has them hiding in Chile, well then I hope that they are happy in such a beautiful country, and what about if they want to kill me if we meet? Well, surely Paz knows that we did whatever was possible. As far as Suárez I will never be convinced that he did not avenge Otero making the bomb explode in the middle of Sheridan Circle against everything that had been agreed to and just a few meters away from the Chilean Embassy, and with other people in the car. I am sure that they implicated Michael so that they could also implicate DINA. Could there be anybody more representative of DINA?

Light-haired, blue-eyed Michael Townley is hardly the symbol of the Chilean secret police. Townley, known in Santiago and Miami as the CIA's "shrimp man," is the quintessential symbol of *American* covert operations.

Callejas did let slip her DINA cover in the confusion after her husband's identification in Chile, just before his irregular extradition.

He had the opportunity to escape. It was offered to him by Major Vianel Valdivieso who wanted Townley to escape to the south. It was me, not Michael, that went to the rendezvous with the major and the major got very mad at me. He told me that he was upset because...Townley could disappear...and after that he blamed the CIA and he said that the CIA could make one of their own men disappear. When Valdivieso realized that Townley would not go to their side, he then exhorted me to make sure that he went into hiding for himself.

The confident Townley, she admits, "wound up hiding in our own house." Then came the Silbert-Glanzer deal and the shock of extradition.

Callejas had also been involved in the attempted assassination of a moderate and prominent Christian Democrat, Bernardo Leighton, in exile in Rome. Callejas had been in touch with Italian Fascists who were to provide support for Michael. In the spray of the automatic weapon, Leighton and his wife were wounded so seriously that Mrs. Leighton still remains paralyzed.

Fascists in Miami and Rome involved in these crimes with the Townleys had discernible links to CIA. The defense was unable to bring these violent acts up during the trial. Legal observers were astonished when Judge Parker allowed Townley to plead the Fifth Amendment when asked about other crimes because of the Silbert-Glanzer plea-bargain understanding.

I can't lie, I don't know how...I had to sell one of the cars. No one is paying me...Michael was extradited without due process of law. I do not like it when the U.S. blackmails Chile and other countries. Pinochet had no choice...that's all I can say. Obviously, the government of Chile cannot help us because that would be an admission of guilt.

According to witnesses, Callejas' well-known charm was not lost on younger FBI special agents involved in the case. Later, Callejas would say, "I liked them. We saw eye to eye. There was mutual respect." There were, reportedly, also many fiery moments during the plea-bargaining sessions in Washington, with Callejas at one point threatening to expose her identity as a CIA contract agent over the years. This was chilling to "opposing" attorneys Silbert and Glanzer because of something Townley had said earlier. In Santiago, infuriated at being turned over to the FBI in violation of Chilean law, Townley had blurted out: There are today executives and directors of the Press who collaborated with me and who knew me and my wife and who we were during that time of our opposition to the deposed government of Unidad Popular.

Sources close to the junta bear out these hints. Ambassador Landau had reason to know that Townley was CIA-connected, that that was why the agency had "lost" the photographs and false passports in the summer of 1976 when Landau suspected that criminal activity involving Townley might compromise United States interests.

On August 4, 1976, the deputy director of the Central Intelligence Agency, Lt. Gen. Vernon A. Walters, had, himself, informed Landau that the agency was unaware of the two Chileans and did not recognize their photographs. *Despite* this reassurance Ambassador Landau had refused to issue travel visas to the United States for Townley and Fernández.

Vernon Walters was the first deputy director in CIA history who was a complete outsider to both the CIA and the intelligence community at large. That is the popular version. In 1964 Frank Carlucci and Vernon Walters just happened to be stationed in Brazil at the time of the coup there. Ten years later, they were both in Portugal at a time when the CIA was working on a contingency plan to set up an independent state in the Azores if the agency should completely lose control of Portugal. Carlucci was the Nixon-appointed ambassador; Walters was there unofficially. During the Quartered Man—Plan Z period leading up to the Chilean coup, Walters was acting director of CIA. In his memoirs, Colby explains that this interregnum came about because James Schlesinger was being made Secretary of Defense and a technicality delayed Colby's swearing in. Who replaced Vernon Walters as deputy director? Frank Carlucci!

The year before the assassination of Letelier, General Contreras, as an honored guest, had called on General Walters at
Langley, Virginia. Walters was close to the Phillips, Hunt, Broe
hard-liners in the Clandestine Services: he had worked with Hunt
in Paris under cover of the Marshall Plan; worked constantly with
both Hunt and Phillips in preparation for the Bay of Pigs invasion;
was closely in touch with the godfather of Hunt's children, William
Buckley; had been Nixon's liaison to Hunt and the CIA as the
plotting against Cuba progressed from 1959 on. Walter's contribution to the Watergate investigation and cover-up was to attempt to
turn the FBI away from a full inquiry by telling the Bureau that the
investigation threatened CIA assets and sources. H. R. Haldeman
has said that he and Nixon told Walters that CIA conspiracies
would surface if the FBI persisted in its pursuit of the money.
Nixon's excuse: "Look, the problem is that this will open the
whole, the whole Bay of Pigs thing. . . . Well, we protected Helms
from one hell of a lot of things . . . it tracks back to the Bay of Pigs,
and it tracks back to some other. . . . This fellow Hunt knows, ah, he
knows. . . ."

The record is fatal to George Bush and the CIA:

1. In July of 1976 General Walters, Bush, and Secretary of State
Kissinger had advance knowledge that a DINA team was in motion,
headed toward Washington.

2. The names Jara, Rose, and Silva (all used at one time or another by
Townley and aides) were removed from Immigration and Naturalization
files. Townley's photograph was removed as well as all paper work about
the assassination teams' several entry attempts into the U.S., and all
computer entries of the event were erased.

In other words the CIA not only had advance knowledge and did
nothing, but must have destroyed the evidence after the fact. The
Agency argues that the State Department must be responsible.
The responsible officer at State? Harry Shlaudeman—David Phillips' covert action aide in Santo Domingo and later in Santiago.
Not one of these men—Kissinger, Walters, Phillips, Shlaudeman,
and especially Bush—has ever delivered an accounting to explain
these damaging facts.

The money chain—Walters was told by the Nixon men that he must convince the CIA and the FBI to join Henry Petersen, Earl Silbert, and Seymour Glanzer in treating the money chain as an untouchable taboo. In a conversation with Helms, General Walters confirms that they agreed about "the agreement between the FBI and the CIA that if they run into or appear to expose one another's assets they will notify one another." This was the man at CIA, Nixon's man, that General Contreras conferred with at Langley in 1975.

In 1976 Michael Townley was given Walters's name and phone number to call while the assassin was in Washington. The information was povided by General Conrado Pappalardo, the head of Paraguayan intelligence.

What Pinochet finally signed off on was a deal whereby his innocence would be featured in the United States theory of the case. For his contribution, General Pinochet promised that he would conduct a serious investigation in Chile and would not implicate the CIA through Townley. This is part of what Callejas meant when she later described her husband as a "small cog in a gigantic wheel", and in jail, as a "talking machine."

So Pinochet was willing to give Washington its "own man" back, change the DINA's name to National Information Center (Centro Nacional de Información, CNI), put Contreras and Espinoza under luxurious house arrest, and ride the storm out, hoping that George Landau and the American Embassy would accept the generous spirit of the arrangement.

The secret pact that formalized the agreement was signed on April 7, 1978, one day before Townley was turned over to Robert Scherrer and the FBI by the junta. The document had been signed by Enrique Montero Marx, the Chilean Under Secretary of the Interior, and Earl Silbert, the United States Attorney for the District of Columbia and Eugene Propper's superior during the entire troubled course of the Letelier-Moffitt investigation.

When, during the trial, attorneys for the Cuban defendants confronted Propper with the agreement's existence, the prosecutor temporized: "Any information we had to be disclosed we said would be used only in the United States court or given to the government of Chile. That is, we would not spread it to the press, and Chile, in turn, said if it came up with any information in the Letelier case it would give it to the United States."

"Only" in the United States or "given" to the junta, and the reverse if the junta "came up" with "anything." Sources in Santiago point to these euphemisms as bearing out their information about the secrecy pact drawn up to protect both General Pinochet and the CIA from any involvement in the crime. "Everybody wins" is how one disgusted assistant U.S. attorney sums it up.

On April 7, 1978, Earl J. Silbert, for the United States Department of Justice, signed a secret agreement with the Pinochet junta agreeing to keep from the public information relating to the other assassinations involving either Townley or the junta. That is why, the record shows, and Callejas supports, Contreras refused to give any money to the Cubans after the murder. Privately, Contreras blamed his Chief of Operations Pedro Espinoza for the disaster.

Before the trial Callejas functioned as a sort of "baby sitter" for her husband (to use an intelligence term and her own apt description). The situation was delicate and required the now almot lethargic Townley to bring off a version of that classic tale *The Spy Who Came In from the Cold* to a world-wide audience. In short, Townley was required to take responsibility for the crime as a Chilean, a "self-taught" terrorist who *had never had any contact with the government of the United States through the Central Intelligence Agency*; a self-taught Chilean who had acted on orders from DINA, orders which he *"knew" General Pinochet did not know about.*

The testimony came through as a rather crude caricature reminiscent of that farce billed as the first Watergate tiral, and popularly loved as the "third-rate burglary." Two of the authors then, as in the Letelier case now, were Seymour Glanzer and Earl J. Silbert.

Silbert and Glanzer had worked together for the Department of Justice in the first trial of the Cubans and former intelligence officers arrested for the Watergate break-in. Now, Townley's

American laywer was Seymour Glanzer. Townley's lawyers make an interesting study.

At first, before the Pinochet-Silbert agreement that paved the way for Townley's unconstitutional extradition from Chile, Townley retained two prestigious Santiago attorneys. Dr. Manuel Acuña was representing Townley before the Supreme Court of Chile when the deal abruptly ended his involvement. In one of the documents presented to the court, Acuña had pointed out: "The missions carried out by Michael Townley are documented in five files which have been placed in five different parts of the world and which will only be opened in the case of having to prove in the memory of his children that he is not a criminal."

A senior lawyer in the same office, Dr. Fernando Rivera, asserted that "The jobs that Townley had were higher, or superior, to the technical jobs that they're talking about."

The statements were made while legal and court circles in Santiago were buzzing about Townley's CIA connections, and they should be understood in that light, according to these court sources. And when Townley arrived in Washington and began to prepare to testify for the government against the Cubans and *some* junta officials, his new attorney became Seymour Glanzer, who had left the Department of Justice after Watergate and gone into private practice. How? Who recommended Glanzer to Townley? Was it U.S. Attorney Propper at Silbert's suggestion? Was it not, in fact, part of the Silbert-Pinochet deal?

It was Glanzer's responsibility to negotiate or plea bargain for his client Townley with the prosecutor, Propper's boss, Earl J. Silbert. Their conversations took place at a series of secret military locations in the Washington area.

Both Silbert and Glanzer had served under Henry Petersen at the Justice Department through 1974. Under Petersen, Silbert and Glanzer focused on the Watergate burglary with a mindless zeal. Together with Congressman Gerald Ford, they were successful in killing the Patman House inquiry into the *money*, the key that the Special Prosecutor's office later found would open wide the door to the White House horrors. They refused to touch on other matters involving such people as Herbert Kalmbach, Dwight Chapin, Donald Segretti. These U.S. attorneys, Silbert and Glanzer, informed the White House at all times, through Peterson, of the progress of the grand jury investigating the Watergate affair. They permitted Nixon aides to testify in secret. When John Dean finally started to talk, in April 1973, they broke their word to him and informed the White House of his defection, thus causing him to fear for his life.

It was Silbert and Glanzer who shielded conspirators such as Egil Krogh and Charles Colson from the grand jury. When Segretti appeared before the grand jury, Silbert and Glanzer carefully avoided all connections betwen the Segretti spy ring and Nixon aides Chapin and Kalmbach. They considered James McCord, they said, "a phony"; this was before McCord broke open the "third-rate burglary" case that Silbert and Glanzer had so painfully constructed out of the Cubans and Gordon Liddy.

When Judge Sirica demanded to know from the Cubans whether any of them had ever worked for the Central Intelligence Agency (they *all* had), they replied, "Not that we know of." At that, even Liddy laughed out loud, but that had been the Silbert-Glanzer position.

Now Silbert and Glanzer reunited for the Letelier drama. Cuban cannon fodder, and in place of Liddy, Michael Townley. From the day of the murder until the free-lance investigation broke the case, Silbert had run the official inquiry along the rails of the Watergate cover-up.

By 1979, independent researchers had learned that the secret police of five countries—South Korea, Iran, the Philippines, Taiwan, and Chile—had conducted systematic campaigns on United States soil to silence dissidents speaking out against the repressive regimes of those countries. According to official leaks from a classified report, spies from Iran and Chile had been sent to the United States to murder critics. And according to the Senate sources, "The State Department actively discouraged FBI investigations of probable crimes in the United States by friendly intelligence services."

The FBI expressed dismay that this information had been leaked in August 1979. Especially painful to the Bureau was this quote from the classified Senate report:

The CIA passed on to SAVAK, the Iranian intelligence agency, information it had received from the FBI on a prominent critic of the Shah who lived in the United States. The critic, *Nasser Afshar*, was later targeted for assassination. The CIA, according to the report, also provided information to the intelligence services of Chile and the Philippines on U.S. residents about whom the governments of Augusto Pinochet and Ferdinand E. Marcos wanted information.

And the report charged that Henry Kissinger made "false and misleading public statements" concerning the extent of such foreign intelligence activities in the United States.

According to William Bader of the Senate Foreign Relations Committee, and Senator Church's chief aide, "it [the report] was not intended to be released..." Bader is a former officer of the Central Intelligence Agency.

Bader neglected to mention the operators in the United States, of Libya's Muammar el-Qaddafi. That inclusion would have raised the name of indicted former intelligence officer Edwin P. Wilson and behind him the AFIO.

What happened to Orlando Letelier and Ronni Moffitt was American secret policy.

Dr. Letelier's mail had been tampered with before the murders. Futher, the Leteliers had reported a series of death threats to the FBI during 1976. What did the FBI files reveal about who might have wanted to kill Orlando Letelier? The defense saw no such Bureau files. The defense was not allowed to question Richard Helms (he refused to appear, the judge refused to force him).

So Townley testified,as arranged, that *both* the CIA and Pinochet were completely clean, and then went off to serve his three years, while the Cubans took the maximum. By contrast, the thrust of this and other investigations should now be clear: Members of William Buckley's ACC and David Phillips's AFIO—acting for the Central Intelligence Agency—should immediately be called before a federal grand jury and compelled to answer to their involvement in the Letelier-Moffit assassination both before and after the fact.

The CIA double agent Otero Echeverria, is a part of the continuing conspiracy from August through the day of the murder. He, Phillips, and Buckley ran a major covert media operation *commencing the day of the murder*. Were Buckley, Phillips and the people they represent in the CIA, the ACC, and AFIO—a part of the conspiracy *before* the murders? Only the Justice Department, with its subpoena and perjury power, can discover the answer to that question by following the bloody footprints between Santiago and Langley.

According to an official of the National Council of Churches, the FBI was on notice that the plot was unfolding. They were informed of the arrival, days before the murder, of secret agents from Chile. the Church official stated: "The high DINA officer was none other than Air Force Colonel (retired) Sergio Crespo, who was the junta's minister of agriculture until he joined the secret police after the *gorila* dictatorship's first cabinet change."

Besides this, former CIA officers state that in 1976 the Agency had some sixty-five agents operating in Chile, not counting seven, besides Townley, who worked directly with DINA.

The IPS in a comprehensive interim report on the case, *They Educated the Crows*, sums up well the CIA-DINA connection by quoting from the Church Committee report, and it then points to a pattern of domestic violence generated by CIA actions abroad:

There seems no reason to believe that the CIA would not have considered killing Letelier a simple matter of helping the government of Chile in "controlling subversion from abroad."

The Letelier-Moffitt murder investigation cries out for the appointment of a special prosecutor.

The Justice Department's team—Silbert, Propper, Cornick, Scherrer—has also become a candidate for obstruction of justice charges. How else can one explain: (1) the refusal to question Orlando Bosch after the Cubana airliner crash; (2) the refusal of the Justice Department to order the FAA to act against Chile Airlines after Townley implicated them in the murder; (3) the constant surveillance of the Novo brothers by the FBI *before* the murder; (4) the Silbert-Glanzer arrangement to sanitize the CIA connection; (5) the handling of the Letelier briefcase and its use as propaganda; (6) the prosecution's part in Townley's covering up his past activities; (7) finally, the foreknowledge of the crime, based on informers in Miami and Santiago and Bonao. As in the Watergate investigation, the FBI and the Department of Justice are radically compromised. And just as then, a special prosecutor is mandatory, according to Justice sources.

The attorneys for the convicted defendants Guillermo Novo and Alvin Ross have now, in 1980, summed up their case for a new trial. This appeal throws into relief the key contradiction in the Silbert-Propper-Glanzer official theory of the case. First and foremost, of course, is the question of the role of the Central Intelligence Angecy.

As a Republican presidential candidate George Bush touted his service as director of the CIA in 1976; he may soon find the experience to have been a liability. According to an investigative book on the assassination of Orlando Letelier, Bush, as head of the CIA, knew more about the assassination than he told federal investigators probing the case.

In *Assassination on Embassy Row* authors John Dinges and Saul Landau say Bush and other CIA officials knew that the Chilean police had sent a team to Washington on a covert mission. But Bush withheld that information from investigators after the assassination while "CIA sources" were quoted in major media as having concluded that the Chilean government was "not involved" in the murder. (The present study puts Bush in Miami involved in the actual cover-up).

The defense had been asking, since their original discover motions, for the CIA files on Townley. Those files were voluminous; it took the trial judge several hours to examine them. However, the judge refused to order that this material be disclosed to the defense because "it would take too long"(4933-37).*

In particular, defense counsel was precluded from asking any question implying that the CIA had a motive for wanting Letelier killed and the fact that the CIA had participated in the overthrow and assassination of Letelier's previous political ally and employer, Salvador Allende. They were also restricted in inquiring into those CIA hiring practices and operations which would have indicated that Townley was likely to have been an agent (4721-22). Counsel were able to establish, however, that Townley had applied to the CIA, and had been granted operational status (4985), and that he had been seen in the vicinity of CIA offices and personnel in Santiago (4657-4690, 4715).

The Cuban defendants—as their theory of defense—argued that Townley himself admitted having had contact with the CIA. Moreover, on September 21, 1976, the day of Orlando Letelier's assassination, Townley attempted to develop an alias for himself by signing in, in Florida, at Audio Intelligence Development (AID), a part of a CIA front organization (the National Intelligence Academy). The defense developed independent information indicating that this company and its president, John Holcomb, were associated with the Central Intelligence Agency (transcript of December 13, 1978 at 76). Consequently, counsel requested discovey of any information in the government's possession concerning any relationship between the CIA and AID or its president (Id. at 74-76). The trial court denied this application, saying simply, "You have sufficient information. You proceed yourself." (Id. at 95).

Defense counsel advised the jury in their opening statements that they would show that the CIA and not the Chilean government masterminded the Letelier assassination. The trial judge, however, decided not to allow the counsel to raise this legitimate defense: "I'm not going to let you put the CIA on trial in this case . . ." (5019). To carry out this threat, the judge first issued a blanket ruling forbidding the defense to cross-examine any of the government's witnesses about CIA involvement in the assassination (1262, 1474; see also 1233).

*All citations here are to the trial transcript.

On the question of whether Townley was a CIA agent, the CIA's official position was that they had interviewed Townley and had in fact given him "operational status" but then had not actually used him because they "lost contact" with him.

Defense counsel sought to attack this claim on three levels: (1) by making inquiry into the hiring practices of the CIA so as to establish that the CIA, in addition to hiring full-time agents, also hired people on a "contract" basis, and that such hirings would not necessarily be reflected in the central office files; (2) that the CIA operations in Chile were such that it would have been impossible to "lose contact" with someone like Townley, who was living openly in the capital city; and (3) that Townley had repeatedly been seen in the vicinity of the CIA's offices in Chile. Both the government and the court substantially and improperly curtailed defense counsel's examination of these legitimate issues (4722, CIA witnesses won't go into where offices are; 4741, CIA witnesses won't confirm whether they have an office in the vicinity where Townley was repeatedly seen in the American Embassy in Chile; 4740, 4979, limitations on questions going to the credibility of CIA officials' claim that they "lost contact" with Townley).

The court likewise prevented defense counsel from presenting any evidence to show the CIA's motive for ordering Letelier's assassination. The CIA had invested immense amounts of time and money into bringing about the overthrow of the Chilean socialist regime and the assassination of its leader, Salvador Allende. Letelier was one of the principal leaders of an international movement working to return Chile to socialism, by revolution if necessary.

Townley's CIA files turned out to be voluminous. After looking at the files on February 8, 1979, the trial judge took form 8:00 to 10:20 A.M. just to review them again on the morning of the ninth (4930-31). The judge did not even understand some of the material in the folder, and had to ask CIA officers to explain it to him. After reading it, the judge apparently realized that defense counsel might have some legitimate interest in the material and so asked the CIA's representative whether any part of the material might be made available to counsel. When the representative said that portions might be declassified, but that it might take time, the

Court responded: "No, I am not going to wait around for that. I am not going to wait around for that" (4937). The court then denied defendant's request for disclosure of the material.

Most crucial to the defense was Townley's admission of his CIA status to a man named Armando López Estrada. The refusal of the court to turn over their López grand jury testimony to the defense was fatal to their case. Who was Armando López Estrada?

In 1978 López stood trial in Miami charged with a number of firearm violations. At trial, López was indentified as a long-time CIA contract agent. Another Bay of Pigs-David Phillips Old Boy. During testimony the agency was constrained to admit that López was, as of 1976, still an employee of the agency. The man testifying was Grayston Lynch. Lynch had been a CIA case officer for the Bay of Pigs invasion and Brigade 2506. Lynch testified about López Estrada's training, particularly with respect to weapons, pointing out that the weapons provided to the Brigade by the CIA in the early 1960s were not registered so they could not be traced. He also testified that although some operations planned by the exiles received express approval, some did not. "There were some that we neither approved nor disapproved...[I]f they didn't bother anything they just ignored them"

On June 29, 1976, there was a meeting at the New England Oyster House in Coral Gables, Florida, involving two Chileans, two Cuban exiles, and an American. It now appears that the participants included Hector Duran, Bernardo de Torres and Armando López Estrada, from the Brigade 2506; General Juan Manuel Contreras Sepulveda, the notorious then-head of DINA, the Chilean secret police, and Michael V. Townley.
This meeting, which was apparently conducted under police and FBI surveillance, and which included an informant (López), centered on the murder of Letelier and several sabotage actions. No police action followed this meeting.

What is more, it is public knowledge that López Estrada was also present at the secret meeting in July 1976 in the Dominican Republic. That fateful meeting organized the Co-ordination of United Revolutionary Organizations (CORU), the heinous bombing of a Cubana airliner in October 1976, and the Letelier murder.

Almost as pressing as the questions concerning CIA are those touching on the FBI. The Bureau's relationship with Townley led to a shocking incident that exemplifies the problem.

The defense was able to document that the government, in it's continuing program to curry favor with Townley, gave him free run of the United States attorney's office and unsupervised use of the telephones located there (4852-55). This included allowing Townley to make long-distance calls over government phones, including personal calls to Chile. One such call, to a Gustavo Etchepare of Santiago, Chile, at 5 P.M. on January 30, 1979, during the third week of the trial, was recorded by Mr. Etchepare and later turned over to the defense.

The tape of this conversation raised serious doubts about Townley's credibility as a witness. First, he indicated his disdain for the jury before which he had just testified, and his belief that any "shit" would confuse them: " . . . the jury is so ignorant that one of the best defenses at this time is to throw more shit in and stir it up." (Appendix at 2)

For the judge, Mr. Townley expressed utter contempt: " . . . they have a cretin for a judge, and on top of that the judge is ill-humored, and on top of that they have a judge who is badly educated . . . [Question by Mr. Etchepare] Is Judge Parker a reasonable and pleasant man? [Answer by Townley] Are you kidding? He can go to hell." (Appendix at 2-3)

Then Townley indicated his willingness to take action, even criminal actions, to subvert the judicial process in his favor: " . . . I offer right now to ask friends all over the world to call [Judge Parker] and threaten him and get him to withdraw from the case." (Appendix at 3)

Apparently, this was not a new thought for this witness. He next explained that he *and some FBI agents, apparently those working with the prosecution in this case*, had actually discussed arranging such threats: "That was one of the things that was talked about *confidentially* with people from *the FBI* . . . how many friends we all had who could call . . . make threatening phone calls to the judge to get him to withdraw from the case." (Appendix 3, Emphasis added)

In a voir dire outside the presence of the jury, Townley admitted making this call (5072-77).

Along with Silbert, Glanzer, Propper, and Townley the FBI went to torturous lengths to keep the Buckley name out of the courtroom.

FBI Special Agent Whack gave the following remarkable testimony during the trial. Whack is describing how Townley cooperated with the prosecution after his extradition from Chile in August 1978.

We met Mr. Townley at Kennedy Airport and proceeded under his direction to the International Arrivals building . . .

The route we traveled was to the International Arrivals building, to the second floor to LAN Chile Airlines office to their first class lounge and subsequently left the airport.

Q: Who was directing the route that you were taking?
A: Mr. Townley was.
Q: After leaving JFK Airport, did you go anyplace else?
A: We went to the vicinity of 42nd Street and Fifth Avenue, New York City.
Q: And would you tell us what happened when you got to the vicinity of 42nd Street and Fifth Avenue?
A: Mr. Townley led us to the specific building of 500 Fifth Avenue.
Q: And what happened when you got to 500 Fifth Avenue?
A: Mr. Townley—we entered the building and we proceeded to determine or he proceeded to determine what office he had visited in the building.
Q: Did there come a time when he pointed out an office that he had visited?
A: He did. He pointed out the office of a New York state senator on the 41st floor of the building.
Q: Do you know an individual by the name of William Sampol?
A: I do.
Q: Where does he work?
A: William Sampol works in the office of a New York state senator at 500 Fifth Avenue, New York City, on the 41st floor.

Q: Are you aware sir, whether or not he has a relationship with the defendant Guillermo Novo Sampol?
A: William Sampol is known to me as the cousin of Guillermo Novo.

The Supreme Court cautioned in *Berger* v. *United States*, 295 U.S. 78, 88 (1935) that an assistant United States attorney is the representatuve of a sovereignity "whose interest . . . in a criminal prosecution is not that it shall win a case, but that justice shall be done." For the assistant United States attorney in this case, however, conviction was clearly paramount. His financial and professional future depended on that outcome.

Consequently, no techniques were spared which would help to produce a conviction. The prosecutor entered into agreements with Chile and the government's chief witness, Michael Townley, which insured that that witness could not be properly cross-examined by the defense.

The defense counsel was not permitted to cross-examine Townley concerning his modus operandi in other assassination plots. Cross-examination as to Townley's assassination activities in Italy and Argentina was particularly important to show the extent of the benefit which Townley derived from his plea agreement with the government. Contrary to requiring Townley to "come clean," that agreement required him *not to talk.* By drafting the agreement in this fashion, however, the government conferred a major benefit on Townley, relieving him of any obligation to disclose the serious crimes which he had committed outside the United States.

The gravamen of the defense is that Michael Vernon Townley masterminded the Letelier assassination, brought his criminal plans to the United States, enlisted others to assist him, went to Washington, built the bomb and planted it in Letelier's car. Even crediting all of the government's allegations, the defendents Novo and Ross on the other hand, played a very minor role in these events. Novo is accused of providing some of the explosives, and Ross is accused merely with having been present at certain peripheral events. Neither man went to Washington, neither built the bomb, neither planted that bomb, and neither detonated it. Nevertheless, Townley was sentenced to only ten years incarceration; he will be eligible for parole in 1981. The Cubans were each sentenced to two life terms, to run consecutively.

We are left, at the end, with the missing briefcase as the supreme symbol, in this case, of a cover-up and obstruction of justice. How could the Letelier briefcase have been moved from the scene of the crime into the hands of Otero Echeverria, Phillips, Buckley, Cline, and their "media assets" world-wide? How did the Washington Metropolitan Police lose control of the Letelier papers?

The Homicide Division of the Washington police department had jurisdiction in the Letelier investigation, including possession of the briefcase.

At the time the bomb went off, Fred Landis was living a few blocks away. Within thirty minutes, Landis was explaining to newsmen at the scene the existence of working relations between DINA and CIA, and a list of political assassinations of Chileans that one or the other agency was involved in. This impromptu lecture by Dr. Landis was interrupted by a burly plainclothesman who identified himself as Detective Stan Wilson. Wilson said he would like to follow up on some of the allegations, and would Landis be willing to put these in writing? Landis spent the next six hours at the homicide bureau explaining to four detectives the facts of recent Chilean political history. Wilson interjected every hour that it was "probably an inside job." Wilson did insist that, given Dr. Landis's suspicions of an interest on the part of the FBI or CIA to interfere with the police investigation (in order to prevent the uncovering of working relations with DINA), he would not allow any outside agency to examine the written deposition. Within one week Landis was called in by the FBI to explain how he happened to know the exact date and circumstances of CIA-DINA liaison. They had a complete copy of the statement to Wilson. Saul Landau of the IPS and other fellows contend that it was Wilson himself who gave a copy of the Letelier briefcase to Rafael Otero Echeverria. Later, Wilson's ties to the White Hand would emerge.

What is certain is that the Rockefeller Commission Report on *CIA Activities Within the United States* states, "the Agency's closest contacts have been with police departments in the Washington, D.C., metropolitan area." According to the Commission findings:

In 1969, arrangements were made with the Washington Metropolitan Police Department to allow the CIA to conduct certain training exercises using police facilities and personnel. These exercises involved the contrived "arrest" of CIA trainees by a Washington police officer and the lengthy interrogation of those trainees at Washington Police Headquarters by Office of Security personnel. The object of the training was to determine whether CIA trainees, scheduled for covert assignments overseas, would "break" when placed under such pressures—and to give them experiences similar to those which they might be expected to encounter on their assignments. . . .

The CIA has occasionally obtained badges and other identification from local police for the purpose of maintaining cover during CIA operations. Such "cover" has been obtained from police departments in Washington, D.C., Fairfax County (Virginia), and New York City, among others. . . .

The accounting demanded of the CIA for its actions both before and after the murders has never been made (1) Did CIA hide Townley's photograph and false passport, after it was sent to them by Ambassador Landau in July 1976? The FBI had a photograph of Townley within *one month* of the assassination but was unable to identify him; (2) Was David A. Phillips an accessory before the fact as he was after it, along with Rafael Otero Echeverria? (3) Did Phillips's relationship with Michael Townley continue *after* 1975? (4) Did the Association of Former Intelligence Officers (AFIO) and Buckley's America-Chilean Committee (ACC) and Cline's CSIS act as fronts for the CIA *before* the killing as they did afterward? (CIA man Volman set up the murder meeting in Bonao in July 1976). (5) Based on the Phillips-Otero Echeverria-Buckley false-leads campaign after the murder, and the obstruction of justice that the Phillips network achieved, why have there been no indictments? (6) Were former CIA men Edwin Wilson and Jack Holcolmb ever questioned concerning the bomb components? (7) Finally, who arranged for Seymour Glanzer to represent the interests of Michael Townley?

Did Townley receive the Fanon-Courier paging or beeping system that was used to trigger the death explosive from the

National Intelligence Academy in Florida? The evidence indicates that he did. Did Townley receive the C-4 plastic explosive detonators from former CIA officer Edwin Wilson? Why, when Wilson's name surfaced, did Langley break off relations with the investigation? And why was FBI agent in charge, Carter Cornick, temporarily replaced by someone from the FBI security Force who had links to CIA?

The fix was in. As Special Agents Cornick and Scherrer flew out of the Pudahuel Airport, with Townley in tow, his attorney, Manuel Acuña, was lodging an appeal with the Supreme Court of Chile. But no justices "were available," and at Pudahuel, Interpol had taken its telephone off the hook so that it could not receive a countermand. Michael had a new attorney—Propper's former superior, Seymour Glanzer.

What is the CIA's connection to CORU, the White Hand, today? They set up Bosch and Otero, but today Roland Otero is free on bail, during appeal, in Miami. His interests are being represented by friends of the old Brigade. One of the demands made on Townley—in September 1976 by his CORU accomplices in the Letelier assassination—had been that the Agency, someone, help Rolando Otero, the CIA's victim in Santiago who had been betrayed by Townley.

Some individuals, of course, are in a better position to cover up their crimes than an Otero Echeverria or a Townley. Chile was the Nixon administration's foreign Watergate, and nobody understood this more clearly than Henry Kissinger. Only six individuals in the world were authorized to know about Track II: President Nixon, Kissinger, CIA Director Helms, State Department Intelligence Chief Ray Cline, General Alexander Haig, and David Phillips.

President Nixon had, himself, been pardoned for all crimes committed as President. Kissinger first moved his "tapes" to the Rockefeller estate and then "gave" his State Department records to the Library of Congress, with the provision that no one may have access to them until have the statute of limitations has run. As soon as the leaks concerning CIA activities in Chile began, CIA was instructed by the White House to delete all references to Kissinger in Chile records, and where this was not possible to destroy them. When William Shawcross, the British author of

Sideshow came to Washington, during the early stages of his research into the secret Cambodian war, he was the victim of a robbery. The only thing taken was his Kissinger file. More recently, Orlando Letelier's colleagues at the Institute for Policy Studies had complied material for a book on the assassination. All of the chapter on the role of Henry Kissinger in Chilean events will not appear because someone broke into the Institute and stole the Kissinger file.

The fact that Phillips and Cline are both directors of organizations of retired intelligence officers may not be coincidental. They may need all the friends they can get.

The files of the House Select Committee on Assassinations, containing the autopsy photos of the head shot that killed President Kennedy, X-rays and other articles, were found to have been rifled in 1979. Sources said that the only unauthorized set of prints the police found belonged to Regis T. Blahut, CIA liaison officer who had been detailed to "assist" the committee.

When Mr. Blahut was interviewed briefly by telephone he stated, "There's other things that are involved that are detrimental to other things." When asked to elaborate, he refused, stating, "I signed an oath of secrecy with the CIA. I cannot discuss it any further." No charges were ever brought in this burglary that dwarfed the Watergate break-in in its implication of constitutional crisis.

There are indications that not only the cover stories are related but the burglaries as well. The agency described Blahut—the agent who broke into the House Committee's most sensitive safe —as having "acted alone and out of curiosity." The *Washington Post* found out that, on the contrary, Blahut had been part of a large CIA operation code—named "MH/CHILD."

According to the *New York Post*:

The House Assassinations Committee discovered that its most sensitive files were rifled and traced fingerprints on them to a CIA man.

The CIA fired the officer in question, Regis T. Blahut.

Blahut failed key parts of three lie-detector tests, said sources quoting the committee's chief counsel, G. Robert Blakey.

"He denied he did it and he flunked that," one source said.

"They also asked him whether anyone ordered him to do it. He said no one and he flunked that. . . ."

The episode reportedly produced a great wave of anxiety within the CIA, which has been claiming for several years now that its era of domestic spying is past...

Asked whether it might have been a matter of conscious CIA spying on a congressional committee, [CIA's Herbert] Hetu replied, "Good Lord, no."

The Howard Hunt-James McCord-Frank Sturgis break-in at the Chilean embassy in Washington in 1972 was a precursor to MH/BABY and an Agency operation, and *no one* was ever prosecuted for it. The Hunt-McCord-Sturgis team had "bugged" the Letelier quarters in 1972. These episodes make a semantic mockery of such euphemisms as "ex" and "former" intelligence operatives.

The same names and faces—from out of the Western Hemisphere Division, as in a recurrent nightmare—from across three decades are gathered together for the Letelier murder as if by invitation. The players all used to proudly call themselves "the Company"; today they are undercover or "White Hand" or "AFIO" or "ACC" or "ex" or they are at Georgetown's CSIS or "acting alone"—but they are all present in the secret war that has been raging behind the scenes of the Carter administration since 1976.

The Assassinations Committee break-in weaves into a sinister pattern. (1) In 1972 Howard Hunt and other "former" CIA operatives were busy breaking into Orlando Letelier's living quarters at the Chilean Embassy in Washington on Dave Phillips's orders. (2) In 1974 the Townley assassination squad rifled General Prats's home in Buenos Aires in search of the manuscript of Prat's book. (3) In 1975 Philip Agee's work in progress was stolen by CIA thieves. (4) The Leightons were robbed in Rome before they were shot by Townley's thugs. (5) The year 1976 brings us to the second illegal entry into a Letelier domicile—this is before the September murders and is obviously connected. (6) In 1978, the MH/CHILD looting of the House Select Committee on Assassinations is discovered.*

*Robert F. Groden, a photoanalyst and former House Assassination Committee staff aide, has stated that four of the JFK autopsy photographs of the fatal head-shots are forgeries. Groden alleges that the Select Committee was the victim of major evidentiary tampering by CIA.

Each and every one of these official and unofficial operations is connected to the Clandestine Services of the Central Intelligence Agency, most of them through Hunt, or Phillips, or Townley or MH/BABY. In almost every case, the raiding operatives are *former* intelligence officers like Hunt, or contract agents like Townley. In every case the thieves are searching for documents relating to CIA. Chile, Kissinger, and assassinations are persistent themes in each episode.

There are a number of organizations like Buckley's ACC, Ray Cline's CSIS, and Phillips' AFIO in secret linkage. Organizations of former secret agents deserve careful study. There are three Old Boy networks of CIA hands active on Capitol Hill and in the media. David Phillips's Association of Former Intelligence Officers was the first (1975) and remains by far the most visible and important. In addition, former Deputy Director of the CIA Ray Cline has set up a National Intelligence Study Center. Cline's group has space at the Center for Strategic and International Studies, at the Library of Congress, and at the National Archives. The principal purpose of the National Intelligence Study Center is to assist former intelligence officers to come to Washington so that they can be assisted in researching, writing, and placing pro-CIA articles, James Jesus Angleton, former Chief of Counterintelligence at CIA, has set up a foundation called the Security and Intelligence Fund. In Angleton's view, half of Congress, the Justice Department, and all the Agency's critics are dupes of a KGB-orchestrated plot to destroy the CIA. Together with superannuated FBI security officers and OSS types he proposes to lead the charge up Capitol Hill to lobby for an American version of an Official Secrets Act.

The Association of Former Intelligence Officers leads the pack, lobbying for "anti-Agee" laws as well as for unleashing of CIA covert operations. The "lesson learned" from the great scandals of the early seventies: never get caught again. The talk of reforms was merely a "fast brush," to use the Howard Hunt's term of art. That is all the AFIO ever meant. That, and finding a presidential candidate, or three, who could be counted on to "close his eyes and take it" in the words of one Southern senator sympathetic to covert action ("Capital C, capital A," to use Phillips's phrase).

Lest there be any doubt about the recrudescent power of secret America's Cold War dependence and obsession, by the presidential election of 1980, candidate Ronald Reagan was openly calling for "an airlift" and "the liberation of" Cuba. Cuba, always the trip-wire to World War III, once again playing a decisive role in domestic politics. Then, in mid-April 1980 came the obligatory editorial in the Hearst press: "The Time Has Come for Us to Liberate Cuba." The author, Patrick Buchanan. is a sometime newsman who has been associated with David Phillips, Frank Sturgis, William Buckley, and the Old Boy network since the 1950's.

The AFIO quite clearly has plans, to use a word. Life member of the AFIO George Bush is featured in the group's *Periscope* brochure mailed to members. And as of spring 1980 Phillips and ultraright-wing Texas millionaire Gordon McLendon were in constant consultation with Langley concerning a television series bearing the Agency's imprimatur. Both McLendon, a life member of the AFIO, and Phillips were quoted by the Los Angeles *Herald Examiner* on March 3, 1980, as wishing to do for CIA what decades of J. Edgar Hoover Cold War horror shows achieved for the FBI. Both men say that they are eager to trade Agency cooperation for Agency approval. AFIO is "into" books and film and polls in America just as the CIA was abroad. But most of all, AFIO is involved with private intelligence for the transnational giants.

In its March 24, 1980 issue *Fortune* magazine lists numbers of former CIA officers who are helping Exxon, Bechtel, ITT, to name a few of the 193 corporations involved, to "not only study key countries in depth" but to "analyze them more astutely." Former DCIA William Colby hails this development of a private industry of political analysis."

Fortune makes the euphemism unnecessary by clearly stating that it is counterinsurgency that the Old Boys are providing. One executive is quoted ruefully to the effect that "the time has passed when we could buy or rent governments."

What ITT did in Chile is now on the multinational drawing boards. The names are: Richard Helms's firm "Safeer" and trouble shooting operations like "Prism" and "Probe": all staffed by former officers of the Clandestine Services of the Central Intelligence Agency. This new subculture of former secret operatives is writ large in the case of Helms's master in Chile, Henry Kissinger. Kissinger sits on the "Risk Committee" for the Chase Manhattan Bank, consulting for their world-wide interests. Thus Helms and the Old Boys behind the scenes, while Buckley and Phillips address themselves to the public through long-used conduits of the Cold War, Ralph de Toledano, for example.

In a syndicated column for the CIA's Latin American News Service, Copley, de Toledano reports on the latest bogus polls Gallup has been commissioned to concoct. According to de Toledano, the polls show that 70 percent of the Chilean people do not want elections, dictator Pinochet is regarded as "decent and humane" by this same 70 percent, while those finding the junta's maximum leader "likeable and pleasant" is, surprise, 70 percent! De Toledano regards these figures as a sufficient answer to "Mr. Carter and the goo-goos in the State Deparment who gurgle about 'human rights'." As if to authenticate the Gallup polls, de Toledano went all the way to Chile and did some polling of his own. The results were that "to a man, they all told me that if the military had not ovethrown Allende, there would have been a popular uprising of farmers, housewives and professionals. . . ." De Toledano seems to be unaware of the fact that these demonstrations did occur, and that Seymour Hersh won the Pulitzer Prize for proving that the CIA was behind them. In a recent telephone interview, William Buckley admitted that de Toledano's trip to Chile, along with those of six other *National Review* writers, was paid for by the junta. Buckley added, "It is absurd to think that someone like de Toledano or William Rusher can be bought by airfare to Santiago, an uncomfortable eighteen-hour trip."

Finally, there is Buckley's superagent Robert Moss. Moss, a key author in the CIA's Plan Z and *White Book* campaign in Chile, has ventured, openly, into fiction, along with Buckley and Phillips. Moss's new work, *Spike*, says Richard Helms from the novel's jacket, "deals with what the Russians call 'disinformation.'" We learn from Helms that the book describes how disinformation may be used by the KGB to "destroy the West without firing a shot." But that is a fairy tale. Psychological warfare, as Helms knows so well—from Tracks I and II, Plan Z and the "Quartered Man"—psywar, includes a number of shots being fired.

The conclusion is inescapable that when Nixon and Kissinger gave Helms the Chile baton, they set in motion a dynamo of evil in the Clandestine Services at Langley. The orgy of savagery that followed from the Centaur plans (September, *El Descuartizado*) was an inevitable spasm of horror at what may be the losing end of the Cold War for the United States. That is, the American humiliation and defeat in Vietnam, which was explained away by the Pentagon because the South's armies were corrupt and cowardly produced a wave of panic. This panic could only be relieved by a formula that would unleash the full potency of the national military in any future "target" country, thus sparing American boys and ensuring a stable anti-Communist client state for the American market and investments.

The nihilism of Centaur and the Quartered Man can be traced to its proximate origins. The Old Boys who destroyed Vietnam and Chile—and, it may be argued, besmirched America—are defined by their heroic experience in World War II. They have never been able to find a contender to follow Adolph Hitler, to take up the moral slack in their lives and so engage them that they could feel good and glamorous again.

Hannah Arendt has reasoned that a ruling group increases secrecy and violence as it *loses* power. From World War II to Korea to Vietnam to Chile there is a geometrically widening structure of secrecy in America. America in the 1960s and the 1970s dared not tell her citizens what her foreign policy was, or that the old philosophy of democratic republicanism had been replaced by corporate anticommunism. The American use of the other country's assassins to do what we were afraid to do in our own name is the inevitable failure of nerve that follows the failure of intellect.

That is why Orlando Letelier had to die in Washington in broad daylight. Both the Cuban and DINA assassins had been created and defined by American power. Because of the assassins' ambivalent but vital connection to that power, through Langley, the killing ground—for once—had to be Washington, the *genus loci*, the place where it all began.

In 1979 independent investigators developed information implicating the national airline of Chile in the Letelier-Moffit assassinations. Evidence of the DINA's use of a LAN Chile airliner—to transport explosives to *replace* explosives used in the Letelier murder—was handed to Federal Aviation Administration Chief Langhorne Bond in November 1979. Despite what purported to be the Carter Doctrine on Chile, nothing happended. Finally, weeks later, Representative John Burton, the powerful Democrat from San Francisco, made a public statement: "No action has been initiated or planned by the FAA, either on its own or at the request of the Department of Justice, against LAN Chile."

And now, according to *Newsday's* John Cummings, sources in the Department of Justice say that Townley's father, Vernon, received "packages" from LAN Chile in 1976.

By 1980 the Washington *Post* was reporting that:

> Chile's involvement in the 1976 Washington murder of Orlando Letelier, considered a potentially debilitating crisis here barely a year ago, appears instead to have become a personal triumph for President Augusto Pinochet and to have bolstered, rather than weakened, his military regime . . .
>
> U.S. diplomats here now say the Administration was never prepared to carry out the threats.
>
> "All right we bluffed," said one high-ranking U.S. official here. "They called our bluff, and we lost."
>
> It was all part of a game, this diplomat said . . .

Within four years the Carter Administration's Human Rights Policy had become nothing but a cosmetic covering for the butchers of Santiago and the Old Boys at Langley.

America now is in what the revolutionary depth psychologist Frantz Fanon called "the third phase of violence," the "boomerang phase." In the Letelier case, what Phillips did for the CIA in Chile was eventually acted out in this nation's captial—execution on American soil by men, *every one of whom had been trained by the Central Intelligence Agency.* But we are discussing more than merely the "moral authorship" of the political execution. The kind of clandestine propoganda and psychological warfare run by Phillips and his successors is not intended to convince rationally or win our hearts and minds, it is intended—what was done in Chile was intended—to prepare the population for violence. And then, afterwards, project the blame, the bloodshed, onto others and onto the victims themselves. The Phillips-O'Leary headline is the stereotype, the scandal that must shame every intellectual in Washington—"MARTYR THEORY PROBED."

When the left wing cover stories were being laid down, George Bush, Vernon Walters, Henry Kissinger, Harry Shlaudeman, David Phillips (and their media assets) all knew the truth, and Bush, Walters, and Kissinger, at least had known in advance. "MARTYR THEORY PROBED"—that hollow headline will haunt American justice.

It was not quite possible to say that Orlando Letelier and Ronni Moffit had killed themselves, as the murderers had said of Salvador Allende's execution, though Otero Echeverria actually tried to do so immediately after the explosion, before the ACC-AFIO "leftist" line had been fully developed and distributed.

What CIA's psywar did to Chile goes on. In this tragedy without God, today, people are starving for the first time in that nation's history, according to international inquiries and Christian Democrat sources who *supported* the coup. And at Colonia Dignidad— where Michael Townley led CIA torture teams using Gestapo tactics—entire families have been brought for torture after being kidnapped from neighboring Southern Cone countries. This is the CIA's SOCO program in action.

Meanwhile, Chase Manhattan Bank and the Rockefeller group have opened new offices in Santiago with more than $2 billion flowing into the economic entrails of the junta, as designed by Milton Friedman and the "Chicago Boys". Senator Edward Kennedy and Congressman Tom Harkin have tried to get aid to the junta cut off.

One of those working behind the scenes to keep economic pressure *off* the junta was the prosecutor Eugene Propper. "Please don't mix politics into this," he is reported to have repeated. Whatever that was supposed to mean. In October 1979 General Pinochet thumbed his nose at the United States by finally refusing to extradite Contreras et al. and laughed all the way to the bank. Then Propper left the Department of Justice and commenced negotiations for the sale of a theatrical film and book on the case.

Ambassador Landau, after he was recalled in 1979, in a Carter-esque gesture, is quoted by the *Village Voice* as telling friends in New York that, "it's a great time to invest in Chile."

Henry Kissinger who had given the go-ahead in the first place to the junta to set up the SOCO murder apparatus promised to discuss Chile in the Second volume of his memoirs.

In Santiago, torture and repression picked up speed, according to recent exiles. In Washington, a purge of human rights activists in the government began. Patricia Derian, Bob Stevens, George Lister, Ralph Guzman: to mention a few respected names who have been muzzled or transferred. Behind the screen of Iran, Chile was once again thrown to the wolves.

What explains the obsession Chile held for Kissinger? Was it the moral example of Allende and Letelier, the moral authority they had among the Third World leaders? That when Allende appeared before the UN General Assembly he received the longest standing ovation in its history? This was the real threat, and not some mythical terrorist threat to Latin America.

This obsession with Chile is reflected in an exchange of letters between former U.S. Ambassador to Chile Ed Korry and his former deputy, now U.S. Ambassador to Venezuela.*

KORRY: "I hope that you at least have washed Chile out of your system and are enjoying your assignment."

SHLAUDEMAN: "No, I have not worked Chile out of my system, and probably never will. One minor problem of the moment is seeing Orlando Letelier at countless receptions (reverting to his normally gregarious habits). Keeps reminding me of the past."

Letelier was one of the "new men" who had to be eliminated.

"We are not just *any* nation," said Henry Kissinger—in all his *prepotencia*, to use the Chilean expression—at still another Man of the Year award dinner in 1979. No, we are not, nor was the author of Track II and Centaur just *any* man when he sat in the 40 Committee, representing both the Nixon and Rockefeller powers, and ordered Richard Helms to make Chile's economy "scream."

*See Appendix for photostats of letters.

History may well judge the failure of armed intellectuals, like Kissinger, who did not recognize that economies do not scream— *people* scream.

Joseph B. Smith had served for years with David Phillips and the Clandestine Section. His epitaph for the good and golden lads of World War II is telling:

We sometimes reported on the intelligence which supported our case. ...We lied to ambassadors who tried to thwart our plans and even maneuvered their re-assignment when they persisted in opposing us. Living lies and inventing self-serving excuses for failures, worse still, believing them eroded the character of CIA officers from the lowest to the highest.

The Quartered Man was, finally, a biological symbol as well as a psychological one. And psychology, as Dostoyevsky warned, is a "knout that hits both ways." The "Madman theory" of Henry Kissinger and Richard Nixon, which began as a private joke, is ending as a world-historical tragedy. People who play at madness, who invent monsters, indulge in the ultimate delusion if they think they can return to sanity at will. This is the moment of the boomerang. Having coldly decided to possess a people, to whip an officer corps up into a blood lust, to make Chile the name of a nervous disease, who can predict when the shadow of covert operations will lengthen inexorably across America itself?

The assassination on Embassy Row was fascism in action. The attempt by the AFIO, CSIS, and the Buckley organization, the ACC, to shift blame from the killers and to mislead the police and public was *in the service* of facism in action—in Chile and in the United States.

During the trial Prosecutor Propper asked:

Q: Dr. Luke, what, if any, major injuries did you find on Mr. Letelier?

A: The major injuries included the fact that his legs had been traumatically amputated or blown off...

THE COURT: Doctor, were you able to make a determination as to the cause of death?

THE WITNESS: Yes, sir.

THE COURT: What was it?

THE WITNESS: The cause of death was exsanguination and traumatic amputation of the lower extremities.

He had been *quartered*! Washington had become the homologue of Santiago.

El Desquartizado had reached the soil of the United States of America at last.

Notes

pp. 4-6 "The chronology of the crime": This is based upon an account presented in a pamphlet, *They Educated the Crows*, by Saul Landau (Washington: Transnational Institute, 1978).

p. 7 "classified USA opinion poll": "Chilean Attitudes Toward Communism and the East-West Conflict," USIA Research and Reference Service, Latin American Public Opinion Barometer, Report No. 4, December 16, 1955.

p. 19 "Newsweek's 'Periscope' column": "Murder Mystery," October 11, 1976.

p. 20 "Blake Fleetwood...did, and Bosch told him": "I am going to declare war," *New Times*, May 13, 1977, pp. 45-53.

p. 20 "according to the Times": David Binder, "Two Nations Report Anti-Castro Exiles Have Plotted Many Terrorist Acts," *New York Times*, October 25, 1976.

p. 24 "It is a horrible and monstrous thought": This statement and others made at the trial are taken from the trial transcript.

p. 28 "an awkward, appealing, alienated youth": Reverend Larry A. Jackson, Greenwood, S.C.

p. 33 Project Camelot shift to CIA: Lyman B. Kirkpatrick, *The U.S. Intelligence Community* (New York: Hill and Wang, 1973), p. 127.

"Johan Galtung...refused": See Irving Louis Horowitz, *The Rise and Fall of Project Camelot* (Cambridge: MIT Press, 1967).

p. 34 Bogus polls: See, for example, *El Mercurio*, September 2, 1970, in which a page one story says that a Gallup poll indicated Allessandri had a 10 percent lead over Allende. The results in the election, two days later, were exactly the reverse—for a 20 percent shift in the electorate!

p. 34 "SAO was a CIA front": Unpublished research by A. J. Weberman, for *Coup d'Etat*. Forthcoming.

p. 38 "The orders to the CIA": Senate Select Committee to Study Governmental Operations with Respect to Intelligence Activities, *Covert Action in Chile*, 1963-1973, pp. 26-27 (Referred to hereafter as the Church Committee and the Church Committee Report or *Covert Action in Chile*.)

p. 39 "The games were exciting": David Atlee Phillips, *The Night Watch: Twenty-Five Years of Peculiar Service* (New York: Atheneum 1977).

p. 46 Veciana testimony: House Select Committee on Assassinations. The Committee published eight volumes, of which four are about Chile: 1/ Covert Action in Chile 1963-1974; 2/ Covert Action in Chile-Vol. II; 3/ Foreign and Military Intelligence; 4/ Alleged Assassination Plots.

p. 52 "Track II . . . 'never stopped' ": *Covert Action in Chile*, pp. 253-54.

p. 52 Plan to kidnap Schneider: *Covert Action in Chile*, pp. 225-27.

p. 53 "On September 15, 1970, President Nixon . . .": *Covert Action in Chile*, p. 227.

p. 58 ITT letters and memorandums: Senate Foreign Relations Committee hearings, Subcommittee on Multinational Corporations and U.S. Foreign Policy, ITT-Chile, March 20, 1973.

p. 61 "John McCone . . . 'not chaos . . .' ": Ibid.

p. 63 "Throughout the Allende years": Ibid.

p. 64 "Do we live by a separate standard": Ibid.

p. 67 Break-in at the Chilean Embassy: NACLA Latin America and Empire *Report*, Vol. 8, No. 6 (July-August 1974).

p. 68 Hendrix: This was one of a series of memos from ITT man Hendrix in Chile to the N.Y. office released in 1972 by Jack Anderson. They were collected and printed by the Allende government in Chile by the publishing house of Quimantu in 1972 under the title *Los Documentos Secretos de la ITT*.

p. 68 Moss - on IGS: "The Tribulations of Chile," *National Review*, October 10, 1975.

p. 68 "When Allende took office": *Covert Action in Chile*.

pp. 69-72 "Who's Who in the Institute of General Studies," *Inquiry* magazine, February 19, 1979.

p. 74 Davis cable: Quoted in Jack Anderson column, *Washington Post*, November 10, 1972.

p. 77 Davis: Ibid.

p. 79 Allende speech to United Nations: December 4, 1972.

p. 86 "The artificial crisis": Oscar Waiss, *La Nación*, October 5, 1972.

P. 86 "Handicapped veterans marched": *El Mercurio*, February 24, 1973, p. 14.

p. 87 "The case of the Descuartizado":Alvaro Puga, *La Segunda*, April, 1973.

p. 88 "Government Studies System": *El Mercurio*, October 3, 1972. "Communism and Spies," *El Mercurio*, October 5, 1972

p. 90 "The unconscious depth-message": Marshall McLuhan, Understanding Media (Signet, McGraw-Hill, N.Y. 1964).

p. 91 "stages in the development of each image": Further details, the results of a content analysis of these themes appearing in *El Mercurio*, are given in Dr. Landis's "Psychological Warfare and Media Operations in Chile: 1970-1973," Ph.D. dissertation, University of Illinois, 1975. See especially "Black Propaganda," pp. 239-265.

p. 93 "computerized letter": In the days immediately after the coup Dr. Landis spoke with 22 persons (including 14 military officers) who received a copy of this letter. In each case it was personalized so that the addressee's name appeared at the top of the list, together with the correct address and correct names of family members. Reference to Plan Z—accepted as genuine rather than as CIA provocations—may be found in the junta's *White Book (Libro Blanco)* and in *Allende: Fin de Una Aventura* a book written by *El Mercurio* journalist Lautaro Silva. Such personalized letters can only be mass produced by using a computer—a technology perfected in mass marketing in the United States.

p. 93 "Beria's Secret Diary": The "diary" was a piece of deception. It never existed.

p. 96 "You don't play with fire": Quoted in Marquez, "Death of a President," *Harper's Magazine*, March, 1974, p. 52.

p. 97 "A remarkable conversation': Taped by Red Nacional de Telecomunicaciones de las Fuerzas Armadas de Chile, September 11, 1973, 9 A.M. to 11 A.M.; subsequently published in *La Segunda* and *Ercilla*. The English version here is taken from a Reuters dispatch.

p. 98 "People of my country:" Ibid.

p. 99 Marquez account: "Death of a President: The Last Days of Salvador Allende," *Harpers Magazine*, March 1974.

p. 102 "Extremists in Osorno": Armando Uribe, *Libro Negro.*

p. 104 Story by Teresa Donoso Loero: *El Mercurio*, January 2, 1973 p. 21.

p. 104 CIA financed book by Robert Moss: *Chile's Marxist Experience* (London: David and Charles, 1974).

p. 108 "Henry Kissinger was stating": Testimony before the Senate Foreign Relations Committee.

p. 108 Ambassador Korry: Korry maintained this pose for a year, denying any CIA involvement in Chile. When the truth began to out, he admitted everything publicly in a vain effort to bring Kissinger and Helms to book and evade responsibility himself.

p. 108 Colby interview with Fallaci: *New Republic*, March 13, 1976.

p. 111 Charles Horman in Chile: Various sources have been used in this account of Horman's life and death, including his father, the *Washington Post, Noticias Aliadas* (Lima, Peru).

p. 114 "Report from Amnesty International": Protection of Human Rights in Chile, A31/253, para. 371, p. 97.

p. 115 "In Colonia Dignidad": Quoted in Konrad Ege, "West Germany Cultist Concentration Camp in Chile," CounterSpy, Vol. 3, No. 3, December, 1978.

p. 115 Amnesty International, "this repressive apparatus"; "a torture and detention center": Ibid.

p. 116 "My name is. . . .": "Confessions of a DINA agent," CounterSpy, Vol. 3, No. 3, December, 1978.

p. 120 *The CIA and the Cult of Intelligence*: (New York: Knopf, 1974).

p. 120 "Marks in his own right": *In Search of the Manchurian Candidate* (New York: Times Books, 1979).

p. 122 "Kissinger Said to Rebuke U.S. Ambassador": Seymour Hersh, *New York Times*, September 27, 1974.

p. 123 "*Time* has learned": *Time*, September 30, 1974.

p. 124 "In AFIO we have": AFIO threefold promotional brochure, n.d.

p. 125 Open letter: In AFIO *Periscope*, Vol. 1, No. 1.

p. 126 "Mr. Phillips said": *Washington Star*, March 22, 1975.

p. 126 "Mr. Phillips, who says": "Reports 100 Attempts," *New York Times*, May 30, 1975, p. 20.

p. 126 "U.S. . . . Plotted": Edward Calimoré, *Baltimore News American*, May 8, 1977.

p. 127 "According to Smith": *Portrait of a Cold Warrior* (New York: Putnam's 1976).

p. 129 "Sturgis never worked for the CIA": *Report to the President by the Commission on CIA Activities Within the United States*, 1975.

p. 129 Phillips essay: "This is About (shh)," *New York Times*, May 25, 1975, p. IV, 15.

p. 130 House Select Committee report suppressed: The report did appear in print in the *Village Voice*, February 16, 1976, under the title "The Report on the CIA that President Ford Doesn't Want You to Read." In the ensuing contretemps Daniel Schorr, the CBS correspondent responsible for this form of publication, was fired. Schorr's account appears in *Clearing the Air* (Boston: Houghton Mifflin, 1977).

p. 131 "It was not surprising": Ernest Volkman and John Cummings, "The White Hand," *Penthouse* (June 1979), p. 76.

p. 132 "It was certainly a tempting asset": Ibid, p. 78.

p. 134 "a thousand assassinations": Ibid., p. 78-79.

p. 136 Townley's movement in 1975: This account is based on Townley's statements at the trial.

p. 140 National Intelligence Academy (NIA): Readers wanting additional information on this organization should read Jim Hougan, *Spooks*, (New York: William Morrow, 1978)

p. 141 "Jeff Gerth . . . monumental study": "Nixon and the Mafia," *Sundance Magazine* (November-December 1972).

p. 144 Robert Caraballa statement: *Que Pasa*, March 30-April 5, 1978.

p. 144 Suarez statement: Ibid.

p. 144 Callejas statement: *Hoy*, May 3-9, 1978

p. 157 American Chilean Council: The account given here is based upon papers filed with the court in the matter. U.S. vs. American Chilean Council, Civil Action No. 78-2379, filed December 18, 1978.

p. 166 *Clearing the Air*: See pages 132-34.

p. 170 Carl Bernstein . . . journalists . . . CIA": *Rolling Stone*, October 20, 1977.

p. 176 Blake Fleetwood: "I'm Going to Declare War," *New Times*, May 13, 1977, pp. 45-53.

p. 179 Ignacio Novo statement: *Que Pasa*, March 30-April 5, 1978.

p. 182 "As regards Paz and Suarez": Cecilia Domeyko, "La Ultima Version de Mariana Callejas," *Hoy*, March 7-13, 1979.

p. 183 "He had the opportunity": Ibid.

p. 185 "This Fellow Hunt knows": *The Ends of Power* (New York: Times Books, 1978).

p. 206 De Toledano report: Syndicated column for Copley News Service, May 23, 1979.

p. 208 Frantz Fanon: *The Wretched of the Earth* (New York: Grove Press, 1965).

p. 210 Korry-Shlaudeman exchange: Private exchange of letters supplied to the Senate Committee by Korry.

p. 211 Joseph B. Smith, "We sometimes reported", *Portrait of a Cold Warrior* (New York, Putnam, 1976).

Appendix

Chronology of Events

1942
December 9. Michael Vernon Townley is born, Waterloo, Iowa.

1950
Chile. David A. Phillips is recruited by the Central Intelligence Agency; takes over ownership of the *South Pacific Mail*.
Mexico City. William F. Buckley, Jr., begins work for the CIA with E. Howard Hunt.

1954
Chile. Orlando Letelier is graduated from college; begins working for Chilean government as copper expert.
Chile. David Hellyer takes over operation of *South Pacific Mail*; Phillips assigned to Operation Diablo (Guatemala).

1957
Chile. Vernon Townley arrives with family as Ford Motor Company employee.
Lebanon. David A. Phillips participates in covert operations against Middle East leftist governments; returns to U.S. 1958.

1958
Cuba. David A. Phillips works under deep cover as public relations specialist.
Chile. Salvador Allende is defeated for president by Jorge Alessandri.

1959
Chile. Orlando Letelier is dismissed from Copper Department and moves family to Venezuela.

1960

United States. David A. Phillips begins working on secret anti-Castro CIA operation.

Washington. Orlando Letelier begins work for the Inter-American Development Bank.

Santiago. Michael Townley marries Mariana Inés Callejas.

1961

Cuba. CIA-sponsored invasion meets disaster at Bay of Pigs.

1963

Mexico City. David A. Phillips becomes CIA Station Chief.

November 22. President John F. Kennedy is assassinated in Dallas.

1964

Chile. Salvador Allende is defeated for president by Eduardo Frei. CIA spends $20 million to accomplish this.

1965

Santo Domingo. David A. Phillips becomes CIA Station Chief.

Chile. PROJECT CAMELOT BEGINS AND IS EXPOSED.

1967

Miami. Michael Townley and family arrive from Santiago. Townley works with SAO and White Hand, Cuban-exile organizations.

1969

Washington. Philip Agee resigns from the Central Intelligence Agency.

1970

Santiago. Townley returns to Chile and begins working with Patria y Libertad. Co-ordinated media operation at *El Mercurio* is launched against Allende.

September 4. Salvador Allende wins popular election to presidency.

September 15. President Richard M. Nixon tells Richard Helms, director of Central Intelligence, to make Chile's economy "scream."

September 22. David A. Phillips becomes head of secret Chile task force; TRACK II BEGINS.

October 22. General René Schneider is assassinated.

October 24. Chilean Congress ratifies popular vote: Allende is officially elected.

November 4. Allende is inaugurated as first socialist president of Chile.

Post-Election. Allende opponents flee Chile; the Institute of General Studies (IGS) is formed to continue Track II; Otero Echeverria begins operating SEPA.

1971

July. Copper mines are nationalized.

December. March of the Pots and Pans. Castro visits Chile.

1972

February. Orlando Letelier returns to Washington, D.C., as Chilean Ambassador to the United States.

May 16. Burglars, led by E. Howard Hunt and Cubans, break into Letelier home in Washington, D.C. Search of Chilean embassy.

September-October. PLAN SEPTEMBER BEGINS.

October-November. Strikes begin among professional groups in attempt to effect coup.

December. President Allende visits United Nations Headquarters in New York City; addresses General Assembly.

1973

Chile. "QUARTERED MAN" CAMPAIGN BEGINS.

March 4. Congressional elections are held; Popular Unity gains at polls.

March 18. Townley blows up government transmitter in Concepcíon, killing a worker; flees to Argentina, thence to U.S.

May. Orlando Letelier returns to Chile from Washington, D.C., and becomes minister of foreign relations.

July 27. Allende's naval attaché, Commander Araya, is assassinated.

July-September. PLAN DJAKARTA BEGINS.

August 23. General Carlos Prats resigns as minister of defense and commander-in-chief of the army. Augusto Pinochet becomes commander-in-chief.

August 28. Orlando Letelier is named minister of defense.

September 11. Military coup succeeds; junta led by Augusto Pinochet takes over the Chilean government. Salvador Allende is assassinated; Orlando Letelier is imprisoned.

October. Michael Vernon Townley returns to Chile.

Post-Coup. Military execute "opponents".

1974

Chile. CIA agents, including Otero Echeverria and IGS, take over all radio, telecommunications, newspapers, economic planning.

New York City. William F. Buckley, Jr., arranges for junta's political lobbying and public relations in the United States.

Washington-Santiago. Formal liaison is established between the Central Intelligence Agency and Dirección de Inteligencia Nacional; informal liaison is established through Michael Vernon Townley.

September 29-30. General Carlos Prats is assassinated in Argentina.

September 10. Orlando Letelier is released from prison, exiled to Venezuela. Subsequently moves to United States.

1975

Washington. David A. Phillips resigns from the CIA, forms first political lobby of spies—the Association of Retired (later: Former) Intelligence Officers.

October 6, Rome. Bernardo Leighton and his wife are shot in apparent assassination attempt.

1976

June. White Hand meeting in Bonao, Dominican Republic, joins planning for Letelier assassination and originates plan to bomb Cubana airliner.

July. DINA Chief Contreras requests Paraguayan counterpart to supply false passports for Michael Townley and Fernández and to secure U.S. diplomatic visas.

Paraguay. George Landau, suspicious, cables U.S.; subsequently revokes visas and asks for return of passports.

Washington. The State Department, CIA, and FBI receive copies of the photographs of Townley and Fernández.

August. Townley and Fernández come to the United States to lay groundwork for Letelier assassination.

August. Michael Vernon Townley returns to U.S.; meets with Letelier assassins in offices of Senator James Buckley in New York City.

Early September. Townley meets with Cuban exiles in Union City, New Jersey, and with former CIA agent Frank Terpil.

September 21. Orlando Letelier is blown up with a bomb in Washington, D.C. Co-worker Ronni Karpen Moffitt, sitting beside him, is also killed.

September 21. The cover-up begins.

Glossary of Organizations

Plan Alba: A genuine plan for a coup by Pinochet, within the Chilean Army. Each branch of the Chilean armed forces had a plan, and each had a different code. Plan Alba, named by Pinochet himself, began originally in 1972 with the title, "Internal Reorganization of the Armed Forces." It was being called Plan Alba approximately three months before the coup of September 1973.

Plan Alpha: The name given by CIA assassins to a part of their own plan to kidnap members of the Chilean joint chiefs of staff, with Alpha (the kidnapping of General Schneider) to be followed by Beta, Gamma, etc. The plan, intended to provoke a coup during "The Sixty Days," did not progress beyond Alpha, because in the process of kidnapping Alpha, they killed him.

American-Chilean Council (ACC): A front set up by William F. Buckley, Jr., and associates with General Augusto Pinochet to do propaganda for the junta in the United States.

American Institute for Free Labor Development (AIFLD): The CIA's counter to Communist labor unions in Latin America. Though ostensibly a labor organization, its sponsors are large American corporations.

Association of Former Intelligence Officers (AFIO): A lobby of former spies founded and directed since 1975 by David Atlee Phillips. Originally called the Association of Retired Intelligence Officers (ARIO).

Andalien: Specifically, an advertising agency formed in 1969 to place CIA ads in the Chilean media during the 1970 presidential elections. As many as 50 percent of the people who worked for Andalien later formed the Institute of General Studies (IGS).

Project Camelot: The name given to a formal contract signed between the United States Army and American University—specifically, a branch of American University called Strategic Operations Research Office (SORO). Camelot was a reference—possibly ironic—to the ideals of the Kennedy administration. Positively, what Project Camelot sought was to establish a stable government, and the original goal was to identify and monitor certain key indices of the spread of "subversion." The intelligence-gathering operation was uncovered in Chile. The formal Army contract was cancelled, but all the components of the program were subsequently carried out by the CIA.

Campaign of Terror: The term used by Chileans to refer to CIA psychological operations during June-September 4, 1970.

Carabineros: The Chilean uniformed police.

Cautín: A province in the south of Chile, center of agrarian unrest and supposed Communist guerrilla training area.

Plan Centaur: A generic term used in this book as a literary device to comprise a series of CIA plans to unseat the Allende Popular Unity government. Centaur includes Track I, Track II, Plan September, El Descuartizado, and Plan Z.

CHAOS: The actual code word used by the CIA for their operation directed at penetrating and disrupting the New Left in the United States.

"Chicago Boys": A group of Chilean economists who studied under Milton Friedman, so called by the Chilean media.

CODE (Confederación de la Democracia): A united slate of opposition political parties.

Copley News Service (CNS): The CIA's eyes and ears in Latin America. Among the CIA agents working for CNS were William Giondoni and Old Man Ira Copley himself.

CORU (Coordinación de Organizaciones Revolucionaries Unidas): Umbrella organization of Cuban exile ultras. Formed at meeting in Bonao, Dominican Republic, June 1976.

Defense Intelligence Agency (DIA): The Pentagon's intelligence arm. It combines and coordinates the intelligence activities of each branch of the armed forces.

DINA (Dirección de Inteligencia Nacional): The Chilean secret police. Formal liaison was established with the CIA in early 1974. Succeeded by the CNI (Centro Nacional de Información).

Plan Djakarta: A divisive CIA black propaganda operation which brought latent fears and hostility between the military and Communists to the breaking point. A card reading Djakarta, purporting to originate from the opposition camp and listing those slated for execution, was simultaneously mailed to military and Communist leaders.

Gallup (Chile): Gallup's Chilean affiliate, Instituto Chileno de Opinion Publica, regularly produced fabricated polls. The vice president was Roberto Thieme of the CIA's underground resistance group, Patria y Libertad.

Institute for Policy Studies (IPS): A Washington, D.C., research institute. The IPS is concerned with national security issues, but it is one of the few of its kind that is not part of the national security establishment; i.e., it does not supply personnel to the top echelons of the CIA or the Pentagon. It maintains a critical stance outside the government, and its point of view is basically socialist.

Institute of General Studies (IGS): A Chilean think-tank set up by the CIA to train and organize the counter-elite that would replace the Allende government.

Junta: The Chilean junta appointed itself; it was not elected by the military. Its members: General Augusto Pinochet Ugarte, Army; Admiral Toribio Merino Castro, Navy; General Gustavo Leigh Guzmán, Air Force; General (Captain before the coup) Cesar Mendoza, Carabineros.

Kennecott Copper Corporation: The second-largest American-owned copper company in Chile. The largest: Anaconda.

"Kunakov Archive": An especially creative piece of disinformation planted by CIA agent Juraj Domic. It was an example of disinformation and black propaganda which appeared in six installments in *El Mercurio* in the week immediately preceding the presidential elections of 1970 in Chile. Its sole purpose was to denigrate, by visual association, candidate Salvador Allende.

Langley: The CIA—so-called from its headquarters in Langley, Virginia. The CIA is also affectionately referred to by its officers as The McLean Agency, The Company and The Agency.

March of the Pots and Pans: Activity of the CIA Women's Action Front, which began during Fidel Castro's visit to Chile in December 1971.

Mercurio, El: Kingpin in CIA media operations in Chile. Cited by the U.S. Senate Select Committee on Intelligence as the recipient of several million dollars in CIA funds between 1970 and 1973.

MIR (Movimiento Izquierdista Revolucionario): Unlike the Tupamaros of Uruguay or the Montoneros of Argentina, the Chilean MIR was primarily an intelligence-gathering organization, not a genuine guerrilla force.

MH/CHILD: CIA code name for a series of agency break-ins.

MW/BABY: Code name for damage-control effort by CIA in each of the Congressional committees investigating the CIA.

National Intelligence Academy: (NIA): A "private" corporation that trains foreign and domestic agents.

October Strike: Also called the Truckers' Strike. A strike by truck owners, in October 1972. In this there were in fact eight separate organizations —*gremios*—basically organizations of owners or proprietors and not just truck drivers. Owners of small business and taxi drivers were also included.

Operation Unitas: Joint U.S.-Chile naval maneuvers, scheduled by the United States for the day of the coup, September 11, 1973.

People's Organized Vanguard: Chilean version of the Symbionese Liberation Army. Killed former Vice President Edmundo Pérez Zukovic because he supervised the mobile units of police that were responsible for several massacres. His assassination had the effect of uniting, for the first time, the Christian Democratic and the National parties.

Propaganda, black, gray, and white: The U.S. *Army Field Manual of Psychological Operations* states (p. 12): "Propaganda is also classified on the basis of identification of its source. White = identifiable. Grey = hidden. Black = deliberately attributed to another source. Grey, white, and black do not refer to anything inherent in the context." A second definition, offered by Victor Marchetti in *The CIA and the Cult of Intelligence* (p. 165) is "telling the truth = white; mixture of truth and half-truth = gray; outright lies = black."

"Quartered Man" (El Descuartizado): 1. A police case involving a man whose arms, legs, and head were severed. 2. A series of false and alarmist stories planted in the Chilean media concerning cannibalism and mutilation, targeted at women. A CIA psychological operation in February and March 1973.

Secret Army Organization (SAO): An organization of Cuban exiles set up in 1968 by Frank Sturgis for the CIA.

Plan September: A plan for a truckowners' strike and coup in September 1973. The name itself was given to the plan by Allende and the Left when they discovered it. The strike was then delayed and Plan September became the October Strike.

SEPA: 1. A humor magazine set up by the CIA to denigrate the Popular Unity leaders. 2. A news service set up by the CIA to launder black propaganda within Chile.

SOC (Special Operations Division, CIA): Same as Covert Action Staff.

Southeast First National Bank: A huge Florida banking conglomerate with connections both to crime and intelligence.

Southern Air Transport (SAT): CIA proprietary airline.

Temuco: Capital of Cautín province, center of agrarian unrest and alleged Communist guerrillas.

Track I: An attempt to overthrow Allende through bribery of the Chilean Congress, propaganda, and political action. It involved economic, political, and diplomatic offensives. Known to and carried out with the cooperation of U.S. ambassador and regular CIA personnel. Involved specifically political action fronts, such as women, youth, labor, etc.

Track II: A secret plan, known only to six individuals in the world, involving assassinations, kidnappings, bombings, and the overthrow of Allende. Operated independently of the U.S. Embassy and CIA station in Santiago. The purposes of Track I and Track II were the same: to permit the CIA to arrange for a military coup immediately to prevent Allende's taking power in 1970. The difference is that Track II involved assassination. The existence of Track II was known—or the instructions that President Nixon gave were known—only by six persons: Nixon,

Henry Kissinger, Richard Helms, Thomas Karamessines, David Atlee Phillips, and (though this was not intended) Ray Cline. At the time Phillips was the CIA officer in charge of the Chile Task Force; Karamessines was Deputy Director of Plans; Cline was head of intelligence at the State Department.

UP (Unidad Popular, Popular Unity): 1. A coalition of leftist parties which integrated the Chilean government. 2. The government of Chile, 1970-73.

Operation Unitas: Joint U.S.-Chile naval maneuvers, scheduled by the United States for the day of the coup, September 11, 1973.

White Book (Libro Blanco): Chilean version of CIA "White Books" issued after the Dominican invasion (1965), in Vietnam, and after the overthrow of Kwame Nkrumah (1966). According to the Senate Select Committee, two CIA "collaborators" wrote the Chilean White Book.

White Hand (Mano Blanca): An umbrella label for a number of armed Cuban exile groups—CORU, Operation 40, Operation Eagle, Commandos L, etc.

Plan Z: CIA black propaganda accompanied by forged documents purporting to show a Red plan to decapitate generals—used in Indonesia, Brazil, and Chile. The name given by the Chilean junta to propaganda and disinformation intended to serve as a cover or provocation for the genuine plans of the military.

Biographical Names and Index

ACUÑA, MANUEL: Chilean attorney for Michael V. Townley. 188, 201.

AFSHAR, NASSAR: Prominent critic of deposed Shah of Iran; targeted for assassination on U.S. soil with full knowledge of CIA. 190.

AGEE, PHILIP: Former CIA officer in Ecuador, Uruguay, and Mexico. Author of *Inside the Company: CIA Diary. Currently*: Living in Germany. 40, 120, 125-126, 130, 135, 137, 176, 203.

AGNEW, SPIRO: Vice President of the United States, 1969-73. Governor of Maryland, 1967-79. 109.

ALEGRIA, PAZ: Alias of Lucia Piedrabuena. 165.

ALLENDE, BEATRIZ: Daughter of Salvador Allende Gossens. 155.

ALLENDE GOSSENS, SALVADOR. President of Chile, 1970-73; assassinated, September 11, 1973. Founder, Chilean Socialist party, 1933. Chilean Senator, 1945-70. Unsuccessful presidential candidate, 1952, 1958, 1964. 11, 16-17, 29, 52, 54, 59, 65, 68, 78, 79-80, 83-84, 93, 96-98, 116, 163, 167, 175, 193, 210.

ALESSANDRI, JORGE: President of Chile, 1958-64. Presidential candidacy in 1970 defeated by Allende. *Currently:* Involuntarily retired from politics. 29.

ANDERSON, JACK: Syndicated newspaper columnist. Author, *The Anderson Papers* (1973). 57-58, 77, 116, 172.

ANDERSON, JAMES: Consular officer, U.S. Embassy, Chile, from 1971. 75, 111.

ANGLETON, JAMES. Deputy director for Counter Intelligence, CIA. 134, 142, 204.

ARAYA, ARTURO: Naval aide-de-camp of Allende; assassinated, July 26, 1973. 95, 164.

ARBENZ CAMPOS, JACOBO: President of Guatemala, 1951-54; deposed in CIA-sponsored coup. 41-42, 161.

ARENDT, HANNAH: Philosopher, political scientist, and author, *inter alia, Totalitarianism.* 207.

ARNELLO, MARIO: Chilean ambassador to the United Nations. 158, 160, 169.

ARZAC, DANIEL N., JR.: Political officer, U.S. Embassy, Chile, from 1971. 75.

BADER, WILLIAM: Senator Church's chief aide; also former CIA officer. 190.

BAEZA MICHELSEN, ERNESTO (Gen.): 104, 105.

BALAGUER, JOAQUÍN: President of the Dominican Republic, 1960-62, 1966-. 50.

BARAONA URZUA, PABLO: 68.

BARKER, BERNARD: Cuban exile. Convicted Watergate burglar. 67.

BARNES, TRACEY: CIA officer; instrumental in coup against Guatemalan democracy in 1954. 41, 46.

BARQUERO, EFRAÍN: Chilean resistance poet. 14.

BELL, GRIFFIN: U.S. Attorney General, 1977-79. xii, 172.

BERNSTEIN, CARL: Reporter for the *Washington Post*, 1966-76. x, 170.

BERRELLEZ, ROBERT: Employee of ITT, head of public relations in Latin America. Prosecuted for perjury and obstruction of justice during Senate investigation of illegal activities of multinational corporations in Chile. He plea-bargained and received a two-month suspended sentence. 55, 58-59.

BINDER, DAVID: Reporter for the *New York Times,* 153.

BISHOP, MAURICE: Mysterious CIA officer, identified as David A. Philips. Liaison to House Select Committee on Assassinations.

BLAKEY, G. ROBERT: Chief counsel to House Select Committee on Assassinations. 202.

CANTRIL, HADLEY: Chairman, Department of Psychology, Princeton, University. Unwitting figurehead of CIA proprietary polling agency run by Lloyd Free. 34.

CARABALLA, ROBERT: Member of 'White Hand' team exiled in Chile. 144.

CARLUCCI, FRANK: Deputy Director, CIA, 1978-. 184.

CARTER, JAMES E.: President of the United States, 1977-. 171-72.

CARTER, MARSHALL S.: Deputy Director, CIA, 1962-65. Director, National Security Agency, 1965-69.

CARVAJAL, PATRICIO. Chilean naval officer. Aide to Orlando Letelier. Foreign minister under Pinochet. 97-8.

CASTILLO ARMAS, CARLOS: President of Guatemala. Installed as result of CIA-sponsored coup, 1954; assassinated, 1957. 41-2.

CASTRO, FIDEL: Premier of Cuba, 1959-. 19, 47-8, 64-5, 97, 128, 142.

CASTRO, FRANK: Cuban exile leader. Participant in founding of CORU. 177.

CASTRO, JUANA: Sister of Fidel Castro. 31.

CHACON, JOSÉ FRANCISCO RENÉ: Head of Salvadoran secret police. CIA agent. Assassinated, 1978. 133.

CHAMOUN, CAMILLE: President of Lebanon, 1958.

CHAMUDES, MARCOS: Editor of rightwing magazine PEL. 68.

CHAPIN, DWIGHT: Personal aide to President Richard M. Nixon, 1969-73. 189.

CHAVEZ, CESAR: Union official. President, United Farm Workers. 35.

CHURCH, FRANK: 53, 56, 64, 122.

CIVILETTI, BENJAMIN: U.S. Attorney General, 1979-. Assistant Attorney General, Civil Rights Division, Department of Justice, 1972-78.

CLARK, RICHARD: U.S. Senator from Iowa.

CLINE, RAY S.: Director of Intelligence, U.S. Department of State, 1969-73. Formerly Deputy Director for Intelligence, CIA, 1962-66. *Currently:* Director of Research, Center for Strategic and International Studies, Georgetown University. 50, 166, 168, 170, 199-200, 202, 204.

COLBY, WILLIAM: Director, CIA, 1973-75. *Currently:* Attorney in private practice, Washington, D.C. 57, 81, 108, 120-2, 124, 127, 137, 170, 184, 205.

COLSON, CHARLES H.: Special counsel to President Richard M. Nixon, 1969-73. 189.

CONNALLY, JOHN: U.S. Secretary of the Treasury, 1971-72. Advisor to President Richard M. Nixon, 1973. 44.

CONTRERAS SEPULVEDA, JUAN MANUEL: Director, Dirección de Inteligencia Nacional (DINA). Indicted as co-conspirator in murder of Orlando Letelier, 1978. 5, 21-3, 26-55, 114, 135, 136-7, 143, 181-82, 185-86, 195-209.

EISENHOWER, DWIGHT D.: 34th U.S. President (1953-1961). 43-4, 66.

ENYART, KENNETH WILLIAM: Alias of Michael V. Townley. 36.

ESPINOZA BRAVO, PEDRO: Chilean army officer; DINA agent. 5, 23, 25-6, 114, 186-7.

ETCHEPARE, GUSTAVO: Companion of Michael V. Townley in Patria y Libertad. 196.

EVANS, ROWLAND: Syndicated newspaper columnist. 152.

FAISAL II: King of Iraq, 1939-58.

FALLACI, ORIANA: Italian writer and interviewer. 108.

FANON, FRANTZ: French writer. Author, *The Wretched of the Earth*. 208.

FERNÁNDEZ LARIOS, ARMANDO: Chilean army officer; DINA officer. 5, 23, 26, 99, 151, 184.

FIORINI, FRANK: *See* Sturgis, Frank.

FLEETWOOD, BLAKE: American writer-journalist. 20, 176.

FORD, GERALD: President of the United States, 1974-77. Member of the Warren Commission, 1963-64. 89, 108, 188.

FREE, LLOYD: CIA agent. Executive officer of CIA proprietary polling agency in Princeton, N.J. 34.

FREI, EDUARDO: President of Chile, 1964-70. Leader of Christian Democratic party. 29, 31, 51, 74, 78, 136.

FRIEDMAN, MILTON: Nobel Prize-winning economist (1976); professor of economics at the University of Chicago. His theories of the value of the so-called free market forces are one of the main bases of the Chicago school of economics. 209.

FUENTES, MANUEL: Chilean journalist; member, Patria y Libertad.

FULBRIGHT, J. WILLIAM: U.S. Senator from Arkansas, 1945-74.

GALTUNG, JOHAN: Professor of political science, University of Geneva. 33.

GAMBINO, ROBERT W.: CIA security director. 25.

GARCIA MARQUEZ, GABRIEL: 96, 99.

GARCIA, ORLANDO: Cuban exile; head of Venezuelan intelligence service. 147.

GENEEN, HAROLD S.: Chief executive officer, ITT. 57-8, 61.

GERRITY, EDWARD J.: Director, corporate relations, ITT, 1964-. 58-60.

GERTH, JEFF: American investigative journalist. Presently with *New York Times*. 14.

GIANDONI, WILLIAM: CIA agent working under cover of Copley News Service. 66.

GLANZER, SEYMOUR: Attorney for Michael V. Townley at trial. Formerly U.S. prosecutor at trial of Watergate burglars, 1972-73. 179, 183-4, 186-9, 192, 197, 200-01.

GOLDBERGER, PAUL: Counsel for Guillermo Novo at trial. 24-5.

GONZÁLES, CARLOS: Former Chilean congressman; detained and tortured with O. Letelier in Dawson Island.

GONZÁLES, MAX GORMAN: Cuban exile. Member of Plot to kill Fidel Castro. 144.

GONZÁLES, VIRGILIO: Member of Cuban "Plumbers" team. 67.

GOODWIN, RICHARD: Assistant to President John F. Kennedy and State Department officer. 49.

GOULART, JOÃO: President of Brazil, 1961-64. Deposed in coup.

GRODEN, ROBERT F.: Photoanalyst and House Assassination committee staff aide. 203.

GUEVARA, ERNESTO ("CHE"): Leader of Cuban revolution. Murdered in Bolivia, 1967.

GUZMÁN, RALPH: U.S. government official "purged" for his advocacy of human rights policies. 210.

HAIG, ALEXANDER M.: Assistant to assistant to President for National Security Affairs, 1970-73; Deputy assistant for National Security Affairs; later, assistant to President, Chief, White House Staff, 1973-74. 201.

HALDEMAN, HAROLD R. ("BOB"): Chief, White House Staff, 1969-73. 185.

HALPERIN, MORTON H.: Fellow, Institute for Policy Studies. Formerly, Staff Member, National Security Council.

HAMILTON, EDWARD J.: Alias of E. Howard Hunt.

HARRIMAN, AVERELL: 123.

HARKIN, TOM: U.S. Congressman from Iowa. 209.

HARRINGTON, MICHAEL: U.S. Congressman from Massachusetts, 1968-74. 121.

HELLYER, DAVID: CIA officer in Chile. Editor-publisher *South Pacific Mail*, 1964-66. 66.

HELMS, JESSE: 153.

HELMS, RICHARD: Director, CIA, 1966-73. Prosecuted for lying about CIA activities in Chile in testimony before Senate Committee. 25-6, 32, 36, 46, 53-4, 81, 106, 122-4, 134, 138, 170, 185-6, 190, 201, 205-7.

HENDRIX, HAROLD: CIA officer working under journalistic cover in Latin America with *Miami Herald*, UPI, and the public relations department of ITT. x, 58-9, 68, 137-8.

McLUHAN, MARSHALL: Media expert. 90.

McMANUS, JOSEPH F.: Political officer, U.S. Embassy, Chile, 1972-. 76.

McNAMARA, ROBERT S.: President, World Bank, 1968. U.S. Secretary of Defense, 1961-68. 63, 123.

MALCOLM X: Black Muslim leader. Assassinated, 1965. 14, 152.

MARCHETTI, VICTOR: Executive assistant to Deputy Director of the CIA, to 1969. Co-author, *The CIA and the Cult of Intelligence*. 119, 120-1, 126, 135.

MARCOS, FERDINAND E.: Dictator of the Philippines.

MARKS, JOHN: Intelligence officer, U.S. Department of State. Co-author, *the CIA and the Cult of Intelligence*. 120-1.

MÁRQUEZ, GABRIEL GARCIA: Novelist and poet. (Colombian) 96, 99.

MARTÍNEZ, EUGENIO: Cuban exile. Member of Watergate 'Plumbers' team. 67

MEANY, GEORGE: President of AFL-CIO, to 1980. CIA collaborator through AIFLD. 82.

MERRIAM, WILLIAM R.: Assistant director, Washington relations, ITT, 1961-67, director, 1967-73. 54, 57, 59, 60-1.

MEYER, CORD: CIA officer, specialist in international organizations. 137.

MILLAS, ORLANDO: Chilean intellectual and member of the Chilean CP. 105.

MIRANDA CARRINGTON, SERGIO: Chilean attorney for Manuel Contreras. 55, 182.

MITCHELL, JOHN N.: U.S. Attorney General, 1969-72. Convicted of obstruction of justice in Watergate burglary. 52-4.

MITRIONE, DAN: AID official working with Uruguayan police on inter-rogation methods. Kidnapped and killed by Tupamaro guerrillas, September 1970. 109, 110, 168.

MOFFITT, MICHAEL: Assistant to Orlando Letelier at the Institute for Policy Studies. xvii, 4-5, 10, 13-4, 16, 18, 151-2, 172.

MOFFITT, RONNI KARPEN: Assistant to Orlando Letelier at the Insti-tute for Policy Studies. Killed by bomb, 1976. xvi, 3, 4-5, 10, 13-4, 16, 151-2, 157, 171, 190, 209.

MONTERO, ENRIQUE: Chilean deputy minister of the Interior, 1978-. 186.

MORALES, RICARDO: CIA and FBI double agent. Residing in Vene-zuela. 147-49.

MOSS, ROBERT: British writer & journalist; CIA asset. Expert on psywar. 68, 104, 162, 165-7, 206.

MUELLER, HERBERT A.: Cousin of Nena Ossa, and CIA asset. 161.

REAGAN, RONALD: Former Hollywood actor; right-wing Republican politician. 205.

RIVERA, FERNANDO: Associate of Manuel Acuña, Townley's Chilean counsel. 188.

RODRÍGUEZ GRES, PABLO: Chilean attorney. Leader of Patria y Libertad. 51, 55-6, 66-7.

ROGERS, WILLIAM: Assistant Secretary of State for Latin American Affairs. 38.

ROMERAL JARA, ALEJANDRO: Alias of Armando Fernandez. 20-1.

ROSS DÍAZ, ALVIN: Cuban exile. 5, 22, 24, 26, 192, 198.

ROSS, THOMAS B.: Journalist. Co-author, *The Invisible Government.*

ROSTOW, WALTER: Special Assistant to President Lyndon B. Johnson, 1966-69. 33.

RUSHER, WILLIAM: Writer. Co-founder of *National Review*, 1955, and publisher, 1957-. 206.

RUSK, DEAN: U.S. Secretary of State, 1961-69.

SAENZ, ORLANDO: Leader of gremios that paralyzed Chile, October 1972. 55.

SALISBURY, HARRISON: Reporter and editor for the *New York Times*, from 1949. 176.

SAMPOL, WILLIAM: Employee in New York office of Senator James Buckley. 160, 169, 197.

SANFORD, R. JEROME: Assistant U.S. Attorney for the Southern District of Florida, 1975-. 147.

SANTANA, MANUEL: Member, Cuban Nationalist Movement.

SCHACKLEY, TED: CIA officer. Head of Phoenix Program in Vietnam. 40, 61.

SCHAEFFER, PAUL: Leader of Nazi sect associated with *Colonia Dignidad* Project in Chile. Presently a torture and detention center. 115.

SCHERRER, ROBERT: FBI special agent in Southern Cone (Buenos Aires). 22, 145-6, 149, 186, 191, 201.

SCHLESINGER, JAMES R.: Director, CIA, 1973. U.S. Secretary of Defense, 1973-75. Chairman, AEC, 1971-73. 108, 134, 184.

SCHNEIDER, RENÉ: Commander in Chief, Chilean Army. Assassinated, October 22, 1970. 52, 54, 62, 94, 136, 163.

SCHORR, DANIEL: CBS television reporter, to 1976. 166.

SCOTT, PETER DALE: Researcher who has advanced a "Chicago Junta" terrorist group theory. 100.

SEGRETTI, DONALD: 189.

SEPULVEDA, EDUARDO: Pinochet's personal representative. 116.

SHAWCROSS, WILLIAM: Author, *Sideshow*. British journalist. 201.
SHAHEEN, MICHAEL: 172.
SHLAUDEMAN, HARRY W.: Deputy chief of mission, Santiago, 1969-73. 50, 75, 108, 185, 209, 210.
SIERO PÉREZ, ISABEL: Member of International Federation of Women Lawyers (CIA front). 31.
SILBERT, EARL: 179, 183-4, 186-9, 191-2, 197.
SILVA ESPEJO, RENÉ: Editor, *El Mercurio* (Santiago). 67.
SILVA, JUAN ANDREAS WILSON: Alias of Michael V. Townley.
SIMONS, MARLISE: Reporter for the *Washington Post*. 135.
SIRICA, JOHN J.: U.S. district judge. 189.
SMITH, JOSEPH ("LITTLE JOE"): CIA officer. 44, 127, 211.
SOMOZA, ANASTASIO: Dictator of Nicaragua, 1967-79.
SORENSEN, THEODORE C.: Special counsel to President John F. Kennedy and Lyndon B. Johnson, 1961-64. 172.
SPRAGUE, RICHARD A.: Staff counsel to the House Committee on Assassinations. 138-9.
STAVINS, RALPH: Fellow, Institute for Policy Studies. 154.
STERLING, CLAIRE: Right wing writer for CIA-influenced organs. 166.
STEVENS, BOB: U.S. government official supporting human rights. "Purged." 210.
STURGIS, FRANK: American anti-Castro leader; leader of Secret Army Organization (SAO). CIA informant. 34-5, 41, 45, 49, 67, 101, 127, 129, 139, 203, 205.
SUÁREZ ESQUIVEL, JOSÉ DIONISIO: Cuban exile. Indicted for assassination of Orlando Letelier. *Currently*: Fugitive. 5, 22, 144, 146, 151, 179-80.
SUKARNO, ACHMED: President of Indonesia, 1945-66. 83.
SUN MYUNG MOON: Head of Unification Church. 18, 157, 159.
SYMINGTON, STUART: U.S. Senator from Missouri, 1953-. 106, 123.
SZULC, TAD: Former reporter for the *New York Times* (to 1969). 176.

TER BEK, RELUS: Member of Parliament, The Netherlands.
TERPIL, FRANK: Former CIA agent and indicted terrorist. 169, 173, 174.
THAYER, WALDO: News analyst for *San Francisco Chronicle*. 73.
THEBERGE, JAMES: Director, Latin American and Hispanic Studies, Center for Strategic and International Studies, 1970-75. 166-7.
THIEME, ROBERTO: Director, clandestine operations, Patria y Libertad, and vice president, Instituto Chileño de Opinion Publica. 224.
TIPTON, JOHN. B.: Political officer, U.S. Embassy, Chile, 1970. 76, 111.

WEISS, PETER: Chairman, Institute for Policy Studies. 171.

WELCH, MICHAEL TOWNLEY: Alias of Michael V. Townley.

WELCH, RICHARD: CIA Station Chief, Greece. Assassinated, 1975. 131.

WHACK, LARRY E.: FBI special agent. 197.

WHEELOCK, KEITH: Political officer, U.S. Embassy, Chile, 1966-. 76-7.

WHITTEN, LES: Journalist, associate of Jack Anderson. 172.

WILLIAMS ROSE, JUAN: Alias of Michael V. Townley. 20, 21, 177.

WILLS, GARRY: Journalist. Former writer for *National Review*. 169.

WILSON, ANDREAS: Alias of Michael V. Townley. (see Michael Vernon Townley).

WILSON, EDWIN: Former CIA officer. *Currently:* Under indictment in Libyan murder conspiracy. xii, 150, 172, 173-4, 200-1.

WILSON, STANLEY: Detective, Washington Metropolitan Police Department. 155, 199.

WINTERS, DONALD H.: Political officer, U.S. Embassy, Chile, 1969-. 77.

WISE, DAVID: Journalist. Co-author, *The Invisible Government*. 127.

YEAGER, JOHN: Alias of Michael V. Townley.

YOUNG, ANDREW: U.S. Ambassador to the United Nations, 1977-79. 171.

YOUNGBLOOD, JACK: FBI special agent.

YOUNGER, JOHN: Alias of Michael V. Townley.

ZEGERS, CRISTIAN: Head of Andalien ad agency, CIA asset for mass disinformation in Chile. 66.

Chilean Victims of Political Assassinations—1970-1980

General of the Army René Schneider	1970
Journalist Elmo Catalan and his wife	1971
Allende's naval attaché, Captain Arturo Araya Peeters	1973
President Salvador Allende	1973
Director of Investigation Eduardo Paredes	1973
Minister of the Interior José Tohá	1973
General Oscar Bonilla, Minister of the Interior	1974
General Carlos Prats, Acting President during Allende's visit to the United Nations	
Chairman of the Joint Chiefs of Staff, Minister of Defense	1974
General of the Air Force Alberto Bachelet, Minister of Commerce	1975
Orlando Letelier, Minister of the Interior, Minister of Defense	1976

1. Before 1970 there had never been a political assassination in Chilean history.

2. *Before* the Letelier assassination, every Minister of Defense in the Allende Cabinet had been assassinated.

3. Before Letelier, three Ministers of the Interior under Allende were assassinated.

4. CIA officers or their Chilean agents were involved in all the above.

5. Michael V. Townley was the principal agent directly responsible for the assassinations of Prats and Letelier, in addition to attempted assassinations of Socialist party leader Carlos Altamirano, President Allende's nephew Andrew Pascal Allende, Communist party theoretician Volodia Teitelboim, and Christian Democratic Senator Bernardo Leighton.

6. David Atlee Phillips was the CIA officer directly responsible for the Chile task force at the time that all these assassinations occurred.

7. Before Chile, Phillips ran what President Johnson would refer to as a "Murder Inc. in the Caribbean."

8. Before Chile, Phillips's assistant Ted Schackley had run a pacification program in Laos, Vietnam, and worked with Phillips in assassination attempts against Castro.

9. These assassinations tend to occur in the Sept.-Oct. period, the anniversary of the original Track II period when Nixon ordered the CIA to get rid of Allende.

10. The *only* punishment meted out in all these cases has been to two hapless Cubans and one American—and this only because the assassination was carried out in broad daylight in Washington, D.C.

Excerpts from a Study by the Center for National Security Studies

TOP SECRET

Cable Traffic, CIA Hdqtrs.-Langley, Va. to American Embassy Santiago, Chile

Regarding threats to U.S. interest, we conclude that:

1) The U.S. has no vital national interests within Chile. There would, however, be tangible economic losses.

2) The world military balance of power would not be significantly altered by an Allende government.

3) An Allende victory would, however, create considerable political and psychological costs:

a) Hemispheric cohesion would be threatened by the challenge that an Allende government would pose to the Organization of American States, and by the reactions that it would create in other countries. We do not see, however, any likely threat to the peace of the region.

b) An Allende victory would represent a definite psychological setback to the United States and a definite psychological advance for the Marxist idea.*

Up until the September election, the C.I.A. had approved "destabilization" plans for Chile that included massive propaganda campaigns in the press, funding workers to stay out on strike, and plans to bribe the Chilean Congress. Working with the C.I.A. and the State Department were the large multinational corporations such as I.T.T., which also had much to lose in the Allende takeover. . . .

One of the obstacles confronting the coup planners in Washington and Santiago was General Schneider, a member of the Chilean Armed Forces, and a strict constitutionalist. He refused to consider a forceful takeover of the Allende government by the military. His strong stance made him the subject of many an irate C.I.A. cable. The following is excerpted from one.

This would make it more important than ever to remove him and bring this new state of events . . . anything we or station can do to effect removal of Schneider? We know this rhetorical question, but wish inspire thought on both ends of this matter. †

*Intelligence Memorandum, "Situation Following the Chilean Presidential Election," C.I.A.'s Directorate of Intelligence, 9/7/70.
†Cable 638, Hq. to Sta., 10/8/70.

246 Appendix

Although plans to promote a coup by destabilizing the country and manipulating the press were in full gear, the problem of how the United States was going to justify overthrowing a popularly elected government remained. The following transcript, extraordinary in its blatant cynicism, is a request from C.I.A.'s headquarters in Langley to its station in Chile for suggestions on how best to argue that the coup is both necessary and worthwhile.

1) It still appears that Ref A coup has no pretext or justification that it can offer to make it acceptable in Chile or Latin America. It therefore would seem necessary to create one to bolster what will probably be their claim to a coup to save Chile from communism. . . . You may wish include variety of themes in justification of coup to military for their use. These could include but are not limited to: (A) Firm intel. that Cubans planned to reorganize all intelligence services along Soviet/Cuban mold thus creating structure for police state. . . . (B) Economic situation collapsing. . . . (C) By quick recognition of Cuba and Communist countries Allende assumed U.S. would cut off material assistance to Armed Forces thus weakening them as constitutional barriers. Would then empty armories to Communist People's Militia with task to run campaign of terror based on alleged labor and economic sabotage. (Use some quotes from Allende on this.)

2) Station has written some excellent prop guidances. Using themes at hand and which best known to you we are now asking you to prepare intel report based on some well known facts and some fiction to justify coup, split opposition, and gain adherents for military group. With appropriate military contact can determine how to "sicover" [sic] intel report which could even be planted during raids planned by Carabineros.

3) We urge you to get this idea and some concrete suggestions to plotters as soon as you can. Coup should have a justification to prosper.‡

Three years after these documents were written, a military coup did in fact take place primarily due to efforts of the C.I.A., U.S. multinationals, and American banks. The year after Augusto Pinochet, the Chilean dictator, took power, he declared that there would be "no elections in Chile during my lifetime nor the lifetime of my successor." The C.I.A. had ended 180 years of constitutional government in Chile, to replace it with one of the most repressive regimes in modern history.

‡Cable 88s, Hq. to Sta., 10/1970.

Support Organizations

Numerous organizations around the country can assist groups and individuals interested in learning more about human rights, U.S. policy, and specifically about the Southern Cone countries. We have listed a few of the main national groups; further information about local groups is available from them.

Argentina

Argentina Information and Service Center (AISC)
P.O.Box 4233
Berkeley, Cal. 94704
  Also publishes *Argentine Outreach*

Anti-Imperialist Movement for Socialism in Argentina (MASA)
P.O. Box 134, Times Square Station
New York, N.Y. 10036

Denuncia (in Spanish), same address as MASA.

Chile

National Chile Center
156 Fifth Ave.
New York, N.Y. 10010

Non-Intervention in Chile (NICH)
151 W. 19th St., Room 905
New York, N.Y. 10011
  Also publishes *Chile Newsletter* (P.O. Box 800, Berkeley, Cal. 94701)

Office for Political Prisoners and Human Rights in Chile
    (OPRICH)
156 Fifth Ave., Room 521
New York, N.Y. 10010
or
P.O. Box 40605
San Francisco, Cal. 94140

Latin America

Community Action on Latin America (CALA)
731 State St.
Madison, Wis. 53703

Council on Hemispheric Affairs (COHA)
110 Maryland Ave., N.E.
Washington, D.C. 20002

Ecumenical Program for Inter-American Communication
    and Action (EPICA)
Wilson Center
1470 Irving St., N.W.
Washington, D.C. 20010

Latin American Information Service
300 East 4th St.
New York, N.Y. 10009
   Also publishes *Lucha*

Latin American Task Force, Third World Coalition
c/o AFSC
1501 Cherry St.
Philadelphia, Pa. 19102

Washington Office on Latin America (WOLA)
110 Maryland Ave., N.E.
Washington, D.C. 20002

U.S. Policy and Human Rights—General

Center for International Policy (CIP)
122 Maryland Ave., N.E.
Washington, D.C. 20002

Clergy and Laity Concerned (CALC)
198 Broadway
New York, N.Y. 10036
   Also publishes *CALC Report*

Coalition for a New Foreign and Military Policy/
    (Human Rights Working Group)
120 Maryland Ave., N.E.
Washington, D.C. 20002

Institute for Policy Studies/Transnational Institute (IPS/TNI)
1901 Q Street, N.W.
Washington, D.C. 20009

A Psychological Warfare Sampler

En Vida Habrían Cercenado El Cuerpo del Hombre Encontrado en Quilicura

En vida habría sido cercenado de la cabeza y de sus extremidades el hombre de 45 años, cuyo tronco apareció en el camino al Cementerio de Quilicura el domingo pasado y que dejó al descubierto el más brutal y espeluznante crimen de los últimos 50 años.

Tan macabra hipótesis comenzó a circular en forma insistente en la mañana de ayer en fuentes policiales, mientras un grupo de detectives de la BH a cargo del inspector Juan Morales Espina realizan infructuosos esfuerzos para localizar a un sastre que podría permitir identificar a la víctima.

Respecto a sus autores —trascendió en forma extraoficial— que éstos serían tres o más, ya que la tarea de descuartizamiento con sierras eléctricas y cuchilleros carniceros, como el traslado del tronco hasta un camino de Quilicura, requieren la colaboración de más de una persona.

Todos estos antecedentes, que pista concreta, son revisados minuciosamente por la policía. Respecto a los móviles de tan horrendo crimen, se presume que podrían ser tres. En primer lugar, el individuo habría sido ultimado por venganza por una mafia de traficantes en drogas o contrabandistas. También se cree que las causas fueron la posible delación que la víctima podría haber hecho de algún importante suceso delictivo o bien, el caso tendría ribetes pa-

Importante pista en caso del descuartizado.—

Policía se Moviliza
Tras Fiat 600 Robado

Toda la policía se encuentra tras la pista que permita ubicar un automóvil Fiat 600, robado, en el cual se habrían trasladado los restos del hombre que apareció cercenado en el camino al Cementerio de Quilicura.

Los antecedentes logrados en el día de ayer indican que fueron vistos cerca del lugar donde apareció el cuerpo descuartizado, dos sujetos conduciendo un automóvil Fiat. Este según testigos tiene la patente DJ.939, de Las Condes y corresponde a un automóvil Fiat 600 color beige, cuyo robo fue denunciado por sus propietarios. El vehículo, que podría significar una pista en el espectacular caso fue sustraído desde la calle La sionales, donde estaría por medio una mujer casada.

PUZZLE POLICIAL

El suceso, que ha sido denominado "El descuartizado de Quilicura", tiene, sin embargo, otros antecedentes que lo complican aún más. La aparición de un paquete con carne humana correspondiente al segundo tercio de un muslo del sexo masculino. Estos restos, encontrados en un sitio eriazo por el comerciante ambulante del Mercado Persa Dagoberto Riveros, luego de ser examinados en el Instituto Médico Legal, resultaron corresponder al cuerpo localizado en Quilicura. Esto hace pensar a los investigadores que los autores del homicidio pueden haber repartido otras extremidades en diferentes lugares de la capital o bien fuera de ella. Sin embargo, se cree que la cabeza, que fue cercenada a la altura del cuello, como los brazos, fueron enterrados con el

"Man Quartered Alive (in Quilicura)."

MACABRO HECHO INVESTIGA LA POLICIA.—

Dueña de Casa Compró Longanizas Fabricadas Con Carne Humana

Expertos del Instituto Médico Legal y peritos de la Brigada de Homicidios se encuentran analizando la procedencia de un kilo de longanizas que una dueña de casa compró en una rotisería de Alameda con Chacabuco y que resultaron estar fabricadas con carne humana.

El macabro hallazgo fue hecho en la noche del martes por la señora Rogelia Cifuentes Bórquez, de 32 años y con domicilio en la manzana 138, sitio 22 de la Población Pudahuel, en Las Barrancas.

La dueña de casa había adquirido en una rotisería de Alameda con Chacabuco un kilo de longanizas. Posteriormente Rogelia Cifuentes se dirigió con el paquete a casa de su hermana Elsa, ubicada en Capitán Gálvez 4563, en la Población Los Nogales. Una vez que abrió el paquete se percató que desde el interior salía un profundo mal olor a carne descompuesta. Rápidamente cogió un cuchillo y un tenedor y comenzó a cortar algunos trozos de longaniza observando que la carne en su interior era diferente, ya que presentaba un color amarillento. Sin embargo, la mayor sorpresa se la llevó la señora cuando entre los trozos aparecieron algunos vellos oscuros y pequeñas partículas de restos humanos correspondiente a la parte de una pierna. Alarmada Rogelia Cifuentes se dirigió con su hermana y una vecina a la Tenencia de Carabineros. Cabo Tomás Pereira, donde llevó el macabro paquete. Los uniformados luego de abrir el paquete se dieron cuenta que la carne era diferente a la animal, a la vez que también sintieron un fuerte olor a putrefacción. Rápidamente se dio aviso a la Brigada de Homicidios constituyéndose en el lugar el inspector Juan Morales Espina, acompañado de varios detectives.

En el lugar los policías pudieron verificar que estaban ante restos de carne humana, razón por la cual remitieron de inmediato las longanizas al Instituto Médico Legal, con el objeto de que fueran analizadas en forma más detallada.

Mientras tanto los detectives iniciaron una serie de diligencias para localizar la procedencia de dichas longanizas, que incluso podrían guardar alguna relación con el caso del descuartizado de Quilicura.

Mañana Viernes, Nueva Constitución De Mesas Receptoras

Mañana viernes 23, a las 14 horas, deberán constituirse las Mesas Receptoras de Sufragios con los nuevos vocales designados para tales efectos por la Junta Electoral.

Como se estima que las nuevas designaciones de vocales enviadas por correo a sus destinatarios no alcanzarán a llegar a tiempo, los vocales que asistieron a la primera constitución de mesas deberán concurrir también mañana viernes 23.

Las listas de los nuevos vocales se publican hoy en "El Mercurio". Hoy y mañana se publicarán en el diario "La Nación".

Primeramente se había informado que la constitución se haría el sábado, pero ayer se confirmó que tal trámite se hará mañana.

EN CERO SE ENCUENTRAN LAS PESQUISAS.—

Fracasó Importante Pista En Caso del Descuartizado

"Housewife Bought Hot Dogs Made from Human Flesh."
"Descuartizado."

"Brutal Marxist Assault at School No. 12."
"Marxists Descuartizar Dog."
"Marxists' 'Lesions' Students."

"March of the Handicapped . . .
Marxist Government Disperses Them with Blows."

¡MENOS MAL QUE ERA CARNE DE PERRO!

El caso de las longanizas sospechosas:

NO ERA CARNE HUMANA; ERA DE SIMPLE PERRO

¿SE IMAGINO USTED QUE LLEGARIAMOS A ESTO?

proteste hoy votando por la

CONFEDERACION DE LA DEMOCRACIA

PARTIDO DEMOCRACIA RADICAL   PARTIDO DEMOCRATICO NACIONAL   PARTIDO DEMOCRATA CRISTIANO   PARTIDO NACIONAL   PARTIDO IZQUIERDA RADICAL

"Hot Dogs Not Human Flesh (of Descuartizado)."
"Just Dog Meat."

"The Other Lee Harvey Oswald"

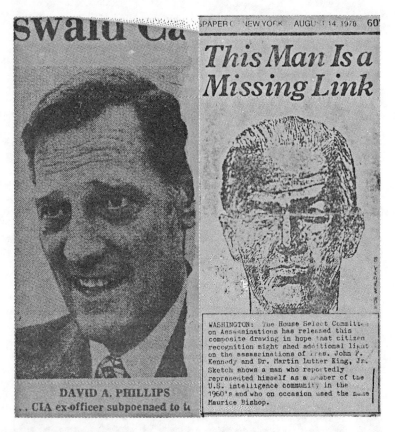

Photograph of David A. Phillips and Sketch of Maurice Bishop prepared for the House Select Committe on Assassinations.